OTHER WORKS BY DANIEL ROBERT SULLIVAN

PLACES, PLEASE! (BECOMING A JERSEY BOY)

PROSPECT HIGH: BROOKLYN

LOCKDOWN: AWAIT FURTHER INSTRUCTIONS

Beginning Inauguration Day 2017, a cynical New Yorker tours thirty cities across America in a struggle to understand the motivations of devoted Trump supporters by capturing their words and stories.
Four years later, will their perspectives change?
Or will his?

THERE'S NO SUBSTITUTE FOR EMPATHY

A Liberal's Journey Through Conservative
America

by

Daniel Robert Sullivan

NEW YORK | LONDON | TORONTO

Copyright, 2020, in the United States of
America
according to
Act of Congress

Library of Congress Cataloging-in-Publication
Data

Names: Sullivan, Daniel Robert, author.

Titles: There's No Substitute for Empathy /
Daniel Robert Sullivan.

Description: First edition. | New York,
Theatrical Services, Inc., 2020.

Subjects: LCSH: United States — Politics and
Government — 2020 | Government Executives —
United States

PRINTED IN THE UNITED STATES OF AMERICA

1 2 5 6 9 12 15 19

THERE'S NO SUBSTITUTE FOR EMPATHY

A Liberal's Journey Through Conservative America

by

DANIEL ROBERT SULLIVAN

THEATRICAL SERVICES, INC.

NEW YORK

A Note on the Title:

Ben Wheeler was six years old when his life was taken during the violent attack at Sandy Hook Elementary School. President Barack Obama grieved with Ben's parents, David and Francine, two days later. David Wheeler was taken with President Obama's sincerity, recalling the moment in Dawn Porter's documentary, *The Way I See It*: "There's no substitute for empathy. It is a foundational relationship between human beings. We are so good at dismissing the people we elect to serve us. We're so good at turning them into things that aren't people. When you do that, then you get the elected officials that you deserve."

THE JOURNEY

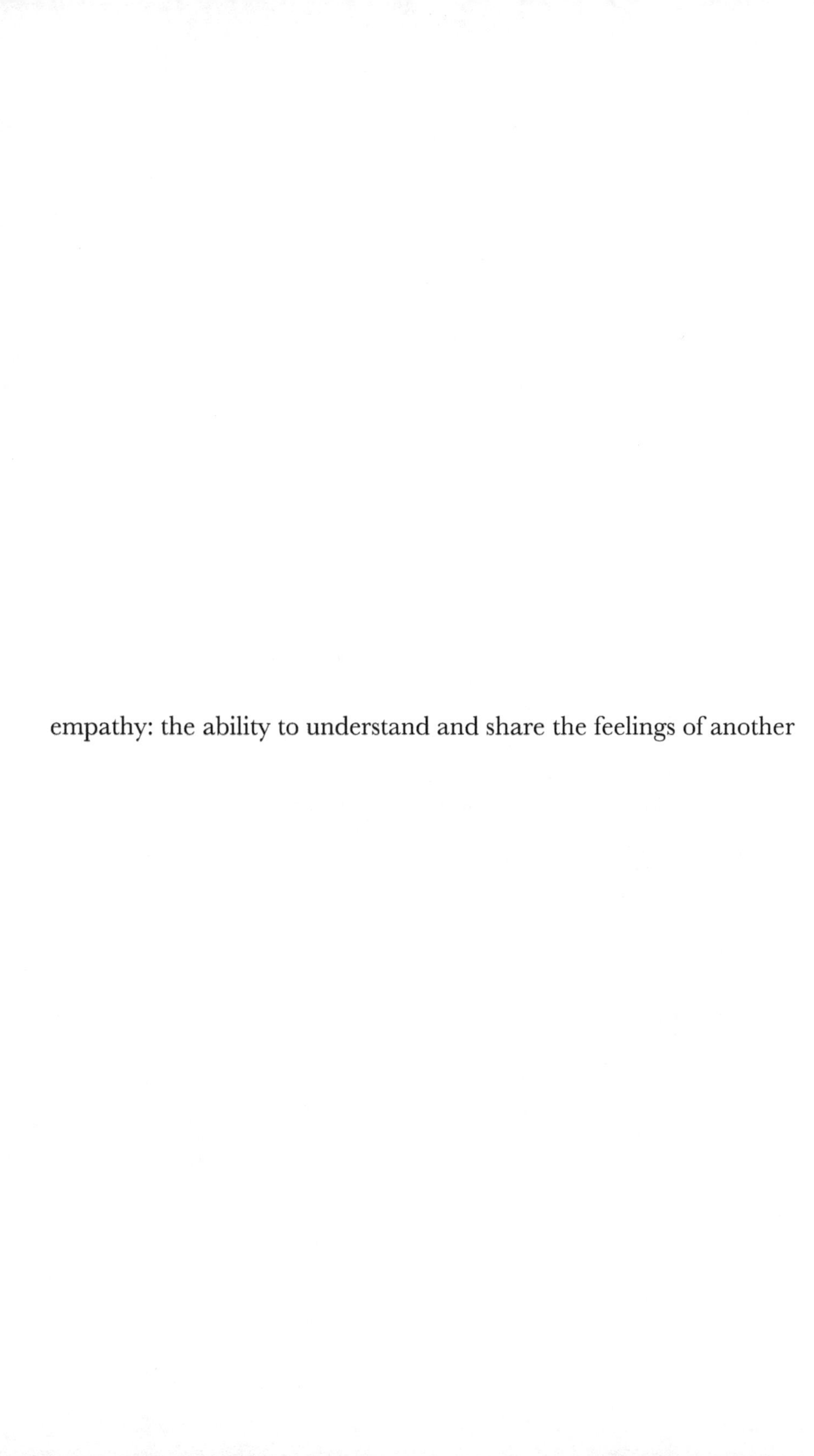

empathy: the ability to understand and share the feelings of another

THERE'S NO SUBSTITUTE FOR EMPATHY

ACT ONE: 2016

My friends are going to #resist this book; I'm certain of it. Many hold a moral conviction that supporters of Donald Trump's presidency are, by virtue of that endorsement, unequivocally erring. Many hold a moral conviction that a vote for Trump equates with ignorance, racism, or selfishness.

Moral convictions, by definition, are "perceived as universally and objectively true, and are comparatively immune to authority or peer influence."[1] That immunity to peer influence is a mighty big wall for me to find a way over, but I'll try. My premise is the title, but my conclusions will be slow to unfurl.

For four years, I've worked on this documentary project. It is epic in scope and far, far too long; forgive me. I'm strengthened by debate and take joy in being a contrarian, and this work has offered space for both. I hope the American panorama contained herein may offer you the same. I cannot hope to convince either side of our divided country to alter their political orientation, but I've come to believe there is tremendous value in leftists giving good ear to those on the other side; there are reasoned arguments there. I've also come to wish that conservatives would confront more of the incongruities in their devotion to Trump; there are unconscionable choices there. This is my contribution to those parallel goals.

Like Obama before him, Donald Trump was the change candidate, and remains a force for change to this day. Conservatives made a deliberate choice to elect a fresh face that they view as a devoted outsider. It's difficult to understand that choice when bound

---

[1] Linda J. Skitka, *The Psychology of Moral Conviction* (Annual Review of Psychology - Vol. 72, 2021)

by moral conviction, difficult for a liberal to look for explanations beyond ignorance, racism, or selfishness. But I have come to understand that such explanations are out there.

I'm a so-called liberal elite. I'm quite privileged, and I'm pretty left-wing. I live in a fancy New York City apartment, have gay family members, and tend to believe entitlements are requirements. In the days following Donald Trump's 2016 election, I joined protests, chanted "not my president" through Times Square, and – yeah, I'll admit it – shed some tears. Are you like me? Or are you one of those conservatives who could feel the pulse and knew there was a different movement afoot?

As a country, our algorithms have split. Our curated newsfeeds reflect only half the landscape, and perhaps it's time for some of us to start listening more closely and with more nuance to the other side. Beginning Inauguration Day 2017, this cynical New Yorker journeyed through more than thirty cities across America in a struggle to understand the motivations of devoted Trump supporters by capturing their words and stories. I sat with them where they live and work, and I listened deeply so that I may learn. Who is it that could vote for such a man?

The most persuasive conservatives I met are represented here, as are a few bold characters further right. The most humble and promising members of the young Republican generation speak here of their inspiration, but so too do their grandparents who vote red out of tradition rather than philosophy.

Yes, many characters in this journey will repeat conservative media talking points that are categorically untrue. But they will do so because the talking points support their pre-existing feelings, and those feelings must be understood if our opposing parties are ever to achieve *domestic Tranquility*. If a liberal reader is open enough to hear the other side, I challenge that reader not to dismiss a conservative's entire story if a supposed fact is deemed false. The conservative media has power to indoctrinate, and we liberals have been unduly influenced by our own media, too. The underlying feelings are what interest me here, and empathy is a tool for understanding.[2]

After nine months travelling the country and speaking at length to conservatives on their home turf, my curiosity only

---

[2] By way of example, I found myself convinced by liberal media that the Tax Cuts and Jobs Act of 2017 only helped the rich. In fact, the vast majority of Americans have had a lower income tax burden since the cuts were made. (We should continue to argue, of course, about a lack of equity in the tax cuts among various income groups, but the fact that they helped more than just rich people is irrefutable.)

increased. As Donald Trump rocketed through policy and economic changes, as he destroyed all established norms of communication, I wondered if he was fulfilling the hopes his supporters had for his term. Following up with these supporters four years later, my tone changed. I'm not going to tell you how just yet, because I'd rather first make a promise: after giving voice and attention to the steadfast Americans who fill the pages of this book, you will be changed, too.

Political commentary in the latest election cycle has never been more robust, but the trend is toward analysis rather than representation. Rather than talk about a group of voters, *There's No Substitute for Empathy* talks with them. With mostly-gentle prodding and ample space for stories, this book introduces the real people behind the trends. Rather than over-analyze, I've let the citizens of conservative areas speak for themselves.

In *On Liberty*, John Stuart Mill writes, "He who knows only his own side of the case knows little of that. His reasons may be good, and no one may have been able to refute them. But if he is equally unable to refute the reasons on the opposite side, if he does not so much as know what they are, he has no ground for preferring either opinion. Nor is it enough that he should hear the opinions of adversaries from his own teachers, presented as they state them, and accompanied by what they offer as refutations. He must be able to hear them from persons who actually believe them...he must know them in their most plausible and persuasive form." What's that mean to me? It means that if I want to continue thinking I'm an intelligent liberal, I have to speak with intelligent conservatives and attempt to truly, deeply understand their point of view. That's what I'm doing here. And I'm doing it in thirty cities across America.

Interpretation is called for. Analytics are called for. We must understand the driving force of cataclysmic change underlying the 2016 election cycle... but all of this is not for me to do. I'm a documentarian. I'm a collector of stories. I would like to understand the deepest motivation of my conservative opposites by listening to them, representing them, and – yes, of course – pushing back at them. That's what this book is all about: discovering the real words and motivations of real people.

My four year quest is to listen fully to those with whom I disagree, and give them abundant space to provide justification. *There's No Substitute for Empathy* documents the results of that quest. Attempting to scale the wall of my own moral conviction, I try to empathize in an effort to learn – and reveal – what I've missed.

Conservatives can use this book as confirmation: there are people from every type of background who feel Trump is the refreshment America needed. Liberals can use this book as a weapon: there are themes in these narratives that explain the enthusiasm for Trump and should be used when your politics are on the offense, for the Trump base isn't going away anytime soon.

I was naïve in 2016. My dinner conversations were about whether Hillary Clinton's win would be marginal or enormous, not whether a win would occur. My election night plan was to open the special-occasion champagne or walk down the street to see Hillary's fireworks over the East River, not to drain my cell battery streaming results in past-my-bedtime disbelief. It took me some time to remember that there are real people behind the rallies, and real stories behind the votes.

Conservatives are part of my family. Conservatives are some of my friends. They are not my enemy, and yet conservatives have voted for a man that has actively assailed other family and other friends (the gay ones, the social welfare ones, the liberal ones). So we are at war, these conservatives and I. But it is a war of empathy, and I'm giving the first volley to the opposition.

CHAPTER ONE
The Apollo Engineer

January 20th, 2017
Las Vegas, Nevada

I'm in Las Vegas on Inauguration Day, 2017. Having previously lived full-time in this neon city while headlining as one of the Jersey Boys, the color and luxury façade no longer fools me. The illusion worked only until I peeked too many times behind the curtain; there's some harsh reality back there. The city has excess poverty, deep addiction, and pervasive desperation behind those shimmery lights. I must confess, however, that the feeling is different today. It's been a year since I left Sin City, and the new W Las Vegas in which I find myself impresses and draws me in. Why? What's that feeling? Ah, yes… It's sexy. The W Las Vegas feels damn sexy. My year away has allowed the façade to fool me once again.

Las Vegas has an allure – fickle as it may be – and I see the appeal with fresh eyes in the lobby of its latest property. This hotel opened within days of the Clinton-Trump election, so it seems fitting to meet my first devoted Trump supporter here; the glamour of richness meets the realism of residents. It's even more fitting when I discover Tom has brought a gun with him. I abhor guns.

Nevada often feels like the Wild West. Cities are spread far apart by swaths of hot, cracked, earth. Guys that live on land in the charred majority hold their guns closely – as is their right – but one of them travelling a gun to this uppity hotel is a surprise to me.

"Tom is smart," I tell myself, "He's making whatever decision suits him best." I know he's an engineer who worked on the Apollo space missions, so my assumption is that he's a sane, normal guy. I don't like that he brings a weapon when meeting me in a public place — what kind of person does that? — but he's my first interviewee for the project, so I suppose I can allow myself a little bit of trepidation. I can allow myself to worry that I may be embarking on a journey through an America I don't actually trust.

###

TOM: I watched the inauguration today and I'll tell you, I'm thrilled. Well, I'm thrilled except for one thing: I think the actions of the left are deplorable. They're out there saying they're protesting. But they're not protesting, they're rioting. They're breaking windows. They set a limo on fire — a new Cadillac limousine, probably costs a hundred thousand — set it on fire. I saw one guy with a hammer actually going along cracking any large window he could find: bang, bang, bang. That's not a protest. That's vandalism.

Some people are already saying the election was illegitimate. In what way?! In what way could Trump be ineligible? He was elected by the Electoral College. If you discount California, he actually won the popular vote. I'm a native Californian, but I hate it there. I left because I couldn't stand the liberal bullshit.

They have really restrictive gun laws in California, and the place is a joke. Listen to this: of all the politicians that refused to go to the inauguration today, and last I saw there were forty-eight of them, 25% were from California. A full 25% were from California! I was born and raised in Long Beach. I was there thirty-four years, but California today is turning into a third world country.

See, I'm a believer in the Constitution. I'm a major fan of Thomas Jefferson. He had some brilliant things to say. He was one of the greatest minds in the history of this country. Trump, to me, represents that train of thought, that kind of action. Obama was a joke. He was only interested in what would benefit him, not the people. If he were concerned about the people, he wouldn't have divided the country so deeply. The division today is worse than it was during Vietnam. I'm seventy-five years old; I remember.

Trump's style is similar to Jefferson's. One of the quotes that has always stuck with me is, "Government has no business being in business." That's an extremely powerful statement. In other words, you can monitor the rights of the people and make sure that everything's fair, but you don't have any business telling me how to run my business. Unless I'm doing something illegal, back off.

Sorry if I seem too passionate. I just really believe Trump represents the interests of the common man. We've had enough of the elites running the country.

I worked on the Apollo program, putting a man on the moon. I was an engineer for forty years. In 1967, I said to bunch of guys, "Our government is really getting corrupt." I thought those guys were going to kill me. They said I was an anti-American, that I was just a crazy person. I was working on a very American mission, so you might assume everybody was patriotic. But they weren't true patriots. They just blindly agreed with everything the establishment said. Not me. See, that job paid good. This is 1967 and we're making five bucks an hour. Do you know what the average was then? You were well-to-do if you were making $10,000 a year, and we were making more than that. So, the Apollo missions drew a lot of weirdos because of the money you could make. Engineers tend to be a little weird anyway, but there were more weirdos on Apollo than most projects I worked on.

Aerospace is not unlike Congress. In both, if you've been in twenty-five years, you don't actually have twenty-five years of experience. I say you have one year of experience twenty-five different times. Just because you've done something for twenty-five years doesn't mean you're doing it right. When I first got hired at NASA, I had already had a lot of other jobs. They said, "You've been jumping around a lot; you don't know what you're talking about." I said, "No, I probably know more than you *because* I have been all around and I've seen lots of different operations. So I know how other guys do things and *you're* doing it all wrong. And I can show you why." I wasn't real popular, but I didn't care.

I was with the Apollo missions until '69 when we landed on the moon, but working there didn't really feel like a big deal at the time. It was just a great paying job. Do you remember the way the Apollo was built, with a curve on the bottom of the command module? That bottom portion was the heat shield and there was equipment mounted in there. The problem: there was not a single flat surface on the entire bottom of that capsule. So how do you measure it? Well, we came up with an economical method using axonometric design. Everything was done in a 3D perspective. It was highly accurate *and* cost-effective. I was proud of that.

My dad was also there during Apollo, and he continued on through the shuttle. I left to go work on the VC10, so I understand what Trump is saying about Boeing contracts being too expensive. He's right, there are zillions of dollars going to waste in aerospace. For example, I worked on a project one time and I needed a bearing, just a simple ball bearing. I was building the prototype, so I ran down to the bearing store down the street and I said, "This is what I need. And I need it to be able to withstand this certain lateral pressure." I got it there for a dollar and fifty cents.

I included that ball bearing in the program and they said, "You have to do a source-controlled search." The paperwork that went with it took me a month to complete! All for a little tiny bearing that was a dollar and fifty cents. They paid out the nose for it; wound up costing like seven or eight hundred dollars per bearing, something I thought was outrageous. Trump says he's going eliminate regulations like that, and that's going to save America money.

Since way back in my Apollo years, I've been saying, "Let's bring businessmen into Washington. We've got to get rid of the politicians." Politicians don't care about anything except getting elected. There's only been two or three businessmen in the Oval Office in all our history; we need more. We need people who aren't just worrying about re-election.

I think the country is starting to accept Trump already. He created jobs before he even got into office. The man: he's brash, he says what's on his mind. And that's what I love about him the most. When he says we can do something, I believe him. He's not going to bullshit anybody. A lot of people say, "Oh, he lies." No, he doesn't lie! Trump actually operates a lot like I do. Somebody asks you a question, you shoot from the hip and clean it up later. Somebody asks you a question, you feel compelled to answer it; you don't want to sound like an idiot and say, "I don't know." So, you say something that makes reasonable sense and you will figure out the details later. I've done that plenty of times.

You know, when I heard Trump announce his candidacy, I said, "Bullshit. You are not going to do it." But then he got into the debate and I thought, "Wait a minute, this guy is serious." I knew it was not a publicity stunt from that point on. And in that debate, he tore them all apart! The man knows how to work an audience. He manipulated the media. He got three times the coverage Hillary did and didn't have to spend a dime. You've got to give him points for that.

I'll tell you another thing. I heard several people today talking about how they're concerned about Trump being a bully from his position. Well, another president that was phenomenal to me was Theodore Roosevelt. What is he most famous for? A bully pulpit. Trump's no different, but in Roosevelt's day it was all right to do that and now it isn't. Political correctness is the destruction of this country. Actually, I think Trump's stand on political correctness got me before any of his business stuff did.

That "grab them by the pussy" stuff was disgusting and he should never have said it, but he said it in confidence when he didn't realize someone was recording him. I've sure said things that I hope never get out publicly. Nobody's ever the same in public as they are behind closed doors. People say things like, "Oh, I'm not a racist." Well they can say that until they get into the voting booth, but it's what they do in there that's the real measure. There have been racist candidates, but Trump's not one of them. He's just says things that people are actually thinking.

I think Trump is an honest man. He's not perfect, but the last perfect man was hung on a cross 2000 years ago. I'm not putting Trump in that category. He's not perfect, and nobody else is. We all make mistakes, we all say things that we regret as time goes by. But let's face it, the man has made billions of dollars and you don't do that by being an idiot. It just doesn't happen.

I've seen people say we have to support Black people, but when nobody is listening or watching, they don't have anything nice to say about Black people! I call them closet racists. They don't publicly announce their racism. So, based on that, I think there are a lot of people who will tell you one thing and do something else when they get behind closed doors. I don't appreciate those kind of people, so I think Trump's fight against political correctness is great. Let's just say what we mean. Let's just say it outright. Political correctness stifles intelligent debate.

I grew up with no political correctness. We used to have what we'd call chop sessions. We would stand around and insult one another for hours and nobody got pissed off, nobody went home to mom, nobody started crying. We were all Don Rickles back in those days! I believe if I can be attacked for my position, it thickens my skin. These chop sessions built character for me when I was growing up.

We've got kids today in colleges that get so offended they have to have time off; they have to have safe spaces. There's crying and counseling sessions, and that's all ridiculous. People their age were fighting the Germans on Normandy! You didn't see them whining and crying about political correctness on Normandy. The liberal mindset goes way too far on college campuses.

In my generation, you got out of high school and you knew that you had between now and the age of twenty-six to be in the military no matter what. I watched this movie, *The Fighting Coast Guard*, and it inspired me to join the reserves. I did not want to get caught in the Army sleeping in mud holes and doing long marches. I like boats, so the Coast Guard was it for me.

Six months active duty, eight years reserve, and it was done. I did sweat it a little bit during the Cuban Missile Crisis because they could have recalled us. I would have been so pissed if that happened! But we made it through that issue with Russia, and we're going to make it through the current one, too.

Did Russia hack the election? I can't speak authoritatively on it, but I think it's probably all bullshit. I spent a lot of years with computers and CAD. I learned, inside and out, how to build computers. I used to be able to make them sing and dance. So, first of all, you can't tell who's been hacking you if you get hacked. And I'm not the only one who thinks that. McAfee thinks the same thing. The guy who builds McAfee Security says, "There's no way to know who did the election hacking."

And if Trump did have some kind of communication with Russia, who cares? I'm a great believer in keeping your friends close and your enemies closer. The morons in Congress think he's crazy, but I don't care what they think. We've got people there who've been in forty years and still haven't proven anything substantial to me.

I don't prefer to vote Republican. I'm really a Libertarian. I'm *registered* as a Republican because that's really the only way my vote can count, and I always want to make sure I vote in committed Second Amendment supporters; gun control is a real serious issue for me. I've been a member of the NRA since 1965. If you're opposed to guns, I'm not in favor of you at all; that's just the bottom line. The Second Amendment exists to protect the First Amendment. We are the only civilized country in the world where the citizens are armed. When Yamamoto attacked Pearl Harbor, they asked, "Why didn't you go into the mainland?" It was because behind every blade of grass would be an American with a gun, and that's powerful. The rest of the world knows we've got guns, and that will make them think twice before they try to invade us. A lot of people speak about their own individual protection, but I'm speaking of national protection.

I came to Nevada because we have permission to carry over here. I'm carrying right now. Here in this hotel, I'm carrying my gun because you never know when something is going to go down. You can't see my gun, though, can you? That's the point. In California, you're not allowed to carry like this, which is just more stamping down on my rights.

I have an old friend who used to be a Democrat. We've known one another since kindergarten and he still lives in California. He *loves* to debate. I tell him, "Art, you are without a doubt the biggest debater I have ever seen in my life. If it's raining outside and I tell you it's raining, you argue with me about it." One day I called him and said, "Art, we got your man for the presidency: Trump." He didn't agree, but I kept working on him until he finally became a supporter. I won that debate. He kept saying, "God, I hope you're right about this guy. You were wrong when you said Obama wouldn't get a second term."

The minute Trump won, I called him and said, "Okay, you son of a bitch, we won!" We laughed about that. It was late at night, but I didn't care. We were so happy.

I must say, I really like Trump's family. He does right by them. I've got family of my own, and it's a struggle with some of them. But I try. I try to do right by them, too.

I have a son who lives here in Vegas and has his own business doing custom cabinets. My daughter lives in Oregon, and that relationship is the one that's a little strained. She's gay, unfortunately. It's not a parent's favorite thing to find out your kid is gay, especially your daughter, because she's the one that would bear any future kids. My son has two boys, so that offset it a bit. She's up in Oregon now and she's really been influenced by that Northwest crowd.

On that political correctness thing, I guess I really do edit what I say around my daughter because I don't want her to get offended. I try to be more politically correct in front of her because I don't want to upset her. My daughter and I used to be extremely close, until I got my divorce and my ex-wife tried to turn her against me. It just all broke down and I lost the relationship I had with her. So I'm careful now. I don't want to destroy our relationship any more than it already has been, but I wish I could just say what's really on my mind like Trump does.

My daughter and I never talk politics because I know she's not going to believe me, and I don't want to listen to her. I suppose I could be mean and just tell her what I think, but she's my daughter so

I use political correctness just a little bit. I use it when there's an advantage to it.

I used to have my own real estate business. Talking about political correctness, there I used it all the time because you have to appease your clients. I just wish that wasn't the case. I was pretty successful, but what ruined my business was Jimmy Carter. He came in and interest rates went to 24%. How do you sell a house to someone and charge him 24% interest on a loan? I couldn't do it, and I didn't do it. Democratic leadership has never been good for our finances.

I was an underwriter for a mortgage company, and I saw this meltdown coming. This company that I worked for was one of the companies that would take these substandard loans, package them, and sell them as class A bonds. That's the start of housing crisis right there. It was still the early 90s, but I was right in the thick of it. I saw what was going on, and I went to my boss and said, "We shouldn't be giving these loans to people. Here's a lady who you want me to approve: she makes $400 a month, has two kids, and her new payment is going to be $275 a month. You want me to approve that? We're going to buy that house back in a year!" My boss said, "That's okay, we won't be holding the mortgage by then." That was their attitude, so I left. I told them, "You guys should be arrested for this." When I saw *The Big Short*, I told people, "I lived that. That was like my life story. Holy shit."

Speaking of shit, do you know how they go to bathroom in space? Well, I helped figure it out. Backing up a bit, when the Mercury went up to orbit, they kept having these electrical shocks and nobody could figure what was going on. When I got into the program, I discovered the reason: it was urine. Urine was floating around these capsules because they hadn't figured out how to properly contain it. If you try to suck liquid through holes in weightlessness, it doesn't go anywhere. The air just comes around it and it starts floating everywhere. We fixed that on Apollo, and even designed a new toilet. It looked like one of those three-pound coffee cans. They'd sit on this can, but the laws of physics apply in weightlessness: for every action there's a reaction! When they'd sit on the toilet and poop, it would go down and then float right back up! It would rest against your ass. So we also invented a kind of toilet paper contraption. It was kind of like a glove. It would slip on your hand and had a little handle on the top so you could flip it and wipe with both sides. Then everything went into this baggie that was attached, and you could squeeze the baggie around the toilet and tie it all off. You also had to have this capsule inside the bag to neutralize the gases. You would squeeze it and work it until it turned gray; the color meant it was all neutralized. If you didn't do that, the gasses in the poop bag would build up and explode. Boom!

America was on the verge of blowing up just like that bag of poop on the Apollo. Thank God we have Trump to neutralize us.

CHAPTER TWO
The Hispanic Pro-Lifer

January 28th, 2017
Reno, Nevada

Back in Las Vegas, Tom's articulation of support for President Trump represented exactly what I was hoping to find: an intelligent, educated conservative with whom I disagree. Moving out of liberal California so that he could be freer with his guns? That's a lifestyle that I don't understand. An aerospace engineer who stands behind a president who doubts established environmental science? That's a man I don't understand. Yet.

Moving a few hours north to Reno, I'm about to encounter another surprise: a Hispanic woman who supports – vehemently supports – building an expansive border wall. That feels like a contradiction, and it's something I'll need explained. Melissa is nervous to meet me. We've scheduled our conversation for 10:30 p.m., so she brings a male friend for her own sense of security. Of course I understand Melissa wanting to feel safe, but she's a self-described "proud gun owner" and that makes me wonder if I'm the one who should be extra careful.

We struggle to find an appropriately quiet location outside these darker, stickier casinos of Nevada's secondary gambling center. Reno has all the desperation of Vegas, but doesn't hide it as well. The slot machines are still ringing in Harrah's, but every bar and restaurant we pass on the block is closed. 10:30 p.m. is late for Reno. A movie theatre lobby sits across the street and we settle there. I offer them popcorn.

###

MELISSA: I was born in Mexico, and that's obviously significant right now in the Trump story. I come from a large Catholic family and I am one of nine. My mother's Filipino, my dad's Mexican. My dad was in the Navy when they met. My parents got pregnant, and I was born in Mexico.

The thing is, my dad was very strict. That's a thing with big Catholic families, of course, they're strict! My dad was always working several jobs, and he was raised in a strict family, too. It's a cultural thing. The bottom line is that my dad ran our household. He brought us to the States when I was really little, so I guess most of my growing up was in Los Angeles. I got married there, had four kids of my own, then moved here to Reno for my husband's business. Ex-husband. He's an environmental biologist and works with the gold mines.

I really didn't want to move to Reno at all. I hated it. I didn't even know where it was; I just figured it was the wild, wild west and I'd live in a trailer or something. It was much scarier than LA, where I feel like I lived on the beach.

Reno's evolved since then, thank God. It's gotten a lot better, and there's finally a lot of diversity. When I first moved here, it was just really white. My ex-husband is a German-American white guy, and with me being Hispanic, people would ask him, "Is that the nanny?"

My upbringing ties right in to my early support of President Trump. I'm still Catholic, and pro-life candidates are very important to me. Trump's not perfect, but he has a lot of the things that I was looking for. For example, one of my core beliefs is that you should work hard for what you have; nothing should be given to you for free. My parents didn't come to the United States for a handout, they came to work and live the American Dream. They struggled for their house, their white picket fence. Trump speaks to that kind of work ethic.

All of my brothers and sisters worked at a very young age. I had a paper route when I was eight. Eight years old! That was tough. Even before school, every day in the second grade, I was delivering papers. And when I wanted to quit, my father never let me. "No, you signed up. You knew what you were getting yourself into. You're not giving up." I've done the same thing with my kids. Trump, too. You don't see his kids making headlines like the Kardashians. Every

Kardashian! The Kardashians are not in a smart type of environment like the Trump family. There's no real work ethic there.

I mean, the freebies these Democrats want to give away! I don't know what a freebie is because I've never had one. A lot of the entitlements that other candidates were pushing for, whether it's a free cell phone, free housing... I don't know what that is because I've always worked. If I didn't have enough, I'd have to work two jobs and go to school at night and that's pretty much it. I can't believe all the stuff Democrats just want to give away.[3]

I would have voted the Republican ticket no matter what, but one of the things that is appealing about President Trump is that he doesn't need the job. He's very well off. He's just choosing to serve the country.

Then there's this agenda that he has: "I want our borders protected." Being Mexican, I know there are a lot of Hispanics who also want the border closed. Yes, my parents came here, but they had to pay attorneys and go through the legal system. Coming here to America, and it doesn't matter what country you're from, there's a process. Currently, that process is out of control. Whether they're digging their way underground or hopping fences, it's out of control. I admit that I don't understand that struggle, but at the same time it is just not fair for the people that are waiting in line to get in. We should put up the wall so it's fair to those that play by the rules, like my parents.

People say to me, "You're Mexican, why would you vote for Trump?!" And I get that. I get that it's a debate. I went to a Trump rally in Lake Tahoe. How many Hispanics or Asians – Filipino like me – do you think were there? Yes, I was the only one! I was like, "Seriously, this can't be." There are many, many Hispanic supporters of Trump; I've talked to them! Maybe they just didn't go to the rallies.

Trump and I have the same beliefs, the same upbringing. I mean, he's a zillionaire and I'm not. But the work ethic, and the desire for security. We have a lot of bad people that want to hurt us; you can see it around you. And I want my family, I want my kids, to be secure. That's one of the other reasons I voted for him. For security purposes.

---

[3] There were no candidates pushing to give away free cell phones or free housing. The Lifeline program has been offering payment assistance for landlines since 1996, but it's worth noting that the addition of cell phones to the program happened first in Tennessee during the last months of the Bush Administration.

Do we even know what vetting process was there before Trump came in? I don't know what there was before. We really didn't know who these people were, or if they had documents, or how they were getting in.[4] And this travel ban proposal is just a holding pattern, right? Until they figure out what's going to work best for our country, we have it in place. Then we fix it up. But for now, I say we should be strict and keep them out. Keep anybody out that's going to be in a terror group.

I'm also a family-oriented person; I love my kids and I don't want them to inherit any more taxes than they already have. We all pay our taxes, but I don't want to leave them a zillion dollars in debt either. Trump will be the most responsible with our taxes and America's budget.

My kids are all millennials and have their own opinions. They disagree with me, but we do discuss things and have some debate. I just can't see things from their point of view. I may be a little more old-school, but I also think they don't always have all the facts. I guess I may not have all the facts either, but I can explain to them how I came to be a conservative. It goes all the way back to their Grandpa Nicholas.

My dad, their Grandpa Nicholas, came to America in laced up bootstraps. "You work hard for what you have." That's just the mentality he had. My dad was a strong man. My mother didn't work. She raised all of us, and we all helped raise each other. The older ones took care of the younger ones, and even in the winter – because it was Los Angeles – I was working. After the paper route, I sold oranges. Bags and bags of oranges. My parents had this friend who would go to the orchards and get a whole truckload of oranges. On the weekends, my father and I would bag them up and go door-to-door selling them. Who does that?! Hard workers, that's who. When I wanted better school clothes, I had to earn that money. That's my version of conservatism.

I guess I should clarify that the actual *most* important issue for me is having a candidate that is pro-life. There are always other considerations, but I'm Catholic for life. It was hard to choose Trump at first, because I know he's wavered on the issue. But when I hear Trump speak now, I believe him. I believe he is pro-life in his heart.

---

[4] We did in fact know who these people are, if they had documents, and how they were getting in. Procedures are outlined in the Visa section of the U.S. State Department's website.

Politicians are going to lie through their teeth, regardless. They really are. Doesn't matter what party they're with, they're going to lie and feed you nonsense just to get the vote. Knowing that, Trump stood out as someone more truthful. He talks about wanting to keep our country safe, and I believe his passion. We've had so many bad things in our nation, and Trump spoke to that. That homegrown terror, the Boston Marathon, the lone wolves. There are bad people here and Trump is going to take action. A couple of days in, he's already doing it.

My father raised the women in our family to be tough. No one will ever tell us we can't do something. We hold our own, and we are independent. Trump's wife is that kind of woman. She's beautiful, but she's also her own strong person. She's a businesswoman. She's very intelligent, she speaks five languages, she's a mother. She's a mom and she stays home with the child, and she just happens to be gorgeous. That's a woman to admire. Strong, like me.

And we need to be strong here in Reno. It still has that frontier feeling, so there are definitely more guns here. I'm for the Second Amendment. I think you need to protect yourself, and I do. I have my own handgun, and so do my sons. We go to shooting ranges together; I feel shooting with them is important.

There's a significant difference between Republicans and Democrats with how they treat the Second Amendment. There is never much talking on the Democratic side about protecting those rights at all. From Bernie or Hillary, I didn't hear much of it. And this is something that Trump is very strong on; he definitely speaks about protecting our rights. He's very vocal about it. Where other candidates were wanting to do away with the Second Amendment, Trump was making his stance clear.[5] We need our gun rights, and they're in the Constitution. It's important for everybody to have those rights... except Chicago!

Just kidding. Though I do think Chicago is where the majority of the weapons are. The illegal ones, anyway.

Trump is making us secure and, even if we don't use it, our military has to be the best. We're being laughed at around the world for being sissies, and strengthening our military is going to fix that. Whether it's actually killing bad guys, or just showing the world our capability, we need that real strength. We need to say, "Hey, we are

---

[5] No candidates wanted to do away with the Second Amendment.

number one. We're not number two. We're not taking anybody's crap."

What is exciting to me today is that Trump is actually making a difference right now. Already! It's not all talk; he's actually doing it. I don't know if the wall thing is going to happen, but he's trying. Even with the controversy, he's doing it! We're going to keep the bad people out. Sorry, you're not going to land at JFK today. You're not leaving Egypt today. You're not going into New York City until we get a vetting process that works for everybody. Trump is making that happen today, in his first week on the job.

CHAPTER THREE
The Bank Robber

January 31st, 2017
Los Angeles, California

I'm moving out to the West Coast now. Opinions of California differ with folks in the last two chapters. Tom from Las Vegas views the Sunshine State as a liberal cesspool, whereas Melissa from Reno was reluctant to leave her home there. I suppose that doesn't surprise me much about Melissa. She's contradictory, isn't she? She prides herself on her work ethic and is devoted to Trump's representation of the same. Melissa doesn't believe, as I do, that Trump was handed an easy life, a Golden Ticket. Melissa doesn't believe, as I do, that it's Hillary Clinton who had the work ethic to study, struggle, build relationships, and dedicate thousands of days to public service. How does Melissa relate more to a man who prides himself, as he says in The Art of the Deal, *on playing it "very loose" in the office, without a briefcase, without deep research, without much structure, and who likes to "come to work each day and just see what develops." I cannot draw a correlation between Melissa's strict, work-centered upbringing and Trump's off-the-cuff business style. Melissa could be convincing herself that Trump is like her, when actually her most valued political issue is much simpler: she will vote for the pro-life candidate, period. By that standard, no Democrat could even be considered. To my ears, Melissa's Catholic views trump any of her other perspectives.*

Here in downtown LA, I'm feeling fancy again like I felt in Vegas. The Millennium Biltmore is grand, elegant, and adorned with the art deco trimmings that keep this part of the city classic. I've invited Robert to meet me here because the location is partway between his graveyard janitorial shift and his room at the halfway house. Robert, you see, is a bank robber. Well, a recovering bank robber. I've never met a bank robber before, recovering or otherwise, and I'm a tad giddy for the adventure.

###

ROBERT: You can quote anything I got to say. First off, know that I've always been a Democrat supporter, but this is the first election I've ever voted in. See, I've done about thirty-four years in federal prison for bank robbery. But even when locked up, I always pulled for the Democrats because I believed they were going to bring back good times. They never deliver on none of their promises, though. I finally gave up on them a few years ago.

Boston puts out a lot of bank robbers, most of them from the Charlestown neighborhood. I'm an exception, being from over in Quincy, but I got the bug from my father. Robbery's hereditary, I think, though my dad was just a cat burglar.

When I got out of the feds and was finally able to vote, the choice was kind of obvious. I certainly wasn't going with Killary – that's what I call Clinton; she is an evil person – because she's taken so much money.[6] She got $25 million from the Saudis who donated to her Clinton Foundation. The Saudis sponsor terrorism! They're against women's rights. What are they doing giving $25 million to a woman's charity? China, same way.

Then the worst one of them all is this leftist dude, George Soros. He gave Killary so much money to maintain control over her, but this guy is a racist. Him and his father, when they were in the concentration camps, were both Nazi collaborators.[7] If you collaborated with Nazis, I figure, they you are the worst of the worst. He's got all this money and he just runs around screwing up shit: he collapsed the Ukraine, he's funding Black Lives Matter, he's funding the protesters.[8]

Trump just isn't a politician at all. I love that. No politician says some of the crazy stuff that he says. He's speaks his mind, whereas other politicians just don't. They're going to promise you everything and then not deliver nothing. Trump may very well take us

---

[6] Robert-the-bank-robber doesn't seem to notice the irony in mentioning Hillary has "taken so much money." I happen to think this is hilarious.

[7] No, they weren't. This accusation stems from a strangely confrontational *60 Minutes* interview in 1998. Neither Soros nor his father were, in any way, Nazi collaborators.

[8] None of these things are precisely accurate, but the truthful parts of them are what I really dig about George Soros.

down to the road of ruin, but at least we'll always know what he's thinking.

Killary was going to bring over 60,000 Syrians just because there would have been 60,000 new votes for the Democratic Party. Yes, that's the reason for open border policies, and it's exactly what Soros wants, too. Soros wants to open borders so he can move his war machines around and make billions and billions of dollars on top of the billions and billions that he already has. You see what I mean?

We can't have an open border. Take a walk around where I live in MacArthur Park. People are sleeping in the middle of the sidewalk there, living in the alley. We got a homeless problem that is real, real bad, but nobody wants to talk about it. With this homeless problem, you want to bring *more* people over here? Everybody comes up here thinking that there's going to be great opportunities, and there's not. They're going to wind up in the street, because where else are they going to stay? There would be Syrians all over the place, and we just don't have room for them. We don't even have room for our own.

Even though we have to have closed borders, I view Mexico differently than the other countries Trump wants to close off. In Mexico, they're basically good people. (I've only known the gang members, but I've got along great with them all.) We should just let them come up. Let them come when they have a place to stay and have a job, maybe when they have a sponsor.

As far as those Muslim countries that are steeped in terrorism? No, we can't have them. Mexico has proven to be a friend, but the radical Islamists are not good. I'm not going to say "Muslims," because I know a lot of Muslims that are good. But if the radical Islamist ones was to get over here, they would have a field day! And the cops would be handcuffed because they can't racially profile. The only way to *find* them is to racially profile! Like the Tsarnaev bombers that blew up the Boston Marathon; they were on the watch list, but police don't want to be seen as racist by checking them out. The terrorists know that. They'll use anything they can – psychological, everything – to destroy us. Radical Islamist terrorists are smart. Trump knows this, and he's fighting it.

But I have to admit, man, Trump's already done a couple of things that I don't agree with. Like his choice for Secretary of State? He put a businessman in there, but for Secretary of State you need a politician. You need a *career* politician in there. Then Trump poses a ban on the radical terrorist countries, but he doesn't include Saudi

Arabia because he's got Trump Tower there.[9] Yeah, that's wrong. If you're going to ban terrorist countries, then ban *all* terrorist countries. Saudi Arabia won't take no refugees because they say it's a threat to national security, but Saudi Arabia *sponsors* the terrorist stuff. I wish Trump could see that; I wish any politician could see that.

I made the transition from thinking, "I support the Democratic Party," to, "The Democrats aren't actually doing anything for me." Obama ruined it. He gave Iran their nukes back and billions of dollars, and the very next day they're out on the streets chanting, "Death to America." That's arming the enemy there.[10]

We all thought Obama was going to do good but he had everybody tricked, especially when he got Osama bin Laden. That capture was conveniently right around the same time as the Iran deal.[11] I think that they knew all along where he was. I really thought Obama would just even things out, bring back good times and all that. But that's just like the Democratic Party, they promise and then never deliver. They know if they dangle that "hope" stick out there to you, you're going to keep on voting for them.

Obama went over to Japan and apologized for Hiroshima.[12] How about Japan apologizing for all of their atrocities? Because they did a lot. Those nuclear bombs actually saved a whole lot of lives because they ended the war.

The job thing is really, really rough for guys like me. I got real lucky when I got a job, but most people I know aren't as privileged. I got my job through the halfway house. Most jobs do background checks, and I'll never pass those, so I have to keep this one I have. I'm doing good now, and I'm going to stay that way.

Housing in California is difficult for guys like me because of the state probation officers; they come crashing in doors all hours at night wearing the Kevlar body armor. Landlords know that, so it's hard to get them to rent us a room. I set one up recently, but when I got there the guy says, "Hey, I really want you here, but my wife says we can't because you're on probation. She don't want nobody crashing through the doors." The feds don't do that, only the state officers. Losing that room set me off; I came this close to going back

---

[9] In fairness, there is actually no Trump Tower in Saudi Arabia. (Yet?)

[10] It is not true that Iran received billions and got their nukes back. The nuanced truth is that sanctions were lifted, enabling Iran to finally access billions of its own money in exchange for *not* building nuclear weapons.

[11] Actually, four years separated these two events.

[12] This is getting tiring, but I'll continue. No, Obama decidedly did not apologize for the U.S. dropping a bomb on Hiroshima. He offered condolences only.

on a crime spree again. I give credit to Volunteers of America and Chrysalis; they helped out a lot. Chrysalis is down on South Main and they taught me how to do a resume. The Volunteers helped me get a new room here downtown; a place in MacArthur Park in the sober living house.

Recovering here on the outside has been the hardest thing I've ever done. See, my whole life was geared towards crime. I've done everything except for murder, rape, and kidnapping. This last time out, I robbed seventeen banks in four months. I've been in the worst prisons because I kept trying to escape, crawling through a swamp and all that. I've been a criminal my whole life. You're born with it, like I said before. It's a genetic thing. My father got twelve-and-a-half years when I was just a year old. He was breaking into houses when people were sleeping. I could never do that. I'm bold, but I could never do that.

As long as I could read, I remember being ready for a life of crime. I've had it where I was so poor, I ate an onion for breakfast before school. The teacher sent me back because I stunk. I guess I had a lot of resentment built up, too. I started off stealing cars, then breaking into houses, and then robberies. Then I went to the banks. Next in line was going to be armored cars – that was always my goal back then – but I got caught first. When I got out the first time and started trying to go straight, the guilt over my past got built up more and more. Ghosts come out every night. I'm seeing a shrink now; I know I have depression.

Voting for the first time... man, that was strange. I actually got a say in the process now. Unbelievable. I go in there and I put down as party: Republican. I'm not *really* that. I don't like the Bushs. George W. and Obama are like the daddies of ISIS. Both were contributors to that. And there wasn't no weapons of mass destruction.

Voting for the first time is just another step closer to legitimacy for me. The next one is getting off of probation, and I've already told my PO exactly what I'm going to do that day: I'm going to sit across from the federal courthouse, roll a big ol' joint, and I'm going to smoke it while broadcasting on Facebook live. That'll feel like freedom.

We're still the greatest country in the world, but it's taking a turn for the worse. All of a sudden, we've got racial problems where we never had them since the seventies. It's getting bad out there. I'm always going to survive, but a lot of people are not. Hopefully, Trump does good. I've got misgivings this week about him, but I would have voted for anybody if it was against Killary. She's just evil as hell. She left them hanging in Benghazi.

Everybody keeps on saying that we're a nation of immigrants. Yes, but our ancestors weren't running around blowing up everybody just because of their religious beliefs. It's *those* immigrants we need to be careful of. But like I said, I feel differently about Mexico. A lot of Mexicans are really honorable. Like the Mexican gangs. You got the 18th Streeters. You got the Sureños. You got the Mexican Mafia. You got the Kaisers. Those are the biggest and most honorable federal gangs. (Actually, let me leave out the Kaisers. They're like little cockroaches; they can't be trusted.) Once these guys give you their word, they're going to hold it. As a whole, the gangs are more of an honorable society than a lot of countries. They've just got their bartering fees. So, they're all good guys, but we still can't actually have an open border because it's ISIS that would come through there. I've seen a YouTube video of a dude wearing robes and carrying a large bottle rocket; he just walks right over the border. So we have to close our southern border to keep the terrorists out, not the Mexicans. Trump has the right idea, just the wrong reason.

CHAPTER FOUR
The Spa Owner

February 1st, 2017
Beverly Hills, California

Robert, who has experienced substantively little life outside the walls of a prison, had quite a different take on immigration than I'm used to. He spoke with so much concern about our border to the south, but not because of the "really honorable" Mexicans that might want to come across. He just fears the border is an open roadway for terrorists to sneak into our midst. I can't get behind that logic, but it is a new perspective. More empathetically, I see his point about the homeless in downtown Los Angeles. Why increase our legal immigration when we haven't yet found a way to house thousands and thousands of Americans? The comparison is not so simple, of course, but it is a point of view that means something more coming from this ex-con who teases the edge of homelessness himself on a daily basis. Has this changed any of my traditionally liberal opinions and support of Obama's immigration policies? No. Robert's argument isn't strong enough for me. But I sympathize. I sympathize with a bank robber.

It's a cool evening here in Hollywood. Grauman's Chinese Theatre is across the street when Liza pulls over to pick me up on the star-embedded sidewalk. She's driven over from Beverly Hills to meet me, facing an onslaught of rush hour on the Sunset Strip. Liza has told me already how enamored she is with Donald Trump, and she's promised to share her story of meeting him and the emotional flush that face-to-face provided. There is a sparkle in her voice as she greets me now, her car warm and humming. We're going to drive Hollywood Boulevard while talking. People work out of their cars all the time here in Los Angeles, right?

LIZA: We're opening a spa and naming it after the city of Lourdes, the pilgrimage city. The spa is in Cougar Hills, which is like the new up and coming city in the Valley. I owned a spa for twelve years in Beverly Hills, but then wanted to change it up. I've been looking at the landscape for a while and trying to pick the right area, the right people, and just weave it all together.

I've always been in the industry. I'm an esthetician, but also an educator and I've always been on outside sales and corporate sales. I started with literally just $30,000 in my personal savings account and took a risk buying out a spa from a guy I met at a trade show. I am a strong believer in risk-taking and just seizing the opportunity. That's probably part of why I fell in love with Donald Trump in the eighties when he was promoting *The Art of the Deal*. He inspired me, just like Tony Robbins and all the great motivational speakers.

I have a very strong intuition about people that was developed by working around every possible demographic while pounding the pavement in sales. I came from Texas and dealt with male chauvinists, Texas cowboys. I've worked in the corporate setting where, back in the old days, women couldn't even wear pants and dangly earrings. Nowadays, women are leading *Fortune 500* companies, but I always believe in working for it. Everything is earned. I get irritated looking at how lazy people are, and people who call themselves victims. Everybody's got a story. I didn't come from a very wealthy family; mine was blue collar and everybody in my family worked. We were all Democrats growing up, but when I moved out to California three decades ago, I noticed a huge discrepancy with people's lifestyles and their attitude of entitlement. I became independent as a voter, and eventually pretty conservative. I just didn't agree with all of the liberal craziness.

Donald Trump was kind of hinting at running years ago. I thought, "This guy is going to go. He's like a horse waiting for the bell to ring." He's very strategic, and he waits. He's very patient, but he's always got a plan. It was no surprise to me when he finally announced.

I met Donald Trump when I got invited to an underground Hollywood group called *Friends of Abe*. It's an elite political group founded by Gary Sinise. Very hush-hush. You'd be surprised how many Republicans or Conservatives there are in Hollywood; they just don't voice their opinion very loudly. So, I was invited by this group to hear Trump speak, and as soon as he walked in... oh, the imagery, the pageantry! He walks in and he's like a tower! He's surrounded by men that are even a foot taller than he is, and it's just so intimidating. I thought, "Oh my God, this guy has got it going on." I shook his hand, and he was very gracious. That brash demeanor we see on television? It's all for show.

This man knows how to work the media like no other person. He rode it all the way, always the headliner. No matter what bit of news was going on, he would provoke it. And that's what you do. If you're in sales, you've got to rattle somebody's cage. And sometimes you go for shock value. That's one thing I've learned: it may seem inappropriate at the time but, at the end of the day, who gets the deal? Trump closes, and that's the difference.

My ex-husband was also a ball-buster businessman. Just being privy to a lot of his meetings – and I'm talking about $70 million deals – they're hardcore, and they sound brash. When I see Donald Trump, I understand that's his nature. It's all for shock value, because that's what gets people rattled. The difference with Trump maybe is that he puts his money where his mouth is; if he says he's going to do it, he does it. That's what's really surprising to a lot of people, he actually follows through with what he says.

Everybody votes from their own personal experience. I don't judge people based on how they vote, because everybody comes from a particular story. If somebody believes in Bernie Sanders, that's great. It's a free country. But for me, I've always believed in pulling yourself up by your own bootstraps. Nobody's ever given me a handout. Trump represents that independence.

I love sales because it's strategy. It's adrenaline rush. It's calculation. It's opportunity. When the odds are not in your favor, that's when you have to affect change. And the only way you're going to affect change in a big way is through government. That's why it frustrates me that people just don't care. They just pay! They pay more hiked taxes, and they sign their checks over to Washington. I'm not like that.

I'm for smaller government because when I opened up my spa in Beverly Hills, I had no idea that I would be the least paid in my company. All my employees made more money than me. I was busting my ass seven days a week to put together a small business, employ people, pay them more, give them more... but at the end of the day, I was making less because I was double taxed. I'm a contractor, so I would perform services; I didn't realize that you pay tax on gross profit for your business, but as a contractor you pay taxes again. Then on top of that, it's so over-regulated. Your massage parlor license, your aesthetician's license, your cosmetology license... all those are taxes. I had to check on where my employees lived, because you need a special license just to work in Beverly Hills. A massage therapist couldn't just take a license for California. He had to have $400 for West Hollywood, $300 for Beverly Hills, $200 for Santa Monica. All those accumulate. That poor little independent contractor who is a massage therapist is not making any money when his schooling was thousands of dollars. At the end of the day, how do you get ahead? You don't. You have people living in multiple roommate situations when they're in their forties and fifties. You have people renting rooms in their homes because they have to pay the bills. That is not normal. Where I came from in Texas – where it's low state taxes, low capital gains taxes, low gasoline taxes – you can live like a king. But with huge governments, everybody's got a hand in your pocket.[13]

Of course, you also have the crazy granola bars who come up with all these great ideas about where the money should go. There's $300 million in government grant money waiting to be tapped into. Saving the whales, studying the effects of pornography on Taiwanese prostitutes, transgender modification for prisoners in San Francisco... That money could be used for a good cause instead of frivolous things, like cleaning up streets maybe? Or housing the homeless? That would be practical.[14]

I'm just a mom and pop business trying to get ahead, but I couldn't qualify for a grant because my business was in Beverly Hills, I own a home, and I don't employ the handicapped. Those three categories excluded me, even though I'm a woman and a minority. I'm half-Mexican, half-Spanish. But everybody from Bangladesh to North Korea can get money and I'm the one paying into it! That realization was the pivotal point when I decided I'm voting conservative all the way.

I was born in Houston, Texas. Again, my whole family was Democrat. But now? Now they're all Republicans! Who would have thought? As you get older, you just start realizing all the waste. As you're young, obviously, you're idealistic and you want to help save the world. But when you're paying the bills, it's different.

---

[13] This year, the Texas state budget was actually much larger than California's. $217 billion vs. $183 billion. So, which state government is bigger again?

[14] I can't say I disagree. Uh-oh.

The things that choke a business are taxes and regulation. Here in California, the corporate tax is $800 a year minimum. Before I even report income, it's already $800. Getting your car registered here is outlandish at $700. There's so many areas that they can tap into, but they're choosing to tap into the middle class. All my life, I've driven luxury cars. Every three years, I had a new luxury car until I realized, "I'm pissing my money for no reason on these registration fees."

With a very strong Republican majority now at the federal level, do I believe all these taxes and fees are going to go down. I already see it. They're actually repealing a lot of the regulations that Obama put in place. I think the EPA got way too bully-ish and impacted a lot of jobs. Here in California, they closed down the water supply up north and 40,000 farmers were out of work because we wanted to save a minnow.[15]

Ironically, who has plenty of water? Nancy Pelosi and her vineyards up there. Do you think it affected her? No. This is what I'm saying, the power and greed from the government getting too big is just silly. Every time I'd see Donald Trump, he'd be seething, smoke coming out of his ear every time. The disdain that this man had, I felt, too! "God," I thought, "He's getting it. He totally gets it." He's a businessman and of course he made things in China; who wouldn't? My ex-husband used to get a lot of things made in China until it started getting too expensive, then he started going to Bangladesh and then to India and then to, I don't know, Quaqua land. Wherever you can save a nickel you go, because you'll get killed on the competition. As a businessman, you've got to be competitive. But why can't we be competitive here? It's just been backwards.

I'm fifty-five; I feel I can speak from a historical perspective because I've voted in every presidential election, and I've voted Democrat and Republican. I voted for Bill Clinton twice. I voted for Bush twice. I can go either way. I vote for who I think is going to be the best. That's why I like Donald Trump. As brash as he is and as obnoxious as he is, I don't think he's a chauvinist. He's shown that from the women that he hires. He put a woman in charge of running his real estate organization. That's not chauvinist. Ivanka built and ran a lot of his companies. The proof is in the pudding. He says obnoxious things, so what? Everybody says things like that. Coming

---

[15] Specifically, it's the delta smelt. A small fish with a large impact.

from the spa business, you'd be surprised what people say in private when they think nobody is listening. It doesn't shock me.

Donald Trump was given a million dollars to start off with, and people begrudge him that? It's what he did with it that matters. How many people employ others? This guy has employed thousands and thousands of people. All these government idiots are fat cats; they got fat from passing legislation, by putting a highway near their stupid farm or acting on stock tips. How is it they are only making $150,000 a year and yet they come out millionaires? Doesn't anybody question that?

I also admire the fact that Trump went to a military school, because military school is hardcore. It's a discipline. It's being regimented and having a pattern of following through. In the end, that follow-through magnifies into something magnificent if you just stay the course. That's what he's done, and what he continues to do in office.

I never considered Hillary Clinton at all. Not at all. Not at all. I cannot stand the rancid, blatant lies that she got caught in. A liar is a liar is a liar. Nobody's perfect, but I would never endorse somebody who is good at lying. No way. They know how to work the system and get away stuff. I would have liked to vote for a woman. I would have voted for Condoleezza Rice, and it's a shame that she doesn't want to run for office. Clinton and Rice are both powerful women, but Condoleezza's got ethics. You've got to trust them at the end of the day. I know people will say, "Well, Donald Trump would fool around on his wife." That's not my issue. I don't really care about that. It's the ethics of what he does for *me*, and I'm not married to him so I don't really care.

Democrats use ideas of racism to divide people. It's like they want to divide and conquer. I told you before that I'm half-Mexican, half-Spanish. But one thing that really irritates me is when people use "being a minority" as an excuse for failure. I used to have a girlfriend who is Black. Again, I have nothing against Blacks. I've dated a couple of Blacks in my life. I know the lifestyle. I have a lot of Black clients. But everywhere we went, my friend used it as an excuse to gain something. She would try to include me in it, saying, "Well, you know what I'm talking about. You and I, we've had our struggles." I'm like, "Honey, I've never struggled. You're implying that I'm a victim, and I'm not." That woman went to Loyola and is a CPA, and she's still playing the victim card?

CHAPTER FIVE
The Salvadoran Immigrant

February 3rd, 2017
North Hollywood, California

You know, Liza really caught my attention with her points about regulating a small business and her concern with the EPA's impact on California farmers' water supply. But her final words, those very last few sentences she said to me, are the ones that stuck. As a devout liberal — so far — I try to speak with a little more political correctness than Liza. "I've dated a couple Blacks in my life. I know the lifestyle." That turn of phrase raises my hackles. That turn of phrase seems to demonstrate racism in its speaker. Am I too soft? Rather, am I trying to force my preferred language on her? Frankly, I guess I'm living in my white privilege just by being able to have this debate with myself.

Today it's even cooler in sunny California, cold even. I'm taking the subway to the last stop, all the way up beyond the hills in North Hollywood. I'm bundled a bit, because I expect to stay outside with Elsa. She's bringing her son for our talk and would like to give him some room to run around. Elsa forwards me many pictures of herself prior to our meeting, all of them with bold proclamations about Trump or proud declarations of her Latinx heritage. She defies my Democratic preconception of her demographic, that's for sure. Wouldn't most liberals expect her to lean left?

###

ELSA: I'm an immigrant from El Salvador and I came here in 1989 to escape violence and terrorism. I was a minor at the time, so I didn't really have a choice, but we did everything the right way, the legal way. We became citizens, we eventually bought a house, and we all worked very hard for what we have. We try not to take advantage of the system; we find what we can do for this country instead of what the country can do for us.

I was thirteen when we left El Salvador. Out in the countryside, houses were being destroyed and bazookas and bullets were flying from everywhere, but we weren't really seeing it for a long time. Then, I remember starting to hear of guerrillas coming into the city, kidnapping women and going inside homes. I remember the military coming in and trying to protect us, but that's when my family decided to leave. My aunt was already in America, and she was able to send for us.

I do home health care now. I work with seniors, and I love what I do for a living because I've gotten to the point in my life where it's really not about money. It's more about what I can do for society, for the people, because the good deeds are all that you can bring with you when you die. I feel like I'm giving back because, to be honest with you, the job that I do doesn't really pay that much. I will never be rich. But it's really rewarding at the end of the day when I know that I made a difference in someone's life. (Especially Holocaust survivors; that's who I usually work with right now.) God has given me the understanding to help my patients go through the dying process.

I'm a religious person, but I'm not really a fanatic. I was raised Catholic. When I had my son – I'm a single mother – I was more liberal, and I was more pro-choice. Once I became pregnant, I realized that it's not a woman's choice to decide if the baby should be born or not; life is a blessing from God. After I became a mother, I realized that people can and do change their views. I used to be a liberal; now I'm just not.

I hold sometimes three jobs. I work sometimes twelve hours in a day. But life is a gift from God, and it doesn't matter how hard I work; I'm doing the right thing and raising my son with values. I'm raising him with love. And we're not rich! Actually, we're poor. But my son can see that we stand for what is right.

As a Latina woman, I feel the rejection from Latino people because of my support for President Trump. When I walk around them, they call me names and want to be mean to me. I don't react in a nasty way because *I've been like them.* I think that everything is about growing up and gaining some knowledge about what's right and wrong. That only comes to you at certain times when God thinks that you're mature enough to understand.

I'm more conservative now because I have to think about the future; I have to think financially about what I'm leaving behind for my son. But I'm also more conservative from just educating myself outside of the traditional media, because the left rules them all. When I see what the media is telling me vs. what I see actually going on at those rallies, I realize that we're being lied to. We're being told something that is not true. The leftist media is brainwashing people into hating, into dividing, into disagreeing with each other.

No matter what, we're always going to have differences. But at this point, we have a president. We have to give him a chance! Right now, I hear a lot about the Muslim ban. What people don't realize is that he just picked up from where the other president left off; those seven countries are places that Mr. Obama suggested are giving us trouble with terrorists. So it comes down to the knowledge: when we have the right knowledge, we're not letting the media brainwash us.

I go to rallies. I listen to Jay Sekulow in the morning. He is not biased; he's for the people. He's for the American people. He doesn't protect one side or the other, he just says the facts. So I try to get my information from him. I listen to him almost every day from Monday to Friday.

I'm wearing an inauguration hat because I went. Oh my gosh, it was the best experience, one of the happiest moments in my life. I think that the birth of my son was the most memorable, but going to the inauguration of Donald Trump is a close second. Being in a place where there are thousands and thousands of Trump supporters; the energy, the feeling, is indescribable. I experienced happiness and love, and I made friends for life. I went to the inauguration by myself – flew there by myself, was staying by myself – but I made friends for a lifetime. I'm invited now to go to Nevada, to all kinds of different places in the United States, because we created a bigger family.

At the inauguration, I saw so many Muslim people that support Trump; the media is refusing to report that. I also saw a lot of Mexicans, a lot of Hispanics, and I was interviewed by CNN in Español. The reporter was telling me that she saw so many Mexicans and so many Latinos, and that was just in the non-ticket section. Thank God I ended up a wonderful ticket!

I felt safe the whole time, and I felt protected. I felt a sense of family and unity. I was always promoting Trump 24/7 when I was there and people were just loving and kind to me, even if some people did not agree with it. And I went to the Women's March! It was four of us Trump supporters, and thousands of them. We stood right on 4ᵗʰ and Constitution, and all we did was bless the women, telling the women that we are proud of them for standing up for what they believe in, because that's exactly what we do! This is not about being against each other.

Right now, the message that I have, not just for those women but for the entire nation, is that we have a new president elected rightfully, and our job is to stand behind that man and work with him for our benefit. If we are against each other, we're creating a sense of violence. People are saying, "Trump is hate." Trump is not hate, Trump is love. But if we continue to destroy the city, if we continue to be fighting against each other, the only thing that we're bringing upon ourselves is martial law. People are very ignorant; they don't think that that could happen. We are bringing that upon ourselves. So, my message is, "Let's lovingly work together. Let's sit down, let's talk about the things that we have in common instead of our differences." I can assure you that with love and understanding, we can accomplish more than pulling each other's hair and calling each other names. If we really care for this nation, we have to sit down and work with each other.

But we don't need a president with a gentle, loving spirit! I don't think that we need a president that is going to be playing to so much political correctness that he's afraid of what people think about him. I think we already gave Obama that chance. We, my family, we've been Democrats all our lives, but we had a need to change that pattern because it wasn't helping us. It hasn't helped our nation; we're in more debt than before.

About the refugees, I was speaking to the Los Angeles Board of Supervisors about how we cannot afford to bring these refugees in and make this city a sanctuary city. These people, they're not legal. We're bringing them in because of wars that Hillary Clinton and Barack Obama didn't alleviate in all these countries. I feel sorry for these people, but as an American I think that my tax money should be going to our own people first. Yes, we can help them eventually, but our people have to be first.

I see a lot of veterans begging for money and homeless, and that really breaks my heart. These people gave everything, and freedom is not free. Barack Obama, instead of helping our veterans, actually did the opposite and helped the enemy in the name of love. All Obama does is say, "Oh, we have to help the Muslims," but who's helping our veterans? Nobody is. When our veterans come home and go to the VA hospital, they have to wait for days to get treatment.

I know some people that are illegal here, and when they go to the hospital, they don't have to pay. I think it's wonderful – don't get me wrong – I think it's wonderful that we provide that. But we have to value what our *own* people are doing for this nation first. If I could, I would give my life for the freedom of this country. Why? Because I love it so much.

Health care is very important to me, and Obamacare is a disaster. A lot of people that I work with had their premiums go double. I have no insurance at this time because I cannot afford it. They said that I make too much money for subsidies even though I am a single mother. Obamacare? It's not for us.

And we were lied to. We were told that if we don't want it, we didn't have to have it... and then it became that we have to have it![16] And now that we do have it, no one can stop these premiums going up. They can go up as much as they want to.

My son goes to a charter school and he is learning Common Core. He is obligated to learn about Muhammad and the Muslim faith.[17] I think, as a Christian, that everybody's entitled to their religion, but religion should not be taught in our schools. He's a fourth grader. I'm going to give you a big example. Last year, he came home with a spelling and vocabulary homework that said Jesus Christ was a Muslim from Palestine. I told my son, "That's not correct." And he says that school says it's correct and if I don't write it down the way they want it, I'm going to get it wrong. It was vocabulary homework! They're brainwashing, changing our history, and I'm very against it as a Christian woman.[18]

We have a Bible that is over two thousand years old and the Bible says clearly that Jesus Christ was Jewish and not a Muslim. Now, here in Los Angeles, they are teaching our children that Jesus Christ was a Muslim and I have a problem with that. That was last year. This year, they have an entire section where they're learning the pillars of Islam.

And the math part of the Common Core is ridiculous. I mean, oh my gosh, something simple gets broken down and becomes really

---

[16] Well, not quite. Obama did campaign against Hillary using the rough idea of a plan that had no individual mandate, but every actual bi-partisan proposal once he was in office included the regulation. Early on, the mandate was actually a concession to conservatives.

[17] The Common Core has no religious education standards whatsoever.

[18] Whatever happened with this strange homework assignment, it certainly isn't related to the Common Core standards.

difficult. We should change that. Common Core, it's a big, big no-no on my list. And that whole thing was Obama's fault.

I'm a proud Trump's supporter, and his conversion to being pro-life is one of the best reasons why I love this man. He defends life. I didn't know much about our vice-president, but when he was giving an interview before becoming the nominee, they asked him what he could say to the American people about our obligations as Americans. He said, "As Americans, our obligation is with the unborn and with the elderly." When he said that, I 100% loved Mike Pence. This man is sent by God to protect the children and to protect the seniors.

I was a lifetime Democrat, but I was in for Donald Trump from the first day. I really wasn't going for the party. My family all voted for Obama twice, but I never voted at all until this last election. And my grandma just became a citizen this year so she could vote for Trump. We didn't vote for a party, we voted for the person. If Donald Trump had said, "You know what? I'm not a Republican," then we wouldn't be Republicans. I am supporting the person and the person's values.

We want the wall. We need the wall. I will start working, putting bricks up for free for him. See, I went to school here in LA, so I know the problem with the drugs. It's very easy for kids to have access to drugs here, and the drugs are all coming from Mexico. Being in a classroom in a public high school, knowing that my friends and my classmates were doing coke in the middle of the class... that's not something normal.

Any country that doesn't have a border is not a country. It's very – what's the word that I'm trying to find? – hypocritical. It's hypocritical for the president of Mexico to say that we're racist when I know that Mexico has a border wall with Guatemala. Does that mean that he's racist because he cares about Mexicans? And what a slap in the face for the Mexicans that now he's saying he's willing to help with protection for illegals here. Why isn't he concerned about the people over there that are dying of hunger? Why doesn't he address the real people in Mexico that supported him, that put him in that position, instead of pledging support for illegals here in America?

I know a lot of Hispanics that are Mexicans and they hate their president. Why? Because he is the most corrupt person in Mexico. When I came to this country, we drove through Mexico to get here. We were legal. We had visas. But because our car had a license plate from Los Angeles, we were stopped constantly and the Mexican police took money from us. When we got to TJ, we didn't have any more money, so you know what they did? The Mexican government took away our jewelry. They told me and my grandma to take our shoes off. We had no shoes when we crossed into America! Everything was stolen by the Federales, the people that are supposed to be protecting Mexico.

We have to stop the liberals from ruining California. You're not from here, right? Okay, this state owed $37 million last year, but it went up to $100 million this year. In one year! If we continue, California is going to bankrupt the whole country. I blame Democrats in California for our own state's debt.

Right now there's a petition out for Governor Brown. I mean, he allowed the illegals to vote! I know a lot of illegals who voted (though I can even tell you one that voted for Trump). I have a lot of friends that are DREAMers. Mr. Obama told the DREAMers all they need in order to vote is a mailing address. This girl said, "Do we have to worry about ICE knocking on our doors because they could track us down?" Barack Obama said, "No. You don't have to worry about ICE tracking you down. I can guarantee you that by voting, that makes you a citizen." My illegal friend said, "If Barack Obama is assuring us that we're not going to get in trouble, then I'm going to vote."[19]

I believe in Trump's conservative leadership. Sometimes we try to promote him in West Hollywood by holding a big sign that says, "Latinos for Trump." We take a lot of heat there. Last Saturday, we had ten people with signs at LAX Airport and thousands of people hating us. People say we're racist. How can we be racist? My ex-husband is Asian. My son is half-Black. We're not racist. We're just people that want what's best for this nation. We're loving people and we just want what is good for us. That's all we want. I'm sure the people crying, "Racist!" also want the same thing: what's *good* for our country. We disagree on what those things are, but we hope to work with everyone. I'm hoping and praying that we're going to eventually get to a time where we can just sit down and talk about how to fix our country together, because we can fix it. Definitely, we can fix it.

---

[19] Obama did not encourage DREAMers, or anyone else, to vote illegally during the Gina Rodriguez interview in question. Rather, he encouraged Latino citizens to vote in order to represent those in their community who are undocumented. He also promised that Latino voter records would not receive any kind of extra scrutiny.

CHAPTER SIX
The Fostered Businessman

February 16th, 2017
Denver, Colorado

Whew! Elsa in North Hollywood is knee-deep in the consumption of conservative media. She's got all the talking points from Jay Sekulow's radio show, and she repeats them with such enthusiasm! I can't get behind her views on the Common Core, and I'm not convinced that healthcare premiums are doubling as often as she claims, but Elsa has such warmth, such caring, such love in her heart. I like Elsa. I like her a whole bunch.

I'm flying over the Rockies now, and landing in the midst of a particularly warm afternoon in Denver. Josh agrees to meet me at the Backstage Coffee shop downtown, though this unexpected piece of sunshine provokes me to move us outside. Theatre and concert patrons buzz about the vast Denver Performing Arts Complex as we wander from venue to venue, bench to bench. Josh is buzzing, too. He's hyped, loud. He has a lot to say.

###

JOSH: I was born in Iowa and raised in Santa Barbara. I'll be thirty-two in about a month. I pretty much raised my older brother because we've both been in the foster care system since we were seven or eight. He's just a little older than me, about as close in age as you can be before you pop out another one, but he needed protection. The foster system can be rough. They were always trying to split us up, but

I wasn't having that. I'd go crazy. This one social worker finally said, "We can't split these kids up. This younger one will kill us." They could take my mom, but they weren't taking my brother. That would be like taking my identity, like taking a fucking leg or something.

We were in twenty-seven different foster homes. That's not normal. We'd keep going back to my biological mom, live with her for six months or something, and then get pulled away again. My mom would leave us home on the buddy system when we were two or three years old. She'd be out at the bars. Neighbors would call, and cops would break in and drag us to foster homes in the middle of the night. Truthfully, we were actually fine; she'd leave us with food and stuff.

Mom would do all the right things to get us back after six months, but then the whole cycle would repeat. That's why I'm so passionate about politics right now, because I was raised in a court, with the court making decisions for my life. So when I see the government doing the same thing to people, I understand the frustration. The courts shuffled us around, making choices not with their heart, but because they got funding from the state to put us someplace. I was raised like a business. The foster parents would say, "If you don't do this, I'll kick you out." You're just a dollar to them. They were getting paid for me to live there.

I got in a lot of fights, because you have to establish your ground when you jump into a new place. Fighting was part of my upbringing, and it was pretty constant. I was fighting for me and my brother, you know? I'd just knock people out when I had to, fighting on his behalf or my own. My brother was like my lifeline.

I don't see my brother now. He made a decision to choose drugs over everything else. The last time I saw him, he was about a hundred-twenty pounds and freebasing.

A career in acting is what I dreamed about growing up. It's funny, I learned most about acting from my mom, because when she was around we would just watch movies all day, like from 8:00 in the morning until 2:00 a.m. When the foster care system would put us in a place I didn't like, I'd *act* my way out of it. "Oh, the parents here are so bad..." We'd get sent somewhere new. I learned to work the system, but it was always just to keep me and my brother safe.

There's no foster system once you turn eighteen. They cut off your foster parents and you're just thrown out into the world like, "Figure it out." Most kids get caught up in the juvenile system, and it's just a spiral. I had to fight really hard to stay out of that system, and I did it by going to college for almost a decade: Santa Barbara

City College and Glendale City College. The one thing the state did do for foster kids is pay for our education. You have to keep a C-or-above average, and they cover your tuition and give you maybe $300-400 per semester for everything else. Of course, you can't get a room in Santa Barbara for less than $1000, so it was tough. But it kept me going.

I had dyslexia and ADHD, and I was working two jobs. It was impossible for me to get the full-time college credits done, so I figured out that I could register for twelve credits, get the full grant money, then drop two classes. I did that every semester, which is stupid, but I couldn't make it work any other way. I have so, so many Ws ("withdrews") on my transcript.

I had two choices to keep me straight: military or college. As unrealistic as college seemed to me, I chose to stick it out because this was right after 9/11 and I felt that 9/11 was a real sham. I would have been a perfect killing machine, but I couldn't support that farce of a war. Just like the foster care system, we were being told only 20% of what was really going on. Like, "This is what we've got to tell the public."

So I didn't even know if I was Republican or Democrat. I did vote for Obama a couple times, but I would punch him in the face if I saw him now. He's just a liar, saying one thing and doing another. He's a great speaker, I think he's really freaking funny, but I think he should have been an actor or comedian. He became controlled by the elites, like the Rothschilds and Rockefellers and those boards who own the Federal Reserve. And by the way, why the fuck does someone *own* the Federal Reserve? Kennedy signed a bill to be done with the Federal Reserve and put the money back into people's power. Then they assassinated him. Greed is the ugliest thing in the world.

I went out to DC this past year and I talked to people; I interviewed them just like you're doing. But I didn't realize I was going into 96% Hillary supporters! I didn't know that until I got there, and I was like, "Oh, fuck." But I wanted to see why people were still supporting Hillary when they knew how crooked she is. I started my own company a few years ago, and I've seen the most crooked, cutthroat things happen with money between the $15,000-a-year range to $100,000 range (because that's how quickly I stepped up the ladder in the last few years). I can only imagine what it's like when politicians controlling millions are trying to line their pockets. They'll do and say anything. All of America was donating money for

Haiti, and it disappeared. The Clinton Foundation was the head of that.[20]

I couldn't believe when Obama brought on Clinton as Secretary of State. "Dude, what the fuck are you doing bringing in the competition?!" But they were both just working for the Rockefellers and Rothschilds and JP Morgan and whoever else the super elites are. They're just draining our country, and one of the ways they're doing it is by opening up the borders, bombing countries, taking all the refugees and telling them, "We're all Americans now," and becoming the one world power. Then the top class can really rule the world. I think that's what they're trying to do. And that's one reason why I support Trump, because I feel that the government itself needs a kick in the nuts. Trump is the only one that has the balls to do that. He's got his money; he's not beholden to anyone. Unless you have your own empire, then there's nothing us Americans can do except hold up our guns and fight, and they're trying to take those away.

Speaking of which, the Second Amendment was designed from the beginning so that if the government got too big of a head and tried to overpower the people, we could defend ourselves. That's why the AR-15 is so important, because that is the one weapon we would need to keep the government from smoking us.

I do auto body; I fix hail or big door dings, and I can do it without paint or Bondo. Today, I made $150 in forty-five minutes. If we get a good hailstorm, I'll make $200 to $300 an hour, for six to ten hours. This is my business. Imagine having an orphan who never thought he could make money in this corrupt world, and all of a sudden I learn a skill and work really hard at becoming the best. The first year I launched, I made about $80,000, which was more than I even knew what the freak to do with. I went to do my taxes and my accountant was like, "Josh, I don't know how to write off $15,000 in bar tabs." I was networking!

I have money now, so I flew to Trump's inauguration. On a whim. Why not?! I met a guy at a strip club once who told me, "Dollar bills are freedom units." Exactly that. Money gives me freedom. I'm a handsome dude, but before I had money, girls would bang me and not stick around. I couldn't keep a relationship, because I couldn't take them out and make them feel special. I just had my

---

[20] Now, now, now. The use of money in Haiti is a complicated issue, but there is decidedly *no* money from the Clinton Foundation that has gone missing.

first serious relationship last year, but then I got all sketchy thinking she's just after me for my money. I tested her by pushing her away and, sure enough, she slept with somebody else. So I learned. Money and power corrupts, and yet I have money now. And our president has money. Is he corrupted, am I corrupted? Am I corruptible? Well, I think anybody can be persuaded.

I don't agree with Trump on abortion, but I also just learned that it's not that he doesn't want abortion at all, it's just he doesn't want the state to pay for it. If you're going to have an abortion, you've got to pay for it yourself, and that makes sense. But I think there definitely should be a choice. Trump has a different point of view because he comes from money. The reason I've had a couple of abortions with girlfriends is because I can't support them, and I know what it's like to grow up as an orphan. Also, there's no way I'm going to be put in a situation where someone uses my genes just to have a child and throw me into child support; I'd kill them. Child support is set up where these girls now look at it as a meal ticket. They'll go out and just hook up trying to have a baby if they think you have money. I'm actually scared; you see the look in their eyes you're like, "I've got to stay away from that one. She may be hot but, dude, she could be the devil."

My biological mother, who I have made contact with, has been homeless on and off for thirty years. She's addicted to the welfare system and was afraid to get a job in case they took away her welfare. That's how they trained her to think, how they want all people on the low end to think, and it's not okay. We want America to thrive. I made my business do really well and it's not that hard. If I had two trillion dollars a year to spend, which our taxes bring in, I would certainly fix a lot of things without putting us ten trillion in debt. It's like our country has a big black card; who even has a limit that big?

Democrats want you to rely on the entitlements. I qualified for food stamps and all that other welfare, but I didn't want it. I didn't want to be like my mother. I didn't want to be relying on anybody. When I was eighteen, I'd just eat a big burrito every two days. I had no money, but I wasn't going to be taking any from the government.

When I was younger, I was stealing toothbrushes for my brother and I while my classmates were movie stars' kids. Everyone around me was wealthy. Jimmy Connors, the tennis champion, has a daughter, Aubrey, who I dated in sixth grade. Steven Seagal's daughter, Anna, had the biggest crush on me. Corey Eubanks – he's a big Hollywood stunt guy – I dated his daughter, Rose. I didn't have any money, but I could see the social classes. In college, everyone was going out partying, and I was working two jobs just to get by. I didn't know my head from my ass.

After all those years in school, I still don't have a diploma. I'm two units short, and actually three units short of three different degrees. I sat down with one of the counselors and he said, "Josh, you got about ninety-five units here; you only need sixty to graduate." But I was going to class to learn about things I'm interested in, not for the diploma. Guys I know who were five years older and had graduated still couldn't get good jobs.

I was attempting to be an actor in California, but I couldn't audition well when I was worried about food and rent. Then I landed in Tucson for a couple years and performed in a show where I played a non-speaking rogue assassin wolfman. That's when I learned I have horrible stage fright! So I learned the auto restoration trade. I became one of the best after just a year-and-a-half and started my own company. I said, "Someday, I'm going where it hails," because that's where the big money is, not in door dings. Then one day a big hailstorm in Denver made the national news, and I've been here in Colorado ever since. You can't imagine what Denver can do to you as a single, white male when you're making way more than you can possibly spend.

Later tonight, I'm going to a Seventh Day Adventist prayer group thing. I grew up in in different religions in different foster homes, but when you party a lot, life loses some of its meaning. I'm trying to tap back in. This group is like my AA; I go there to check in, people throw a verse out there, then we pray. It's keeps me sane, because I don't have to answer to anybody in my life, really. No one expects much from me because I had such a hard upbringing, so if I was a drug addict, kicking rocks like my brother, people would still love me. But I have really high expectations for myself. Plus, my ex-girlfriend is in this prayer group and I'm still trying to woo her back.

I had the same opinion about Trump that everybody else did at first, like "Oh God, what a fucking joke." Then he started talking, and I realized how much we agree about big government coming and trying to take away our rights. A lot of people around here were into Bernie Sanders. I got nothing against that guy morally, but he's a fucking socialist. He wants to suppress our country. He wants to share everything, where I'm all about working my ass off for my own shit. I am not going to let someone waste my money. When you don't earn your money, you don't spend it well. Politicians are just given a lump sum from us, but Trump earned his money, turned a million into a billion, so he understands what a dollar is worth.

I have a lot of respect for people who work hard. You can start just waiting tables and work up to starting your own company. The hardest part is getting from ten thousand a year to hundred grand a year. But you can do that. And then you can turn the hundred grand into a million. In school I hung out mostly with ESL students because they were only people I related with; they were on small budget like me. I have friends that have gone back to Japan, South Korea, France, South America, and all of them think Trump is a son of a bitch because that's all they hear in the media outside of the U.S.

My friend's mom who helped raise me didn't want to talk to me because of my support for Trump. She's president of a bank and pretty much a badass. I told her, "Susan, I understand how he has treated women, but I'm not asking him to marry my daughter. I'm asking to run a fucking country." America's business has always been *business*. Now, why wouldn't she want a businessman at that top spot?

Back in the eighties, Trump said, "If you are a successful in business, you stay out of politics." But I think he got really upset at all the money being wasted, the big government contracts, the wars. They are just wasting money.

The beautiful thing that really inspires me about Trump is that as soon as he got in, he said "Boeing is taking us for a ride with Air Force One." Four billion dollars for that fucking plane, are you kidding me? Boeing say, "Okay, we understand that we are totally fucking you. Can we renegotiate a deal?" Shit like that is *happening*.

I support Trump because I believe in his character. And I believe he hires people with experience. He'll juggle around with his advisors. When you are in a high enough position, you have assistance; that's just the way it works. If you have any questions, you say, "Hey, do some research on this," and they come back to you with information and options. That's how he'll manage the country.

There's allegations about Russia, but Trump has been doing business across the world for a long time. To him, it's all just business. He certainly doesn't want to start wars. I know Hillary wanted to, Obama wanted to. Obama was like, "We can make a change." Obama, you didn't make a fucking change at all. You jumped on board with those super-elites and you kept bombing countries, then bringing people that survived your bombs into our country and calling them refugees. Don't fucking shit in the box and stamp it legit.

With Trump, it comes down to money and trust. Who do you trust with your money? What are their real intentions as politicians? If you are just working for the lobbyists, it's going to be really hard to make moral decisions for America.

I grew up in southern California where it was hard to get carpentry jobs because Mexicans would work under the table. People would hire them, because that's just business. I'm not going to knock anyone for that. If I could hire someone for next to nothing, I would do the same. But it's obviously taking jobs away from legitimate Americans.

I tried to go get health insurance because they were going to dock me $1,000 or whatever on my tax return. "That'll be $300 a month for the insurance." Are you fucking kidding me? For the bottom coverage. I was like, "I'm a healthy person. I don't even need insurance. I'd just be doing it so that they don't charge me a fee, just giving my money away." I chose not to go on insurance because of that. It didn't make any sense. Then my ex-girlfriend slept with one of our friends in the prayer group, so I punched a wall and ended up breaking my fist. I probably needed to go see the doctor, but I didn't because it was too expensive.

As long as I'm writing checks to the government for my taxes, I'm going to be passionate about how they spend it. Money and trust: those are the themes of my life. I thought I would never make money. That was ingrained into me until I changed my perspective; I decided to *choose* to make money. Now I want to start a foundation to help people, mostly kids coming out of the foster system. I want everybody to thrive. I'm already stronger than most people, and I'm pretty fucking handsome. But I'm not trying to have one up on other people. I want everybody to work together. Have the American dream. A couple of cars. Own your house. We should live in peace, not be struggling and fighting and bitching and hating on each other.

I was in Washington for election night drinking whiskey with an Australian friend. Hillary was winning at first and I just couldn't look. The more she won, the more girls and dudes were going crazy in the bar. Hundreds of people saying, "Fuck yes!" Now, I'm very much about my Second Amendment. I'm thinking, "If Hillary takes away the Second Amendment, what militia am I signing up on? I'm not letting the government overtake the people."[21] Finally, Trump

---

[21] Hillary Clinton has been forced to deflect this accusation too many times. She has *never* expressed any interest in getting rid of the Second Amendment. Many conservatives choose not to believe this.

won a state, everyone goes silent, and I whistled... loud. My Australian friend is like, "Mate. You fucking blew out my eardrums." I yell at everyone, "With the shit Hillary's gotten away with all these years, you should all be ashamed of yourselves!" My buddy says, "You're going to get us beat up." But I don't care at that point. I tell him, "Watch me. I'll take ten of them."

CHAPTER SEVEN
The Former Democrat

February 20th, 2017
Sierra Vista, Arizona

Back in Denver, Josh didn't want to spend $300 each month on health insurance, but then punched a wall and couldn't get his hand treated. That, combined with his fanaticism about owning guns to protect ourselves from our own government, puts him beyond my realm of understanding. The story of his upbringing is moving, though, and I admire his strength in keeping his brother close while in the foster system and managing to avoid the drugs that brought his brother down. He also pushes Trump as a conduit for change. That, I could come to respect. Josh voted for Obama, the former quintessential "change" candidate. Now, he looks to disrupt the system again by supporting Trump, the latest outsider candidate. What surprises, though, is that Josh is doing very well. His business is booming. Why disrupt a system that seems to be working for you?

With a new resolve to compare Obama's platform of change to Trump's disruption, I head to drier Sierra Vista, Arizona. It is a land of retirees and transplants, of warmth and routine. I'm to meet Charles, a political junkie who supported Hillary over Obama, then planned to vote for Hillary again until Trump came along presenting a bold option. It's a busy day for Charles, and he's finding a hard time fitting me into his schedule. He spends long days volunteering for a food bank and doesn't want to shortchange that time.

###

CHARLES: Okay. I'm sixty-five years old. I was born in a little hick town in Oklahoma, then spent half my life in Texas. Now I'm retired in Arizona where the weather's a lot better. No tornados!

For twenty-nine years I worked for a company called Deluxe Check Printers. When they folded and I lost my job, I didn't receive any good benefits. I moved on to working quality control in a Cardinal Glass plant, and that was killing me. It was working twelve-hour shifts and rotating days to nights every two weeks. My body never got rested. And I'd be coming home as my wife was going to work; we never got to spend time together. After seven years of that, my wife and I used WorkingCouples.com to find jobs together. That's what landed us here in Arizona.

We only got married in 2003. I had been married once before, but my ex-wife thought the grass was greener on the other side of the fence. I find myself working part-time as the door guy at a sports bar in Texas when this woman and her sister come in. I started talking to her, and we ended up getting married. I got very lucky.

We live about ten miles from the Mexican border, but that doesn't actually impact my life much. Most of the people who come across the border don't want to hang around here.

I work with a food bank as a volunteer. They bring the food down in semi-trailers and we unload the pallets of food off the trucks. It's mostly for disabled seniors, low-income seniors, folks living check to check. We also get some young people with multiple kids coming through; they need help, too. In one spot I volunteer, people just drive up in their car and we load food right into their trunk. They don't even have to get out. We'll help about five hundred people in a day. I've had a lot of good things happen to me, so this is my way of paying it forward. Even though I'm a senior, you see a lot of seniors that are in much worse shape than me.

I was a Democrat. I was behind Hillary when she ran against Obama. Then I was starting to get behind Hillary again! But when Trump signed up, I dropped her automatically and went to Trump. I admire Trump because he's not a politician. He's a regular working man, never been into politics. When politicians are filling their pockets with money from everybody else, Trump can turn the country around by doing what the *people* want instead of what the lobbyists want.

I got a Christmas card from Trump when he was running. The card thanked me for being a supporter and wished my wife and I a happy Christmas. That made me feel pretty good. I've got this bedroom in the house that is my political room. There's pictures of all my favorite presidents in there. There's a letter that Reagan signed "to a fan." So I put the Christmas card from Trump in there next to a letter that President Carter wrote to my dad.

See, my dad was disabled. He wrote to President Carter talking about the difficulty he had trying to vote for him; there were so many stairs to get into the precinct. Carter wrote back thanking my dad for his support, but then he also called him at home to talk about the voting challenges. My dad really appreciated that. Nowadays, we have early voting and mail-in voting and other accommodations that make it a lot easier for those who have trouble moving around.

My wife and I went to five or six Trump rallies. These were my first-ever rallies, and my first time supporting a Republican. I was so excited to see a person running for president actually there in front of me, getting everybody all worked up. The last one I went to had protesters interfering with people trying to get into the building. That was kind of scary, because it was close to getting violent. Some of the protesters were able to sneak in and hold up their vulgar signs like, "Fuck you, Donald. We don't need you." I didn't care for that.

I thought Hillary would have been a good president, but as her campaign went along, I really was pleased that I switched sides. Donald Trump was making good promises. And now, look! He's actually doing what he said he was going to! How many presidents have you seen promise they're going to do something, but then you never hear any more about it?

Trump is working to control immigrants from coming in. I'm afraid somebody's going to sneak in with a dirty bomb and blow it off in a big city. I'm afraid of anthrax or some other disease affecting millions of people. Trump doesn't want that to happen. He wants to stop that, so he puts a blockade up. A temporary ban. What's it going to do but weed out the bad from the good? He wasn't saying it would be a permanent thing. If we had something stricter, would 9/11 have happened?[22] It may have happened, it may not have happened. Those people were able to be sneaky; we even trained them to fly the jets.

Do you know there are sections of Arizona where there is no fence or anything between us and Mexico? There's a lot of drugs coming across that area. Whether he gets a wall built or not, I'd be

---

[22] It is worth another simple reminder that the 9/11 hijackers weren't from any of the countries included in Trump's travel ban.

thankful if he at least puts towers up every half-mile, then man those towers. Trump's not a racist person, he just wants people to come across legally, without having to sneak.

Congress has got too many old fogies. They need to get out. I'm all behind Trump getting term limits across the board.

Our son's is not a fan of Trump, I don't think. But I just don't talk politics with him at all; the arguments get too heated. He says he's an atheist. He was brought up a Christian like me, but he turned it around. I still believe heavily in God, and Trump does, too. I'm a devout Christian. I believe in prayer, I believe in the Heavenly Father, I believe that when we die that our soul goes to heaven, and I know that when the rapture comes, He's going to come back and take us all to heaven. But Trump is not pushing any one particular religion. He just says, "We need to pray for this." Carter used to lead his fireside chats with a prayer. Nothing wrong with that.

I think Trump appeals to everybody. Sometimes he might step on the toes of the mighty rich, but that's just because he wants to put America back to work. The blue-collar part of the world, that's where America is. The ones on the assembly lines, the ones that come out to your house and repair things… not just somebody who goes and sits in an office. You're not going to get some suit coming out of an office to come fix your washing machine. The blue-collar worker is the backbone of America.

Obama put all the miners out of work. My nephew used to work in the mines. Not anymore.

The trade deficit? We have been really stupid on that. We pay countries to export our stuff, but we've been bringing in their stuff free of charge. We bring in people from refugee camps and set them up in business. Take an immigrant and a little guy who was born here in America. The immigrant has a better chance getting money to open up a convenience store! Motels are getting bought by immigrants and ran by them. How is that fair? We've got little kids starving here, but the government sends $25 million over to this other country for starving people. Let's take care of our starving people first.

I'm a veteran. I served during Vietnam. And I see a lot of things going wrong with the veterans. I've got disabilities from the Army, but I've never been able to get any compensation because my records got lost and they want me to prove that. They say I wasn't approved for disability, but they've actually just lost my records and I want them to admit it. I've given them sworn statements from people that knew me in the service and knew what happened to me, but they say that's not good enough. My story is not unique; it happens all the time. I've been fighting this since 1976. After all I gave them...

At Thanksgiving, we open our house to veterans in the military's Acquisition Intern Program and have them over for dinner. They're away from family, so we try to give them a little bit of family surroundings for a day, get them away from Army food, give them a good home-cooked meal. It gives me good, uplifting feelings inside, and my wife loves it.

Oh, by the way. These Russia allegations? Any possible revelations wouldn't be a deal breaker for me. I'm behind Donald Trump 100%, and my wife is too.

CHAPTER EIGHT
The Anti-Hillary Christian

February 21ˢᵗ, 2017
Tucson, Arizona

Over in Sierra Vista yesterday, Charles told me he was a Hillary Clinton fan until Trump came along. What?! How?! He shocked me. I need to learn from that. Let me see... Charles is a calm man, devoutly Christian, and not at all extremist in his views. He presented small and tidy reasons for supporting Trump's immigration policies, a moderate viewpoint about terrorism and drug-control. He's also concerned with America's job market, agreeing with both Clinton and Trump that NAFTA needs to work better or be overturned. In brief, Charles likes Trump as a stronger, more-promising version of Hillary's general policy ideas. Charles feels Trump and Hillary are both acceptable, with Trump representing a bolder plan of execution.

Not too many miles away, Bill sees Hillary as the polar opposite of Trump. Hillary is a killer, and Trump is the savvy savior. I walk six miles to visit Bill at his home in the outskirts of southern Tucson. It is true desert out here, dry and bland. Neighborhoods of gated, cactus-laden gardens peel away to become dusty, cinder blocked houses, most having some rusty vehicle resting in their dirt yard. Bill's front door is wide open, and he's got a fire roaring out back. There are three teenage boys milling politely about, curious but standoffish. Bill has business charts stuck to his interior wall, a spider's web of pushpins, string, and numbers. He dives into an explanation of how these lines on the wall will help his business expand, but it's too speedy for me to follow. The fire out back seems more appealing than the dust bunnies inside, so I ask that we sit out there.

###

BILL: If we can get just two houses on each of these blocks, we'll be at the sixteen hundred customer mark. That's my goal. We're in the business-building stage, and we need to ramp up our customer accounts. Right now, we're not quite making enough for us as founders to live. We have less than fifty customers. But with each account, we are building to the point of being able to hire more than just ourselves. We're putting a third of our income directly back into the company now. Our purpose is not to make money; it's to create jobs. This is Diamond Yardmasters. We do high-quality yard work with heart.

I love that you're a liberal who is willing to listen to us devoted Trump supporters. This is a movement; a new movement in this country. I knew some people were going to start working on providing a bridge between our two ideologies. You're absolutely a wonder. It's an awesome idea.

To give you some perspective on me, for the better part of ten or twenty years, I was dirt poor and street-preaching in Chicago. I was studying theology, passing out fliers, playing guitar, and moving with this really radical, cult-like church where I was saved. It was jolly good fanaticism. I was dumb, I was young; what can I say?

Later, I met my wife while living in northern New York. I was working a job where we were laid off every winter because we couldn't the work in the snow. My wife's father was in Arizona and was always wishing we would move out here. I never talk on the phone, but one day he calls while she's at a women's retreat and he says – again – how we should come out to where the weather's better. With the economical place we were in, I said, "If a door opens up, I'll move tomorrow." Next time he calls, he says he bought a four-bedroom double-wide that we can stay in until we get on our feet. We boxed up what we could and that was it. Tucson's been home ever since.

We started this company as a family: me, my wife, and our kids. Our kids went to college, lived here, and we provided everything. In exchange, they said they'd help us get the business up for a couple years. We're in our third year now, and they still help out a bit. Those first couple of years, whew! We learned a lot. Gained customers, lost customers, figured out how much work we could handle.

I turned eighteen during the second Reagan administration, but nobody has earned my presidential vote until this year. I never chose to vote between the lesser of two "Who cares?" candidates. I choose to grant my vote only where it truly belongs. This year I did that for the first time. Donald Trump is the first person I've voted for in a presidential election.

My wife reads the tabloids and stuff, so she follows stars and the big names. She knew a lot about Donald Trump before I did. I never watched an episode of *The Apprentice*. I lived reality instead of watching TV! My wife was the one talking about Donald Trump first.

So when I'm hearing he's running, the only thing politically that I'm thinking is that the Butcher of Benghazi cannot be allowed to win. I wasn't necessarily impressed by Trump yet; I was just feeling committed to making sure Hillary didn't get elected.

As a Christian, we have this Litmus Test of the abortion question. If you're pro-choice, it's not even an issue; my vote is off the table. I thought Trump was pro-choice because he is just a New York guy. But my dad always said, "Young liberals grow up to be old conservatives." And my dad was a sixties Democrat in Albany! He grew up to see that corrupt government run by the Democrat mafia was just normal there in New York.

So my wife looks into Trump and sees that he changed his mind about abortion, and she read his testimony about it. He made sense. He sounded about right. See, there are "tells." You can tell when somebody's politicking you, but Trump seemed sincere. So now I'm feeling good, because he's also a business-quadrant person.

My introduction to Donald Trump came through Robert Kiyosaki, the guy who wrote *Rich Dad, Poor Dad*. He also wrote this book called *Cashflow Quadrant*, and that's my inspiration. I see that Kiyosaki and Trump have the same, quadrant-style business mind. I now trust that Trump truly understands business. This is big, because I understand that business and government are no different. Government is political business and business is non-political government. They're a good check on each other. I knew then that Trump could go in and get things done through the gridlock that's enveloped Congress. Ask a kid today what gridlock in Congress is like and he may not know, because there's never been anything else! Don't ask a fish what water's like, they don't know.

So Trump's is pro-life, has a business-quadrant mindset, and is running against the Butcher of Benghazi. That's it. Those were the only reasons I needed.

That locker room talk? Who cares? I've met women who are just as bad as Trump with their talk and can be the worst misogynists on the planet while tearing each other down. I'm sorry, they all purchased how many copies of *Fifty Shades of Gray*? Don't even give me that. That locker room talk with Trump is just a smokescreen for liberals who are doing a daddy-kid rebellion thing. Sorry, but there's more of *us* this year.

I started my yard care business after twenty years working crap jobs for other people. I've got a solid business plan, but I'm still calling audibles! That said, if you ask my guys what we provide now? We provide happiness. That's our product. Customers don't want yard work done; they can do yard work themselves and get it done cheap. They want *service*. They want yard work the way you want to go out to eat. Steak is cheap. Steak in a restaurant is not cheap. You're not paying for the steak, you're paying for the ambiance, the service, the prep, and you're paying for the waitress that touches your forearm. (Don't tell me that doesn't work. They teach waitresses to do that to boost tips.)

When I was working for other people, I'd enjoy a job for a couple of weeks, but then I'd master it. After that, it was just a daily grind. I like *creating* jobs. I don't like working them. Creating a job is interesting. Creating a job is looking at the yard worker and saying, "Okay, how can I make this the best job in the world?" My guys pick weeds, they're not even landscapers. The hourly equivalent is $11.77 an hour, and I call it an hourly equivalent because if you take what they make in a year and divide it by 2080 – forty hours a week, fifty-two weeks a year, working about four to five hours a day, five days a week, four weeks a month – they are getting the same as an $11.77 an hour job, but they're only working twelve hundred hours a year. That's a great deal for them.

Once I reach fifty customers, my freshman clients go free for life. Those people who signed on early to help me grow my business are getting free lawn care for the rest of their life or mine. We're not there yet, but when we hit fifty, Dora Ramirez is free, Rebecca Dickens is free, David Foster is free. Monthly yard maintenance for life! Because they were the tip of the sword. They took us on when we didn't have references. The first fruits of your harvest go to the Lord.

As we were entering into winter, when Trump got elected, I knew this spring was going to hammer us and we were going to make some real money. I've been watching what they're calling the "Trump Effect." Stock market, businesses, everything's getting better. I see a ton of trucks on the road that weren't there. The trades, the painters, roofers, all that.

During Trump's campaign, we started noticing political signs going out on lawns. Now, we don't have much money. My wife and I were both thinking, "I wish I could send a contribution." We're broke. We rent this house; we're poor. But it occurred to me when I saw a Trump sign on a lawn that happened to need work, "Wait a minute, here's something I can do." If these people were willing to make their house a target by putting out a Trump sign, I was willing to overhaul their yard for free. I knocked on the door and asked them if they'd let us trespass! We cleaned up that yard, then started putting the word out: anybody with a Trump sign gets free yard work! There weren't a lot of Trump signs around here at the time, but this was what I could do to help; I could make the signs look better in their surroundings.

It helped them, and it helped me. We don't really do any real advertising, but when you're doing work out there, people come over and inquire whether they can hire you.

There was a rally here in Tucson where Trump called a woman up on stage who was carrying a "Latinos for Trump" sign. She said she had a restaurant up in Catalina. So, on primary day, I took my guys up to that restaurant and we spent three hours weeding outside in their front area. I sent my wife in to tell them what we were doing; it was just a gift of appreciation. And we weren't the only ones checking out her place! They actually sold out of food that day. One customer asked us what we were doing, then insisted on paying this woman to feed us. That's just the community that Trump has been building.

We were doing a yard and the guy across the street comes out with a weed eater. We all cringe at the sound of it. We don't use weed eaters; we get the weeds out by the root. But this is a guy who owns his house and he's out there doing his thing and it occurs to me that I should appreciate this. Instead of thinking, "This guy is not hiring me," I realized that he's there cleaning his yard, and so his neighbors are going to be interested in keeping up with the Joneses. So, really, this guy with the weed eater is working for me. People see me across the street from him every month, and now they might get interested in having their yard work done. Maybe everybody on earth works for me, somehow? And that isn't pompous or arrogant, because they also work for themselves. I own this company, but I'm also just one part of the company. A company is just a system of systems (thank you Robert Kiyosaki), and we are all connected.

The fuel that drives my company is human greed. We don't discourage it; we teach you how to apply it properly. What's the difference between greed and self-interest? Greed sounds bad; that's the only difference. It's survival; you have to survive. Nobody begrudges you self-interest. I don't call myself an entrepreneur, because entrepreneurship includes a lot more things. I label myself as "businessman." What do I do for a living? I create jobs. The thing that's interesting about creating jobs is that we create them by *never showing a profit, ever*. As long as I own Diamond Yard Masters, we won't pay taxes because we'll never owe them; we'll never have any money left. Our employees will pay taxes because they'll get paid enough. Can you imagine pulling weeds for a living and getting paid enough to owe tax and not be on welfare? That's a gift.

I'm glad we have a president that's pro-Christian, but he didn't have to be for me to like him. Is there evidence that maybe Donald Trump has been saved? Yes, there is. Has he been? I don't know. It doesn't matter. Here's a crazy one: God is the one who put Hitler in office, put Obama in office, put Mr. Clinton in office. Thank you, God, that you didn't put Hillary Clinton in office! That's just me being funny. Seriously, the Bible says God puts kings in office. He put Nebuchadnezzar in office, he put all the wicked kings in office. He put all these people in office and none of them are good; none of us are good! Jesus didn't come to make bad people good, he came to make dead people live. Whether Trump is dead in his sins or alive in Christ, I don't know. Politically, I see it as irrelevant. The question I look at is this: "Is he saying what I think needs to be done?" Yes.

CHAPTER NINE
The Adoptive Mom

March 1st, 2017
Albuquerque, New Mexico

I remain unmoved. Bill's arguments for Trump center on business skills and a new proclamation against abortion rights. Much like Bill cannot see himself voting for someone who isn't pro-life, I find it hard to support anyone who is. Ah, but a flash of memory... I debated in favor of a mock pro-life bill at the Rhode Island statehouse during a "Model Legislature" event in high school. I won a $500 scholarship arguing that Abraham Lincoln's income-stretched mother may have aborted him if given the chance, and where would the country be had that happened? My views have since changed. Bill's views could change. I cannot comprehend a pro-life stance now, but there was a period during which I certainly could.

It's time to leave dry Arizona and head up into the higher altitudes of New Mexico. Here in Albuquerque, a mere five hundred miles away, I find a liberal enclave. This is a college town — stadiums and sports bars at every corner — and progressivism typically finds an easy home in academia. The people riding their bikes around are more likely to agree with me than any Trump devotee. It is here, on a university campus, that Amber agrees to meet. She's frustrated with how her conservative voice is being silenced, even after Trump's win. My book project, she says, is a gift that allows her to speak aloud ideas to which her city isn't willing to listen. That, of course, is my personal aim: to listen. We stroll around campus, but her two (tall) sons trail us twenty yards behind. They feel it's safer for her that way. They're her protectors.

AMBER: On the ground right here is some chalk that says, "Hate speech is not free speech." The University of New Mexico is a sanctuary campus, but this is where we've had people beaten and spit on for having voted for Donald Trump. That's a first in my fifty-seven years. A sanctuary campus means that it's a safe space, but Trump supporters are not safe here. This is a campus that is going to keep holding protests, and those protests are going to turn violent. There's going to be burning, there's going to be looting, there's going be rioting, and that's not a sanctuary for anybody. It happening in Albuquerque already.

I've seen that rioting happen in other cities while traveling to where my father was dying. You think you're going to stand in the road blocking me so I miss my flight? You think I'm going to let you make me miss the last chance I have to see my father alive? Are you kidding me? I'm running your ass over.

Right when we were having a memorial for my father is when Trump came on and started talking about the vetting process for these seven countries. "Let's just hold off," he says. "Let's give it ninety days and let everybody cool down. Let's make sure that we're just not opening up a floodgate." What's wrong with that? Why do you need these large-scale protests because of some cooling off period? I'm against the protests; I'd prefer to have a conversation.

I don't think protesting should be about shutting down streets. You shouldn't shut down businesses. I experienced some backlash from the pipeline protests in Bismarck, North Dakota. The people there were throwing Molotov cocktails, starting fires on the street, throwing rocks at the police. My nephew is a police officer there, and the protesters realized they could start attacking families of the officers. They'd find out so-and-so's wife owns a hair salon, so they'd show up at the salon talking about what a shitty person she is. I had to change my name on my Facebook because they came after me there, all because I'm related to one of their police officers.

I'm pro-choice, I'm pro-gay. If you guys want to get married and pay double your taxes, who am I to say no? If you want the same wedded bliss – and I say that tongue in cheek – as all the rest of us, good luck with that. I knew someone who was gay and he had the same partner for sixty-some years. They met in high school and were together until he died in his seventies. They couldn't be themselves until they moved out of their parents' homes, but I think their relationship was kept alive by the fact that they never did get married! That piece of paper changes a lot of people. They think, "Now you're really going to have to go through it if you want to get rid of me; now I can be bitchy or I can be this or that." It's like marriage changes your perspective. But anyway, I'm pro-choice and supportive of LGBTQ rights, big time. Trump has already made moves to give states more control over whether they want pro-gay legislation to exist. I'm for these things. I think it'll be easier for people to impact these social policies at a state level. Basically, I'm picking my battles, and it's easier to battle at the state level. You have better access there. You know where the governor's office is, you know where your mayor is, and it's easier to vote them in and out.

My bigger concerns are about safety for my kids, safety for my country, and fixing the horrible healthcare we have now. It's these bigger issues that got me to turn from being a Democrat to an Independent, and then to Trump. I didn't go full Republican, and I don't think Trump did either. During the Obama years, I came to realize that I hate all politicians. I can't stand it when you ask them a yes or no question and you get, "So, with positive reinforcement we take this and we go around and circumvent into the area..." They tell you bullshit! It's like, "What the hell was that, yes or no?" I'm done with it. I'm done with you taking money and getting rich without having a product. You're not selling anything except power, and I'm done with it.

Then Trump comes in and says, "You know what, I'm going to keep you safe, because you and I have children." I have two children that I gave birth to, and five others that I took off the street. I've taken in a child whose mother had to go to prison because she knifed somebody. I've taken in a child who had no one feeding him at home, and he grew up to be a train conductor in Chicago. I knew they were all good kids, but I also told them, "This is the way it's going to go. You screw me over or anything goofy happens, you're out." I can turn my back just as easy as anybody else. But I like to provide them with an opportunity.

I'm not actually fostering these children, because do you think the crack-whore mother is going to give away their f-ing debit card?! These kids didn't even know that their mom gets a debit card for food. They had no idea. Actually, she never even kept the card. She sells it for 50% cash. A $500 debit card goes for $250, and because there is no fingerprint, they get away with it.

No, we never got any money for taking care of the kids. It's just me doing my part from my part of the world, and I can make a difference here. My biological son actually asked me to take in the first kid. He said, "Mom, can we help my friend? His dad's selling drugs." I said, "How do you know that?" And my son goes, "I went to put a dish in the dishwasher, but it was full of drugs." That's how it is around here. Another one of my kids asked me if a friend could stay for two weeks while his parents were away. The kid shows up at the door just like he is: shorts, tennis shoes, a shirt. "Where is your tooth brush?" He says, "Well, I don't have one." "Where is the rest of your stuff?" He says, "I don't have anything else." He had nothing. Like no socks, underwear, anything, no.

I told him, "You're going to be treated like one of ours for two weeks. We have rules, we have regulations. This is it; you either do it or you can leave." He did really good, was perfect, and when it came time for him to back to this other place, I'm like, "We bought you some clothes, a toothbrush, toothpaste, mouthwash. Gargle it; don't swallow." And he starts crying. I said, "Oh my god, what's wrong?" He goes, "I never knew people lived like this. I want to stay." How do you say no? John has been with us ever since. He's twenty-two and just got his application to be a police officer.

I'm religious, and I'm also a minister. I was ordained over the internet, but I take it seriously. I'll talk to God every day. I will ask for help moving in the right direction, and God talks to me. You can't tell too many people that, because right away it's like, "Holy crap, she's crazy." But He guides me and has led me to take in these children. Spanish children, Black, Native American, everybody.

I'm an atypical Trump supporter. You see why. I have a couple of liberal views, but it's the big picture items that got my vote. For instance, I grew up on a farm. I can grow sugar beets. I can pick whatever you need me to pick. Nothing's going to happen if all of the illegals were gone right now; there would be people for those jobs! There *are* people for those jobs. We don't need illegal immigrants in the U.S. for any reason.

Here's a big thing about illegal immigration: our prisons are full of about 30 or 40% illegals. We're housing them. We're feeding them. I say, "Get out." I'm done. Open that prison space up so that maybe we can get some mental health in there.

I used to do massage therapy, the mommy massage. After ladies have their babies, the next day I would go in and give him a little back massage or shoulder massage before they were released. In there, "Is this your first baby?" "No, it's my tenth."

Ten babies! Come on! In the hospital, you also have access to their date of birth. You're thirteen years old and giving birth? How nice. You're fourteen? How great. Your baby is shaking in the basket, he's detoxing. And these are the people who get the entitlements. My vote now is if you are going have ten kids and beyond, there's no reason why you can't work in a daycare. We should be able to force you to work in a daycare, not just stay at home and collect money. Obviously, what we're doing in America with these people is not working, but nobody on the left will have a conversation about getting people to do something other than throw money at it.

We shouldn't necessarily have smaller entitlement programs in the welfare system, but we *should* have work requirements. People say, "I have children; I can't work." No, they keep having children so they don't *have* to work. But we can change that. Let them have money, let them have housing, but make them go to work five days a week in a daycare and bring their children with them. Make them do that until they realize it sucks, then they'll start looking at working in fields they actually enjoy. Everybody benefits.

Lots of people are saying free education would be great, but I can tell you from personal experience that when somebody paid for my education, I had the best party. If you would have known me in college, oh my God. But when I had to pay for it, it changed me. I see it with my son. In high school, he'd say, "I got a D, but it's passing." Now that he pays for school, it's a whole new ballgame.

And speaking of education, I think having more police presence in grade schools could help change our culture. Officers making more visits, playing basketball with kids, that kind of thing. I can remember watching TV in '79 or '80 and the commercials would say, "If you are stopped by police, you put your hands at ten o'clock and two o'clock on the wheel, and you look straight ahead until the officer knocks on your window." What happened to those commercials? I don't think people know how to do a police stop anymore.

I'm a massage therapist and naturopathic doctor, with a master's in Herbology. Some of my clients are illegal and they're scared. I tell them, "Do you got a record? No? Then don't worry about it." ICE is not going after them; I've called to make sure.[23] When I went to France in the eighties, they hated Americans. They spit on me. So I know what it's like to be on the crap side. We should be judged on what's in our heads and our hearts, not on our colors. I don't think that anyone should be saying whites not allowed, Blacks not allowed. And that's another thing I have first-hand knowledge of: One of my nephews has a four point plus average and is trying to get into a surgical school. They only take so many white guys, and then they get C students of color. Is that the guy you want doing surgery on your loved one? That guy who got a C? No, I want the A+ guy. I want everyone who worked that hard, no matter what color. I want every single one of those A+ guys to get in because they deserve it, and I don't think that's a bad thing.

Obama wouldn't even call terrorists what they are: terrorists. He wouldn't call ISIS by its name. He was just so out of touch. Trump, on the other hand, is doubling down on our safety. I know firsthand the shit that's in Chicago, because my son's there. You're telling me you've had thirty-some years as a Democratic city and that's all you got to show for it? I've been to Indonesia, Guam, Morocco. All the way down Guatemala and Belize. In all of these places, they're so proud of their country, and it's like a shit hole. There's no hot water. You can't drink the water. People are dying on the street. You're stepping over people dying, and they're so proud of their country. Then you come here, and liberals are like, "It's awful, it's awful, we have to help everybody." No, they don't know what awful is. I'm all for offering a helping hand, but if you're not going to take some initiative, then I'm done with you.

I don't mind paying taxes, but I do know that my sons have had to pay the $1,600 penalty because of Obamacare. I'm a naturopath. When they need something, I get it for them. If they need penicillin, it's garlic.[24] We have insurance, yes, for vehicle accidents, but they don't need insurance for their health. I was absolutely livid about that penalty, because they had motorcycles with insurance. If they got into an accident, they were insured that way.

My insurance used to have a deductible of $250. Now it's over $7,000. Thanks, Obamacare. Where am I going to take my family on vacation? We're not going to go on vacation. My son, on the other

---

[23] In these first few weeks of Trump's presidency, ICE arrests of immigrants without criminal records has, in fact, more than doubled.

[24] In WWI, only 25% of soldiers healed from infections. In WWII, a full 95% of soldiers healed from infections. Penicillin made the difference. But alas, should we have used garlic instead?

hand, had a Medicaid card until he was eighteen. He got all of his stuff free. So, I do know that that part of the system worked really good.[25]

Trump's got a great work ethic. And I'd like to think that I do, too. All of my childhood was on a farm in Minnesota. Nobody asked if we felt like working today. You want to eat? The tomatoes aren't going to pick themselves. The peas aren't going to pick themselves. My father, my brother, and all of us would work every day. The minute your feet touch the pedals, you are driving the equipment. I got my license at fourteen. My dad actually paid me to work the farm, but I never saw any of that money. He put it away, and when I was fifteen I was able to buy a brand new Camaro with it. It was $5,000 and I still have the receipt. I was so proud. It had never occurred to me that you could take money out of the bank.

I see people in my neighborhood needing jobs, but there's so many kids today who just refuse to be flipping burgers. Who didn't flip burgers in the seventies and eighties?! But that's beneath them now. Well, not my kids. They will work. We have tried to instill in every one of them that sometimes you are going to be shoveling shit and it's going to suck, but nobody is going to hire you right out of school with no experience. You have to build your skills and your reputation.

I'm so happy about my kids. They see somebody, like an old lady with problems carrying groceries, and they'll go help her. And they'll stand back and ask first before ever approaching her! In a hardware store, my son had a shirt on that was the same color as the employees. A lady asked him to carry something to her car, and he just said, "OK." He loads it up and then I'm going out with my cart and I find him. The lady says, "Oh my, I thought you worked here!" She turns to me, "Did you raise this boy? Well done. You should go buy him a steak dinner."

My biggest fear, because I've experienced it, is what Muslims can come in and do to us. Overseas, I have been called a lesbian while walking with my friend, been knifed during a purse-snatching, been yelled at by police for not walking with a man, been yelled at by police for not wearing a thing on my head, and even been drugged with PCP. All of this to say, I'm afraid of Sharia law coming to the United States. We already have no-go zones here in Wisconsin.[26]

---

[25] Obamacare expanded Medicaid coverage to millions. These millions are likely to lose Medicaid coverage under the proposed Republican health plans.

[26] No, we don't. (And even FOX News says we don't!)

That is unbelievable in my eyes, and I don't want it to go further. I don't even believe that Muslim is a religion.[27] If you look at it, it's a cult. I can remember going to Saudi Arabia, and it wasn't too bad. But in these other countries, we were told don't go over there, don't do this, don't do that. Remember cassette tapes? We'd see cassette tapes all ripped up and hanging on a stick; that was a reminder that there's no music and no dancing allowed. No talking to men who aren't your husband. There, if you have no male person in your home and you have no kids, you can't even go out to get food. I don't want my daughter growing up with that. I'm going to start learning Arabic because the translation of the Quran to English is watered down so people will think it's really not a bad religion or cult, but the actual words seem pretty harsh. I want to be able to translate it myself.

I signed up for the Women's March, but they said I couldn't go because I'm a Trump supporter. Really? That's actually just dividing us further. And I don't like any politician that the Democrats would ever put up. When Bernie Sanders sold out to Hillary Clinton and all of a sudden buys another house and a sports car like he's going through his mid-life frickin' crisis, I'm done. Bernie knew she was evil, and he sold out. We don't need lifelong politicians in office, we need real people like Trump. I will be at the gay pride march, I will be at the civil rights march. But when you exclude me out of a women's march, I'm not going to vote for your people. And I'm going to convince everyone in my circle not to vote Democratic, and I'm going to teach my kids not to vote Democratic.

I want a global world. To be global, you better start talking to Russia, because they're more like us than you would ever imagine. You better start talking to China. Once you get Russia, China and the United States and all of our allies together, we have a major shot at globalizing the world.[28]

Some liberals have started to compare Trump to Hitler. Really? Six million people died; is he anything like that? No. He's brash, and he's got a lot to learn. But he's also not a politician, and that's what I like about him. I understand everything he says.

My dad fought in the Second World War. He went in when he was sixteen. That war was necessary for our country, and I'm so proud of my father. Thank God Japan didn't attack the United States fully, come onto our shores, because everybody here has weapons. We

---

[27] It's not. Haha.
[28] Wait, isn't Trump against globalization?

have our own little army. Nowadays, I see boys choosing to serve again, serving so their wives don't have to wear veils, so their daughters don't have to get mutilated. Where is the outrage on mutilating female genitalia? Where is that outrage? [29]

I was talking to a veteran from two tours in Iraq and Afghanistan under the Obama administration. He said that their interpreters were Iraqi and Muslim, and that the Americans were told whatever the interpreters do, as long as they weren't stealing their ammunition or shooting at them, they were to stand down. Then these Marines were crying in their tent because they had to stand down as Iraqi Muslims were raping a ten-year-old boy. The boy would be begging for help, but the Marines had to stand down.[30] See, the Muslims think boys are for fun, women for procreation. My Marine friend still has nightmares about that and will never vote for a Democrat again.

---

[29] Hillary Clinton has that outrage: "We cannot excuse this as a cultural tradition... It is, plain and simply, a human rights violation."

[30] According to the New York Times, non-intervention during some forms of child abuse in Afghanistan really was our military policy, sickening as it may seem.

CHAPTER TEN
The Engineer Veteran

March 10th, 2017
Oklahoma City, Oklahoma

During my chilly campus walk with Amber back in Albuquerque, a pair of her boys wandered behind us to keep an eye on her. (Not the first time my interview subjects have prepared some kind of protection against lil' old me.) Probably due to our tendency to duck into building lobbies to warm up, we lost the boys at one point. Finding us again, one of them shouted, "You should have told us where you were! We've been walking around looking for you. I was about to shoot up the fucking place!" Honestly, that comment kind of negated many of the ideas I was trying to hear from Amber's perspective. When you talk guns, I shut down. I've always considered gun control to be my most important personal political issue, so I acknowledge that it weakens my ability to listen when guns are supported by you or – um – actually present on the scene.

Oklahoma City, here I am. I'm travelling to the far outskirts of town. Scott tells me that the tags on his car are expired, so he's not willing to drive very far to meet me. We agree to stop into a Burger King near his house. "I've got some groundbreaking engineering ideas for Mr. Trump," Scott mentions in advance. I make it clear that, while I certainly don't have our president's ear, I'd love to hear what plans Scott has come up with. We split an order of fries.

SCOTT: I'm a veteran from a long line of veterans, and father of an active duty soldier with two tours in Afghanistan. My father served in Korea, my grandfather in WWI, two uncles in WWII, and my cousin in Vietnam. Mr. Trump is pro-military. In this post 9/11 age, people are waking up to the fact that the United States is no longer safe. It's a whole new ball game.

For our own protection, we have to be very careful about who we allow in the country. This is obvious to me, and to Mr. Trump. We have to take more precautions.

I like Mr. Trump because he understands that the capitalist system is the only system allowing people to flourish and be the creative, innovative human beings that they are. See, I am in favor of building the southern wall. Strong fences make good neighbors. However, we don't want to cut off the flow of water to our neighbor because he has to feed his livestock, too. To that end, I have proposed to Mr. Trump in a letter the construction of a water pipeline from Canada to Mexico, with each country building its own section of the pipeline and manufacturing its own pipe. This will create jobs in all three countries while providing more water for Mexico to produce its own goods, mostly agriculture, for export and consumption.

I draw a Biblical parallel here in the story of Joseph. He went to Egypt to buy wheat because there was a drought in the holy land. Mexico has a similar problem. Canada has just about more water than any country on earth, so we start the pipeline there. The U.S. can charge a toll on the passage, Mexico buys bulk water from Canada at fair rates, and Mexico flourishes. I've written up this proposal and sent it to the White House. Two years ago, I also sent it to President Obama, the President of Mexico, and the Prime Minister of Canada. Only Canada responded. They referred it to their interior administrator.

The water plan is not really entrepreneurial, it's merely an observation from reading the Bible. Egypt experienced a rapid growth of the Hebrew population, who eventually they enslaved. *We* are Egypt in the sense that we are experiencing a rapid influx of illegal immigrants from Mexico, and it's primarily because of the lack of water. Rome could not have become a powerhouse without aqueducts. I am hoping Mr. Trump will be open to this idea.

In my military career, I was security police in the Air Force. My job was to guard nuclear weapons. I know that Mr. Trump understands the priority we must put on national defense. After the Air Force, I took advantage of the G.I. Bill and tried to pursue a law degree, but I got sidetracked into electrical work. I studied the way we consume massive amounts of water in the production of electricity. Coal, gas, and nuclear power plants lose over three billion gallons of water a day. The country needs to be looking at alternative energy sources.

Iran is claiming the right to nuclear power for peaceful purposes, when they're actually developing nuclear weapons. The Iran deal is an important issue. They are an ever-growing danger, and Trump is handling them harshly and well.

As a leader, Trump understands the guiding principle of setting up strategies, choosing good people as advisers, and letting them do their jobs. There's naturally going to be resistance from people who don't care for some of Trump's specific picks for advisors, but once he can explain his strategies in a sensible, logical fashion, it's more likely people will get on board.[31]

I am divorced. My ex-wife is a bipolar schizophrenic. Things are a little unsettled for me right at the moment. I'm between jobs, but I'm trying get back to work. All Americans need jobs, but capitalism has its faults when unregulated.[32] Teddy Roosevelt began the renaissance of the rights of the common worker in this country, but things are still progressing, both in civil rights areas and in the rights of workers. It's a slow process. Humans don't seem to have the capacity to be more progressive. The presidencies of Clinton and Obama have stagnated us economically. When people become too reliant on the government, particularly socialistic-type entitlement programs, they cease to be innovative and creative. I believe God gave us brains to be creative.

I would never automatically vote for the Republican candidate. When Ross Perot was running, I supported him even though I felt it was going to split the Republican ticket. And it did. But I felt he could be more progressive in developing this nation to its fullest potential. I could see he really cared for the little guy, and I get that same sense from Donald Trump. I mean, we need economic safeguards for people to ensure that they're fed, housed, and taken care of medically, but we also have to be more self-reliant as a people. We have to be more self-responsible.

I was born here in Oklahoma City. The southwest portion of our city seems to be the most drug infested, the most gang infested,

---

[31] I guess I'm still waiting for Trump to explain his strategies in a "sensible, logical fashion."
[32] Democrats would wholeheartedly agree.

but our entire area has become a center for drug distribution. It wasn't like that when I was growing up. Coming up out of Mexico, the drugs pass through here before expanding east and west.

I've admired that Mr. Trump, who was born with a silver spoon in his mouth, has gravitated from living his own lavish lifestyle to taking care of this country. Franklin Roosevelt and Teddy Roosevelt were also born with silver spoons in their mouths, and they gravitated toward public service, too. What I saw in the Clintons and Obama was the stagnation of our nation while they rose to power. Plus, their histories are shady and crowded with more controversy than Mr. Trump. We all have things in our past that we're not proud of, but the degree of vagueness about the Clintons and Obama is disturbing.

I think if Trump had any dealings with Russia, they would've been on a business level only. I don't think they would have been detrimental to this country. I could be surprised down the road, but that is my opinion for now.

I will say this one thing on immigration that I've never heard anybody say: very wealthy people who wish to immigrate to this country should be forced to pay large fees to live here, offsetting the financial burden poor immigrants place on our government. This is a way that immigrants can take care of their own. I came up with that thought yesterday. It's not Trump's idea, it's mine.

And you know, we've got to watch out for this expanding globalization. Businesses were pretty global prior to World War Two and look what happened. Texaco, Ford, and GM all had subsidiary companies providing war goods to the Nazis. GM owned Opel, and Opel built vehicles for the Nazis. Texaco sold fuel to the Nazis. AT&T provided communications equipment to the Nazis. A lot of people in this country don't realize that. Worse, after World War Two none of those companies suffered any repercussions.

I'm not your average Oklahoman. Most people here in the Bible belt are conservative, but it's because they're not widely traveled. That's changing. People are becoming more environmentally aware, more economically intelligent. They are becoming more knowledgeable of the global economics that Trump has already mastered.

CHAPTER ELEVEN
The Insurance Agent

March 10th, 2017
Oklahoma City, Oklahoma

Up in the northern part of town, Scott told me about his engineering plan to move water from Canada to Mexico. He supports Trump for a couple of the of the now-typical reasons — business skill and border security — but he also believes it is reasonable to send the White House a massive public works project idea. Is that a little bit crazy? Or am I just shooting down ambition? Or, hmm... Is this an example of Trump inspiring people to dream big, to think outside the box, to upend the norm?

I'm hanging out in Oklahoma City for a while, and it's a sunshine-filled day in the Bricktown entertainment district. Karin meets me in front of the Bourbon Street Café and we walk the canal. It's a busy restaurant area, bustling in the day nearly as much as it does at dinnertime. Walking to meet her, I was worried about this lively atmosphere interfering with my ability to record a conversation with Karin. But you know what? She's loud! She has more uplifted energy than I ever expected to experience during a conversation about health insurance. There's another thing: I know we are going to be talking insurance because it's Karin's business, but boy do I hate talking on this subject. I'm notoriously confused when trying to interpret health insurance policies. I was grateful to Obamacare when I signed up because healthcare.gov answered some of my silly, basic questions. (For reference: I didn't qualify for subsidies and paid about $320 per month for a Bronze plan. Seemed like a great deal with all the preventative services that came free. I had a really high *deductible, of course. I suppose that could have hurt me if I hadn't been healthy that year.)*

###

KARIN: My daughter was editor-in-chief of the law review at Michigan. I always say she's had too much education; it made her a little too liberal. She still lives in Michigan, and when I go there I can see she's not touched by the problems we see here in Oklahoma City. She is one of the most giving, generous, loving people you would ever want to meet, but she has no idea what's going on in the real world because it doesn't touch her daily.

In my younger days, I worked as a Playboy Bunny in Baltimore. I was also a disc jockey, and a stand-up comic for the USO. Finally, I landed in a great job at Time Warner, and quickly moved over to the America Online portion of the company to work in retention. I had two kids at that point, and the company paid for me to go to school at night. My work was more technical than you'd think. I'd get the calls when people were saying, "Cancel, cancel, cancel" after they came from tech. These tech guys were the people too arrogant to even ask basic questions like, "Is your computer plugged in?" You laugh but I can't tell you how many of the problems were resolved that way. The tech guys didn't go through the basics because that was beneath them. America Online learned that it's easier to take a customer service rep and teach them technical skills than it is to take a tech person and try to teach them customer service skills! Which came first, the chicken or the egg? Actually, they've resolved that; it was the chicken. Just in case you didn't know.[33]

My work at AOL ended when they moved the call center out of the country, so you can see why I might have a certain sympathy for people whose factory work is being contracted out overseas.

Worked in Seattle for a while, then moved my family to Oklahoma City for a job in insurance sales. My oldest son was in a bit of trouble then. I like to say he was majoring in video games; he was your basic D and F student and could have ended up in hubcaps and drugs. I knew I couldn't meet his needs, so I sought counseling to help me with my parenting – just couldn't change those dynamics alone. It was a huge culture shock for my kids moving from Seattle to

---

[33] I do know, actually. Karin is wrong; the egg came first, not the chicken. As Neil deGrasse Tyson put it, "Which came first, the chicken or the egg? The egg – laid by a bird that was not a chicken."

Oklahoma. So much different. They weren't used to being in the minority. They were the only white guys on the basketball team. It was difficult for them. My daughter, on the other hand, had no problem because she played baseball in Seattle and was the only girl on the team. She was used to being in the minority. She had better skills to handle it.

Anyway, I asked the school to talk to them, the coaches to talk to them, and I even went to the village police. (They're kind of a pretend police department within Oklahoma City. The rinky-dink ones.) I said, "I need some help here. If this kid gets in trouble – which to me is inevitable – you've got to let me know right away." Well, I got very little help. The system won't help you if you need help, but then if you're in trouble, a judge says, "Why didn't you get him to go to school?" You know what finally saved my oldest? Military school. I couldn't get him to go two blocks to class, but the military could teach him to *fly*. That changed everything; he made honor roll his first year there. He's fifty-two now and has had an entire career in the military. That school was the best money I ever spent.

I'm seventy years old. I'm older than I look, and that's always a good thing! I've had creative success and business success in my life, and that mix of creativity and business sense plays into my politics. Freedom, choices, having some control, being able to create your own scenarios; these ideas are all very important to me. I was raised Republican, and those are Republican ideas.

I guess in the sixties I was a little liberal; I may have even registered as a Democrat at one point. But like they say, "If you're not liberal when you're young, you don't have a heart. If you're not conservative by the time you're forty, you don't have a brain."[34] I think there's a lot of truth to that; when we're young, and especially in the creative field, we want to believe that everybody can be saved. That explains the kids doing the burning and the protesting; all they've known is Obama! They've never paid any taxes. They're either in college or mommy and daddy are still supporting them. God knows I'm guilty of that, too. Kids have no idea what comes out of a paycheck.

This one girl has said to me, "Free tuition would be nice." I said, "You have a grant that's paying your tuition." People who make very little money already have free college. I said, "Nobody's going to

---

[34] I turned forty the year before this interview. Uh-oh.

pick up your student loans for you because you want to live in an apartment instead of commuting back and forth, because you want a lifestyle where you don't have to work. Why should somebody else pay for that?"

I work in insurance now. I do think it's fine that people pay $450 for Part B if they make over ninety grand a year. Other people pay $109 because they don't have any money; the state picks up their Part B premium. I think that's fine. I think means-testing for some of that is fine. I'm not saying conservatives should be cruel, just that we can make things much more fair.

I hate the Affordable Care Act, but the new Republican health plan is almost as bad. It's Obamacare Lite. To me, nobody should get a tax credit. They should get a tax deduction, but they shouldn't get a credit. Having Medicaid will help some people. That's okay. But there isn't any reason why somebody that's making a million dollars a year should get a $33,000 credit.

The reason the Republican plan isn't absolutely as bad as Obamacare is because they are going to end the Medicaid *expansion*. I have a booth in Wal-Mart doing open enrollment; this one guy comes in and appears to own a home and have two jobs. He says, "No, I don't work that job anymore. It's just this one," and so he gets a $1000 per month credit. He chooses the Bronze plan instead of the Silver because if you're subsidized and you don't use all of your credit, they give you the difference back when you file your tax return. Now, really?! This guy is going to get $2,400 back when he files his tax return. We've paid for his insurance and we're bonusing him $2,400. What's wrong with that picture?!

We have a Blue Cross/Blue Shield plan in this state that had a 70% increase in premiums. 70% across the board. Unless you're subsidized, of course. There's definitely something wrong with that math.

Now I admit I've encountered a few circumstances where Obamacare is legitimately helping people. There are people that did go in to get a check-up and found they had diabetes or other things, and then got treatment. That doesn't mean these people couldn't have gone to a free clinic or gone to the emergency room and found the same thing. It's not that people didn't have *coverage* prior to that, they just didn't have *insurance*. There's a difference, and it's a psychological difference.

A lady called me yesterday and said that another insurance salesperson had just hung up on her. See, the commission is so minuscule on these things that no one in my business wants to bother. I may as well be a social worker.

Anytime somebody has a special election – that's if you age out, you get married, you have a baby – I will never get a commission on them, never. Blue Cross made that very clear. Here's why: it's all of the special elections that are really bankrupting the insurance companies. These people usually have some kind of pre-existing condition. Well, you can't wait until you have a car accident to buy car insurance! States used to handle this with high-risk pools. If people were denied by insurance companies, they could enter the pool and have premiums that were controlled by the state. When I tell people about that, they say, "Well, no one ever told me that before." That's frustrating. Every state had a plan for those people, and also for people that didn't qualify for Medicaid but were still poor. Here, that one's called Insure Oklahoma and it's paid for by the tobacco tax. I think the income limit on those plans is in the $20,000s.

So, those plans can't help *everyone*, but they do work. Some people here, like teachers, complain when they're making $40,000-50,000 compared to the $90,000 they could make in Chicago. They say we're one of the lowest paid areas of the country, but we have the cheapest places to live, too! It's not that I don't think teachers deserve to be paid well; it's fine to give them some more money if it's there. But they should have to buy their own supplies and not be given all these deductions. If you're a mechanic, you have to buy your tools. Every job you have to buy something. I always say, "Get off the cross; somebody else needs the wood." Sure, teachers are underpaid, but so is everybody else.

The public-school teachers face an uphill battle with all the testing and everything they have to deal with. And still, kids on the whole are not prepared. They don't know how to write. The difference between public schools here and my son's private military school was amazing, so I'm absolutely a supporter of the voucher system. School choice is the only shot these kids have in inner cities like Oklahoma City.

There are two schools I know of in the state of Oklahoma that make the best hundred public schools nationally, and I don't know how kids are getting in there fairly. One of them is like Little Mexico. I don't think there's a white kid in the whole school. It's unbalanced, though I guess if the school was all white, it wouldn't be a good school at all. I had a Hispanic say to me once, "I'm just another dumb Mexican," and I say, "I haven't met a dumb Mexican yet!" I've seen kids come in from Mexico and they'll have them in the first, second grade, but maybe they should be in the sixth, seventh grade. By the end of the year they're top of the class. I've seen three-year-olds translating for their parents. The dual-language trains the brain, probably. All this to say, let's use the voucher system to balance schools out and give everyone a chance at being successful.

Ok, so I've been talking about financial and health care reasons for voting Republican, but I also just don't like big government. I don't want government in my business, telling me what I can do. I don't care what anybody does as long as they're consenting adults, but that doesn't mean that I think people should get *extra* rights. I'm not a devout Christian, but if I had a bakery or a flower shop, I don't know... How hard is it to find a gay florist or a gay baker anyway?! I don't think a Black baker should have to make a Ku Klux Klan cake, do you?[35] Florists and cake decorators are artists, and since when do we have to sell our art to anybody that wants it?

Now, it's a whole different deal if you're talking about serving somebody. If they come in and you've got a public place serving, that's completely different. If you're renting to them, it's completely different. And it's not even really about religion. People that keep saying, "God, God, God," and I wonder who they're trying to convince. If you have faith and you believe, you don't have to keep saying it.

You know, I did spend some time protesting against Monsanto. You might be surprised at that.[36] They're killing us. They're creating all of these health problems and, again, the chicken or the egg; is it the pharmaceuticals or is it Monsanto? I went to the Capitol to protest them. That's the only time I protested, because I knew that one would be peaceful. I'm a child of the sixties; I can't deal with that rioting and shouting down. Most protests these days are just anarchy. We need to allow everyone to speak, whether we agree with them or not. We don't have to break windows or destroy property.

I'm not sure I would have voted Republican no matter what; I'd like to think I give it more thought than that. It really did just come down to Trump. But there's no way I would've ever voted for

---

[35] I thought this was a valid argument until a friend pointed out that the difference lies in whether the "oppressor" is doing the buying or the selling. I wouldn't ask a Black person to make a cake for an organization that has oppressed Black people for years, but I would ask a baker to make a cake for a gay couple so as *not* to oppress the couple.

[36] I'm not surprised that Karin protested Monsanto, though I'm disappointed we don't have that in common. I'm a GMO fan because, as stated by Michael Shermer in Scientific American, "It's the only way to feed billions of people."

Hillary. And I didn't like Obama. First time I saw him, I thought, "Charismatic guy." But, like I do with all major candidates, I read his book so I had a proper view of him. And I didn't care for that view. My son loved him at first, until I said, "What is it that you like? That he's young? That he has the glitz, the glamour?" Of course, he didn't have a clue; he just liked him. I started asking him questions, but he didn't like that. My thing with Obama is that I don't know where he was born.[37] His half-brother just came out with his birth certificate from Kenya today. I don't know if it's real or not,[38] but he came out with the birth certificate.

Anyway, Obama just doesn't like this country; he doesn't like the American Way. From the prayer breakfast when he said, "Let's just not get our high horse," and, "Don't forget the Crusades." Yes, I remember them, but did you guys ever look at history when Michelle said our Founding Fathers weren't born in this country? You got a Harvard education and you don't know the Founding Fathers were born here?[39] Does anybody even fact-check these speeches?

The Crusades were because of the Muslims, right? I'm not against them. Every Muslim that I've known has been a great person. Guy that runs on my corner liquor store is Muslim; he's from Iraq. But is there a pattern with Muslims, or extreme Islam? (I think that would really be a better term than "Muslim.") It's been going on for generations. The reason why we have a *navy* is because of the Muslims! The shores of Tripoli, the Barbary pirates. Those pirates were Muslims, and we started our navy because of them. So I don't think it's by chance or by accident that when ISIS beheaded all of those people in 2015, it was on the shores of Tripoli. It's not by chance. It was retribution.

They say it's about 2% of Muslims that are extremists, but 2% of all of the Muslims in the world is more than the population of the United States! That's what is so scary. You only have 2% that are radicalized, but when it's the second largest religion in the world 2% is scary.[40] A lot of it is just brainwashing. It's just like the Vietnamese. We have a huge Vietnamese settlement here. The Vietnamese – now

---

[37] I do.

[38] It's not.

[39] Michelle Obama, graduate of Princeton University and Harvard Law School, *does* know that most founders were born in the colonies. Her remark on this matter, while speaking at a swearing-in ceremony for new citizens of the United States, pointed out that the founders too became Americans by choice. There *was* no America when they were born.

[40] It is quite difficult to put a real number on this kind of thing, but the Pew Research Center does regularly survey the number of Muslims around the world who view ISIS and other groups favorably. That percentage is above 2% in nine countries as of this writing, but varies each year.

this isn't scientific, of course – are either doctors or they're in a gang. You do not have an average Vietnamese person out here in Oklahoma. I've met a lot, and it's one extreme or the other.

Trump is not a bigot, and he loves his country. It's interesting to me that no one ever called him a bigot before he ran for office, and now that's all I hear from liberals. I think he could care less about somebody's gender, their sexual habits, or what their color is. All he cares about is whether or not he can do the damn job. And he's having trouble doing that job right now. He's got to fix healthcare, but it isn't looking good, so he's probably better off just letting the whole damn Obamacare implode.

We need Trump to drain the swamp and build that damn wall. A lot of people here in Oklahoma City have trouble getting jobs because they can't compete with the illegal Mexicans. The illegals are underbidding Americans on the bricklaying or whatever job it is. When I was managing a restaurant, I couldn't give my grandson a job as a busboy because he couldn't compete with the thirty-two-year-old illegal alien. And the illegals are abused in the workplace, no question! They're underpaid to bring down the market.

The real culprit with illegal immigration is the Chamber of Commerce and the insurance companies. See, roofing jobs are good jobs in Oklahoma, because there's always a hailstorm or tornado. But the Chamber of Commerce lets the insurance companies get away with hiring illegals. Each roof would cost $5000 or $10,000 more if they were using American workers; that's why they do it, and it undercuts the market.

Then I go to my deli on the corner in the morning to get a cup of coffee and there's ten people in front of me paying with the food stamp card, getting in their $80,000 vehicle, and talking on their free phone. Do I have a problem with that? Yes, I do.

CHAPTER TWELVE
The Domino's Deliveryman

March 13th, 2017
Tulsa, Oklahoma

Karin over in Oklahoma City didn't have quite as much to say about health insurance as I expected, but the points she made about fraud in the current system are valid complaints. She is on the front lines enrolling people at a booth in Wal-Mart, and she witnesses people scamming. Ok, fine. But then she finished our conversation by inferring that people on food stamps can afford an $80,000 vehicle? Am I crazy for thinking that is just not true? I mean, of course there is abuse in the system, but claiming that people receiving those benefits are financially well off? I don't see how this is possible. The USDA recently reported a 1.5% rate of fraud in the food stamp program. If we are helping people who need it, my liberal assumption is that a 98.5% success rate in feeding our citizens is something to celebrate.

Food is on my mind, then, as I travel to dusty Tulsa and schedule a meeting with Chris, a pizza delivery guy. I ask him to speak with me in the lobby of the opulent, historic Mayo Hotel. When Chris enters (sans pizza), he laughs while greeting the doorman; they happen to know each other. I overhear Chris attempting to explain the nature of his meeting with me, and he struggles! That's good. His challenge explaining himself reminds me that it's still not ordinary for devotees of the right and the left to agree to speak calmly with one another. This is a reminder that I'm on the right path. We need not agree, but I believe more than ever that we should listen for understanding.

CHRIS: Let me start by saying that I believe we Trump supporters have a message of love. We believe everyone is equal, we believe everyone should be included. We want everyone to participate. And we accept everyone. Democrats have been creating division, we are trying to create equality.

I was born in Woodward, Oklahoma, which is a couple of hours over, but I lived in Texas most of the time I was in school. I graduated high school, but I'm trying avoid college. I personally hate school. I did not do good in school. I don't like sitting in a classroom and have some guy tell me, "This is what you learn and this is how you learn it." I don't like that environment. And I don't want to be thousands of dollars in debt just to do it again. For the career I want, I most likely will have to go back to school, but I'm still trying to see if there's a way around it. I'd like to be a police officer.

In Texas, a lot of the people I hung out with were heavily into drugs. I was not partaking in any of that. I didn't like that environment. So I left Texas to get away from them, and because I wanted to get out and do something with my life. I wanted to see the world. I wanted to get a new job and explore what's out there. I went to Indiana and worked construction, then came here to Tulsa where I became an assistant manager. I actually work right up the road. It's Domino's Pizza.

I see the military and law enforcement out there trying to better everyone. These are not careers that you go into saying, "I want to make as much money as possible." No, these are careers you get into to help the community. You're doing it for a greater good.

Almost every single child on my father's side was a Marine. Yes, almost every one, including the females. Then on my mother's side, a lot went Air Force and Army. My main thing is law enforcement because I'd prefer a more regular lifestyle. My parents actually think I should hold off, because of all these riots, police shootings, and the whole, "we hate cops" movement. They think it's a bad time for law enforcement, so they tell me, "Maybe stay at Domino's."

I gravitate to some of the issues Trump brought to the table, like, how do I explain it? Our social classes. No, not our social classes – how we see each other socially. For years, we've had this "death to cops" mentality, and it's now gotten to where we hate white people, we hate Black people, we hate this race or that race. We try to alienate groups, we don't want them to participate, they're bad. That's not a good culture. We should accept everyone. The country is finally stepping up and saying, "We may have been wrong before, but we're doing better now." This is the mentality Trump has. No one is remembering how it used to be! It's now this idea that we're all equal, we're all in this together, and it's not us against them.

I assume you're either a supporter of Bernie or Hillary. If we go by that, and if it was proved that Hillary rigged the primaries, I could say, "You agree with lying and cheating." But that's not how it should be! Just because you agree with her political views doesn't mean you have to agree with what she's done *personally*. That's the same way I am with Trump. I will say it flat up: Trump's an asshole. Trump says dumb things constantly. But I like his political views and what he's trying to do. Personally though, he's not a friend. I wouldn't be like, "Let's hang out in public with this guy." It'd be more like, "Hey, I see you once in a while at work, but let's keep it like that — just two professionals getting our work done."

Did you know that most of the chairmen of the NRA are Black or female?[41] That shows they have the same ideas and they agree with us, too. It's not just a bunch of rich, old, white men trying to keep you down. It's inclusive, not just us against them. Conservatives, NRA members, we're inclusive. We're trying to bring everyone together. And, no, I'm not currently a gun owner.

I would like to own firearms in the future, when I'm a little more stable financially. I think we should have access to firearms, but we don't need everyone walking around with so many guns on their back. That's complete anarchy. But at the same time, if someone wants to carry a personal sidearm for protection, then by all means. I see no problem with it.[42] The small Oklahoma town where I was born, people have land and ranches and farms. Obviously, you're going to have a firearm with you there. I grew up with that and didn't see it as strange. It wasn't demonized in any way.

I want to see the working class brought back to life. I'm a working man; I don't like people doing things for me. There's this giant gap between the poor and lower-middle class, and the upper class. We have to make it to where it's more accessible to be middle class, rather than just be poor or really well-off. Make it easy for

---

[41] This is categorically untrue. If Chris is talking about the NRA Board of Directors, they are 86% men and 93% white. If he is talking about past presidents of the NRA, there have been only two women in the organization's entire history.
[42] Wasn't this Hillary Clinton's position, too?

someone to have a decent career and just get on with their life. Now, Trump won't be able to fix that himself. No one person is going to make the country do a complete 180 and say, "All right, we're good. We're good to go!" I believe it is a stepping-stone, and Trump can put us on the right path.

One way is to fix taxes. There's a lot of taxes. I came from Texas where there wasn't a lot of taxes. I think had to pay property tax and that was it. There was no big income tax that you got taken out. Here in Oklahoma, I look at my paychecks and see they take out $200-300 out of my $1400 paycheck and I'm like, "Where is that going?" Because I don't see it in the streets. Maybe cut back on the taxes a little, give us a little more money to save up and buy a new car or get a new place to rent, rather than just be almost struggling paycheck to paycheck.

We've got so much government interference. Like with Obamacare, where everyone was *forced* to do something. When everyone is forced to do something, it never ends well. That's why the premiums shot up, and even if you did have health insurance, it was terrible. I have health insurance because of my parents. My father is actually paying $800 a month to keep me on his health insurance through work.[43] I'm tempted to tell him, "Just take me off." Then I can see if there's some cheap little plan that I can get, so I won't get hit with the taxes of not having health insurance.

Let the people live. You don't want to buy health insurance, so be it. I'm not going to force you to buy health insurance if you don't want it. I'm just going to highly recommend it, because it is a smart investment. But it's terrible to just force people to do stuff.

When I decided to move away from my parents, I was rolling the dice. I was moving out on my own for the first time, and I'd never had to worry before about things like food. It was the first time I couldn't say, "Hey mom, can I have a meal?" I have to say, "What am I going to do for food?" The first month I was actually living out of a motel. And I had to make smart decisions because I was doing construction, hard labor. I couldn't just eat chips all night and call it a day. I actually had to have a good meal. It was costly trying to figure it out. How can I set myself up to eat better and start living a better life, not staying up all night, doing whatever I wanted? That threw me off. I was not used to that at all.

---

[43] Thank you, Obamacare! Due to his age, Chris is only allowed to be on his father's insurance plan *because* of the Affordable Care Act.

It got a lot easier. Now it's just very cool.

Looking at me, what would you say I am, ethnic wise? Most people wouldn't guess that I'm actually 50% Hispanic. My mother grew up in Juarez, Mexico. That being said, I do agree with the closed border, and I do agree with getting rid of illegal immigrants. Remember, I was working construction. A lot people in that business are paid cash. We all reported it, but it's cash. With that, companies can say they paid a crew to do this job for so much money, when actually they just hired a bunch of illegal immigrants and paid them half price. People like me had to work twice as hard making lower wages just to compete with them. I said, "Well, I'm an American. I need a wage to live off of. I'm on my own, doing all of this." They said, "Well, why would we pay you this much, when we have this guy here who just wants to stockpile his money and doesn't even have his family here yet? He'll work for half."

On construction sites, you see these guys walking around who can't speak a lick of English. We would actually lose tools to them. They'd actually take stuff and put it way over in their section. Where'd it go? We look all around the site. We find it over there hidden in the corner under tarps. This happened fairly regularly, actually. Regular enough where it's a legitimate problem.

One of my uncles on my mother's side cannot legally enter the U.S. We have to go down to Mexico to visit him; he can't come visit us. I might say my uncle is not a bad person and I don't think he should be barred from the U.S. but at the same time, he is not special. I may love him, but we're all still going to play by the rules.

Trump's super-expensive wall, however, would not help with our immigration problem. Most of the bad stuff, and bad people, come over in planes. But the wall was a selling point for him. It's something he could say to get more eyes on him, but in the end he'll be smart. Trump's too smart to actually build a wall.

I would definitely consider a Democrat. I'm not your average person who says no Democrats, always Republicans. If a Democrat were to come forward with policies I agree with, and they were stronger points than the Republicans had, I would definitely choose the Democratic side. I'm more of the swing vote, I guess you could say. But I'm very pro-life, *very* pro-life. If I were to have a significant other or family member or close friend get pregnant, I would at no point in time say, "Hey, you should get an abortion." All life is valuable; we should give the child a chance. At the same time, legally speaking, I'm pro-choice. Because if we didn't have pro-choice, we would go back to coat-hanger abortions, pushing people down stairs, real brutal acts that would hurt the mother more than anything.[44]

----

[44] So, he's pro-choice. Right?

CHAPTER THIRTEEN
The Liberal Feminist

March 15th, 2017
Tulsa, Oklahoma

My meeting with Chris a couple days ago has been plaguing me. He's an ambitious young man who led with his ideas of equality and inclusion. We liberals are not inclined to think "equality and inclusion" when we think of the conservative movement. But Chris was honest, kind, and engaging in his truthfulness. He's struggled to find his path, clearly, but is successful in his exploration. To him, the ambitious individualism of conservatives does not push away equality and inclusion, but lifts them. To Chris, the social problems on which we liberals often focus can be rendered moot by encouraging more individualism. Self-reliance equates with inclusion because it encourages people to do what they wish with no interference from government or others. To Chris, President Trump represents this centrist version of conservatism.

But now things are getting weirder. I'm still in Tulsa, and I'm contacted out of the blue by one of Chris' co-workers. Diana, or "Babs" as she prefers, also works delivering pizzas for Domino's. Introducing herself via email, Babs says she's a liberal feminist who voted for Trump. Yes, that's right: a liberal feminist. She's sees no contradiction with her descriptor and her vote, and I need to understand why. "When can you meet, Babs?"

Because she works until 2:00 am with the pizzas, she suggests meeting after-hours at a well-known late-night spot, Hurts Donuts. I've passed the place and have so far managed to avoid the bacon-laden creations I can smell from a block away, but

###

BABS: Thanks for meeting me this late, and thanks for the doughnut! It's 2:30 a.m., but I'm used to this because I've worked the late shift a lot the past couple of years. I used to live in cities that closed down at 10:00 p.m., but finally I'm in a place where things stay open. Any twenty-four hour place is awesome, but I like Hurts Donuts because it still feels lively at this time of night. It makes me feel like I'm back in college. You know that magical feeling that happens in a place that doesn't sleep? That doesn't exist much in Oklahoma.

I graduated from college in 2013. I'm twenty-five years old and grew up in Alexandria, Virginia. We were only about two minutes outside Washington D.C., so I was always talking politics. My dad is extremely liberal and, even though my mom comes from a conservative family, she's pretty liberal, too. I grew up with liberal views, but also with the idea that a lot of people are conservative out of fear. Like, they're not necessarily conservative because they have a particular view that they support, they're just afraid of all the things liberals are doing! I personally identify as an independent, though I did work for a while canvasing for Democrats here in Oklahoma. I'm very socially liberal and for a long time I never even had an opinion on anything other than social politics. Now I understand there's much more to consider when casting a vote.

I voted for Obama twice, my first two elections! And I got to go to one of Obama's first inaugural balls. That was one of the most amazing things I've ever done. I had lunch at the White House soon after because my friend's dad worked in the Office of Management and Budget. I was really into Obama but to be clear, I strongly considered John McCain. Even though I disagreed with him on some social issues, I thought that he could be a really good leader. It was Sarah Palin that ultimately turned me off.

I grew up always thinking deeply about elections. This last one was no different, so I've got a lot to say! My parents trained me well to consider the choices carefully, making sure I understood it is a thoughtful process.

This is a transition time in my life, and that impacts how I'm thinking about Trump. See, I grew up with this idea that you go to school to get good grades to get into a good college to get a good degree to get a good job to make a lot of money so that you can pay it forward and send your kids to college. And my dad did a really good job at that! I was always a "goody two-shoes," the one that teachers liked because I actually wanted to be there in school. I got the idea that the more degrees I had, the more successful I was. I thought degrees wouldn't just open doors to success, but that the degrees themselves would mean I was successful. So my sights were set on getting a PhD... in anything! If I didn't get a PhD, then somebody with one would get to look down on me. I'd be inferior to them in some way.

I spent four years in college, but got five years' worth of credits. My two majors were in Planetary Science and Math, and I got a minor in Mechanical Engineering. That was a custom minor where I specifically emphasized thermodynamics, fluid mechanics, and heat transfer. Basically, I took the most difficult classes I could find.

College in St. Louis is the first place I ever heard a tornado siren. I realized that I *love* storms – they excite me! – so I thought that meteorology might be a good fit. I just wanted a PhD for prestige anyway, the actual field didn't matter too much. I got recruited to the University of Oklahoma, which has the National Weather Center. It is arguably the number one Meteorology school in the country, and I was specifically recruited by the director as the number one choice in the country. I point this out because, once I got there, I realized I was really unhappy.

Part of the problem was that I had just worked my butt off in college, and here I was back at square one not knowing anything about meteorology. I didn't even know more than three types of clouds! So I was learning introductory meteorology while learning a whole new programming language. I had never done computing with a gigantic, billion-dollar server, and the learning curve was steep. I wasn't making progress, even though I was working very hard. For the first time, I asked myself, "Is this what I really want to do?" I'd never questioned that before. "Is getting a PhD because your dad has one a really good reason?" No, it wasn't. And that's when it hit me that there is only one thing I really want to do with my life: I want to change the world.

I was president of the Gay-Straight Alliance when I was in high school, I was president of the BDSM and Kink club when I was in college. (Don't get weirded out by that. It wasn't because I have super kinky desires in bed, but because it was important to me that when people do want to explore those things in college they have a way to learn how to do them safely.) These are social issues that I care about, and they were just the beginning of my attempt to have a real impact on the world.

I've always known that I want to be special. There's this desire to have everyone look at me as an adult with the same awe they did when I was a little girl. When I was young, it was, "Wow, you're so special, you've got so much potential." Let me tell you, I hate the word "potential" because it just means you haven't done anything yet! And I don't want to be thirty-something, forty-something, fifty-something years old, go to a high school reunion, and say something like, "Yes, I'm an accountant now." I want to do something that actually makes people excited!

Meteorologists don't change the world, they just report the world changing, so I decided it wasn't right for me. It was scary to leave because my dad had always told me to have a plan. I had no idea what else I was going to do, I just knew that I wasn't happy there.

I took a break. At twenty-three years old, for the first time in my life I got a real job. I worked as a waitress. All my friends had gotten jobs in high school or college, but I never did because my parents told me, "Stay in school, focus on your work. If you need money, we'll give you money. Just make sure you're doing everything you can to get these degrees." Being a waitress was the most rewarding experience. I really, truly enjoyed it, but I had left when they couldn't give me enough hours. That's when I went to the political firm and canvassed for Democrats for ten bucks an hour. I was on Claudia Griffith's campaign when she got elected to the Oklahoma House of Representatives, and they said that I was one of the most important people on her campaign.

I thought that the military might be good for me, but I was rejected because I'm ADHD. (I would've enjoyed the discipline in the military, because I never had it growing up. My parents were so liberal that I got grounded only once in my life, but two days into it they stopped enforcing.) I found a job at a multi-level marketing firm knocking on doors selling TV service. They emphasized, "We do sales, but we don't want you to think about it like that. We'll teach you the basics of sales, because it's really not that hard. If you just talk to enough people, you will make money." So what they were really emphasizing was entrepreneurship, and that's what I'm into now. That's the part of Donald Trump that I really connect with.

My whole life, I'd always been the teacher's pet and just wanted a pat on the back or a good grade at the end of it. Now I was deciding that I'd rather take ownership and do things for myself! I'll give myself a pat on the back! This is my new capitalistic mindset: I put in the work to get what I want for *me*.

Co-workers at the sales firm exposed me to the financial side of conservatism. They never changed my views about being a social liberal, but they showed me how fair financial conservatism can be. "You get what you earn. Period."

When somebody takes on more responsibility, it gives them more power. I live in a super low-income area and I'd love to become a real estate investor. I thought I wanted to invest there, where I live, but these actual real estate investors are telling me that the area I'm in will never be worth a lot of money. You know why? Because there's a mentality in that part of town that you get whatever you can however you can get it. "Do unto others before they do unto you." It's just very primal, very animalistic. As a group, that tends to be how people behave when in a low-income setting. And that impacts the value of the neighborhood, because there's always a risk that your car's going to get stolen or your kids aren't going to be safe or there's going to be drugs and things like that. If people where I live would embrace responsibility, it would lead them to power.

I am still very much a social liberal and want to help people, but I recognize that the problems in my neighborhood are not things that we can change on a grassroots level, they're systematic. We have problems like people making more on unemployment than when they actually have a job. It's a system that rewards people who work less. I don't have a solution for how to change that, and I'm definitely not in a position to change it even if I had a solution. But that's one of the reasons I want to be stupid, fucking rich! It's so that I can actually try to change the system, because the system is so broken. Trump sees that.

Liberal friends wonder, "How could you possibly vote for Trump?" But these are the same people who, at the beginning of this election cycle, were agonizing that we didn't have *any* good choices. What I ended up balancing was, "If I vote for Hillary Clinton, what's the best that can happen, what's the worst that can happen? If I vote for Donald Trump, what's the best that can happen, what's the worst that can happen?" A lot of my vote came off of faith in the answers to those questions. I listen to a lot of opinions, but my first trusted source that encouraged me to vote for Donald Trump was the author, Robert Kiyosaki. He wrote *Rich Dad, Poor Dad.* That's the basis of most of my financial education, and I believe in it so much that I'm taking classes through his company about how to become a real estate investor and financially free. Kiyosaki released a video where he said, "If you want more of the same, vote for Hillary Clinton. If you want change, vote for Donald Trump. You're not going to *like* all of the changes, but he will bring change."

Even Robert doesn't agree with everything that Donald Trump does, but there's a lot of the political system that really does bother me and I think Trump is poised to change those things. Even the bad changes won't end up bad in the end! For example, let's say he starts actually enforcing these immigration laws and deporting people back to Mexico. I don't actually think that's cool, but it would force the issue. People will either realize that we don't actually care who gets deported back to Mexico, or the whole country will come together and say, "Okay, that's actually not cool. We've realized we don't want you deporting people, Mr. Trump." Then we'll change the laws appropriately. Either way, we win.

And in his defense, Trump wouldn't actually be doing anything but enforcing what's already on the books. He's not changing laws. I understand that it's much easier for a president to just stop enforcing a law than to actually try to get something through Congress, but when you put someone as volatile and exciting as Donald Trump in the presidency, it forces shit to get done! What I'm hoping is that the right shit will get done, shit that moves us in the right direction. Donald Trump is shaking things up, even though I disagree with some of his social politics.

Our governor here in Oklahoma is super anti-gay. I don't agree with her, and I don't agree with Trump when he speaks against gay rights issues. But I also know that the gay rights movement has come so far already that it's not going to stop. If we leave certain rights up to the states to decide, and states like Oklahoma say we're not going to give protection to gay couples, then there will be an uprising!

I'm pro-choice, too. So I disagree with Trump on a lot of levels. I've been giving to Planned Parenthood for a long time. So you see, ultimately, I did not vote in this election based on social issues. It was all about economics.

I am not an expert in economics, and I could be very misguided, but I'm taking advice right now from people that I trust, like Robert Kiyosaki. He pretty successfully predicted the financial crash in 2008, and he's predicting another crash next year. America is not secure. The U.S. dollar isn't as strong as it was, and any day there's potential for some political move to completely devalue our currency. And we know that one thing Donald Trump has proven for sure is prowess with money. Most politicians do not have substantial amounts of money. But Trump does! It's very evident that politicians are not economists. Wasn't it Obama who doubled the U.S. debt?[45] Trump can restructure the government in such a way that it's more efficient.

People say, "Well, Trump has lost millions of dollars." Anybody who's a business owner has lost money! The point is his *net*, the fact that he has made more than he has lost. I know people don't want him gambling with the U.S. economy, but when we're already billions or trillions and quadrillions of dollars into debt, it seems like there's no such thing as losing money with the U.S. government.

Trump's big thing is to take care of America first, and then worry about the rest of the world. Hillary Clinton was more like, "We need to take care of these refugees right now." Now, I think it's awesome that America has always been a place where people could come and be safe, but we have to first make sure our country is strong! That doesn't mean, necessarily, that we have to secure our borders. I'm not saying that we need to prevent Mexicans from coming in and trying to find a better life for themselves. I think it'd be *great* if we made them citizens! I'm not talking about *people*, but about our economy and political system. We are so polarized right now. We're not in any shape to take care of other countries' problems. I think we really need to take a harder look at ourselves first.

Whew! That's actually hard for me to say! Because I really *do* want to take care of the rest of the world, and I think the way Trump is looking at our country is not the way that I would look at it. Our president is not super-inclusive of the gays, the immigrants, and everybody else that I would want to help take care of. But he can take care of us financially, and I care *more* about that. If China buys us or

---

[45] Technically, it was the Republican House and Democratic Senate serving during Obama's years that enabled the debt to double, and a large portion of that increase was due to tax cuts. President Trump's proposed tax revisions, at time of this writing, are predicted to double the debt again.

Japan buys us, which at this point I think they could do – they've bought enough of our debt that at any point if they want to cash us out they would literally own our country – if they do that, we're screwed.[46]

I admit that I'm still unsure about all of these economic things, and I did not do as much research as I really wanted to about China and Japan owning our debt in order to buy our country. My dad would say, "No, it's never going to happen, it's not likely." But is he saying that because he's a super left-wing liberal? Or is he saying that because it's actually not possible?[47] What I do understand is that America's economy is fucked right now, and if we continue to work on just the social issues, it's like we're worrying about trim on a house when the foundation itself has problems.

The 2008 housing crash proved to me that even things that *seem* unbreakable can crash spectacularly, and I can see some alarming similarities between what that market looked like right before it crashed and the U.S. economy today. Trump is out to protect us from that kind of catastrophe. The crash the Robert Kiyosaki talks about happening very soon would make the 2008 one look insignificant, and the more I learn about that situation, the more I wonder why no one else seems scared! But then, maybe a lot of them are, and maybe that's part of the reason why Trump was elected; not so much because people hate Muslims or Mexicans or Blacks or gays, but because they're scared of a financial meltdown.

I should also admit that I got turned off by Hillary Clinton. I hate to bring this up, but the whole email thing! I don't understand the details, I really don't and I'm not going to pretend that I do, but somebody that I trust told me that if anybody else had done what she did, they would be in prison for the rest of their lives. There was a five-star general or something – I don't think they have five-star generals anymore, actually – but someone very high up in the military that had a dishonorable discharge and was thrown in prison for doing something similar to what she did with those emails. Perception is very powerful, and I don't want to be in a country that is *perceived* by the rest of the world to have elected a criminal.

Hillary Clinton is a damn good politician. Donald is a businessman and a TV celebrity. Hillary could probably accomplish

---

[46] It is, of course, completely untrue that the United States could be purchased by a country owning our debt. Even if China began to "cash us out," it would be done slowly so as not to disrupt their own economy.

[47] He's saying it because it's actually not possible.

whatever she set out to accomplish, but at what cost? If Hillary ever tried to do anything that the public might not be so keen on, we also might never *know* about it until far too late. On the other hand, if Donald tried to do anything the public might not like, he probably wouldn't even try to hide it! We would all be able to hold him accountable. There's a big difference between the two of them: Hillary can hide things, Donald can't.

I didn't vote on social issues because I figured the media is liberal enough at this point to make sure no social wrongs go unnoticed. Trump wades hip-deep in social faux-pas; he will always be held accountable by the public. I believe too few people understand any political issues besides the social ones, and I honestly haven't heard very many arguments in favor of Hillary when it comes to anything other than social issues.

Let me give you an example of what's going on with liberals right now. This whole "Trump is starving seniors" debacle over the Meals-On-Wheels program is embarrassing to me as a liberal feminist. I looked it up, and there are many reasonable and believable accounts of what really happened. He's was never trying to take food from the elderly. As a liberal feminist, I need to hold other liberals accountable in getting their facts straight. I don't want them crying wolf. We shouldn't be sinking to the level of our political rivals who we hate specifically for their tendency to manipulate facts in grotesque ways, but that's exactly what the liberals seem to be doing with this debate over Meals-On-Wheels. It's not that Trump supporters are against social liberties, any more than I believe Hillary supporters are anti-American. People just care about different issues.

So many liberals with a desire to help people trade their time on a small scale and never make enough money to help on a big scale. I want to be that liberal that saves my money right now, who works my way up, who plays the game by the man's rules, so I can become the one who changes the rules. I'm a capitalist, and I'm going to be financially conservative so that I can be as rich as the Koch brothers. And when I support causes like the Koch brothers do, they will be the liberal causes.

The news is difficult to watch. Fox News deliberately manipulates things to be conservative, and CNN is always so negative. I feel like I don't have a news program that represents my views in a totally nonpartisan way. But I have a dream to fix that. One day, I'd like to have my own news station that is 100% positive. Not to ignore negative things that happen, but to always find the solution associated with them. There is a book called *Broadcasting Happiness* by a woman who, while a newscaster, got a major news corporation to do "happy week." For one full week they only told positive stories. This was during the 2008 financial crisis, but they were committed finding positive stories. One of the examples she gives is the story of two estranged brothers who were both about to lose their homes, but they pooled resources to save one house and live together. They've rekindled their relationship. Isn't that awesome?

During that happy week, the station was convinced they'd lose their audience. Instead, they had record high viewership; record high! But they've never done it since.

My original thought was that I want to be stupid fucking rich so I can buy Fox News and just change it into something more fact-based, but the more realistic option is for me to start a news program online. I'm working three jobs right now, so I put a lot of stuff on the back burner. But this news program is my dream. I think of myself as an entrepreneur. My core values are independence, selflessness, and shamelessness, which I don't think are contradictory. I'm shameless in who I am. I'm unapologetic for who I am, just like Trump. But I have much gratitude. I know that any help I offer right now is on a very small scale, but I'm trying to make people happier than they were before I arrived, and that's something. I try to make at least one person smile every day, and as a pizza delivery person, that's easy!

Psychologically, when you tell positive stories, you empower people to go out and do something. When you tell the doom and gloom stories, it makes people shut down and they feel helpless. That's one of the reasons I wish liberals would stop focusing on what they hate about Donald Trump and look to the *good* he can do for our economy. That positive spin is something the liberals lack right now. They're not giving him a fair chance.

CHAPTER FOURTEEN
The Proud Mother

March 15ᵗʰ, 2017
Tulsa, Oklahoma

In the wee hours of last night (this morning?), my talk with Babs in Hurts Donuts made clear to me that her personal values revolve around being independent, entrepreneurial, shameless, unapologetic, and grateful for what she has been given. I like this. She still maintains her identity as a liberal feminist. I like this, too. One of the last things she said was that she does not want to be paraphrased; only direct quotes allowed! I have no intention of twisting her words, of course, because many of them made sense to me. Obama was a change candidate; Trump is the new change candidate. If nothing else, I can completely understand that Trump equals change.

I'm sticking around Tulsa for a bit. Back here in the pristine lobby of the Mayo Hotel where I met Chris two days ago, I'm about to see Heather. She confides in me beforehand that this conversation is very important to her, so important that her husband has taken off of work (a rare occurrence) to accompany her and keep an eye on their toddler. Heather identifies as a feminist too, but without the "liberal" moniker that Babs was so proud of. Over there at the grand entrance I see Heather, her husband, and a bubbly child approach.

###

HEATHER: I do social media for ministries. I manage Facebook pages, Twitter, YouTube. I never thought I would get married. I grew up in the church, went to Bible college, and was planning a move to Kenya to work as a missionary. I wasn't interested in a typical lifestyle. I was fascinated with travel abroad, fascinated with different cultures, and felt like I was going to make a difference in other people's lives. But life happens. I met my first husband a year out of school, and never moved out of the country as I'd planned. Now here I am with my second husband, happy and busy with five children. All boys!

My dad was a Marine, my brother was a Marine, and my mom was in the Air Force. I was not ever in service, but patriotism is a huge part of who I am. Patriotism and family. I actually work from home now, making three times less, so that I can be present for my children when they need me. I wake up pretty early, just to have a little bit of time by myself.

I feel like I never really disconnect from the social media work. I love it so much and these pages are really exploding. If there's a message that you care about, social media is an amazing way to get the message out. I'm constantly answering messages, moderating. It's pretty all-encompassing, maybe four or five hours a day looking at the screen. Plus, I manage multiple properties that we own. I just make myself always available.

We have family dinners together. I try to feed my family organic as much as possible. I think there's a lot of toxins in the world, and I think most kids are getting a lot of garbage. I'm not perfect at controlling that, but I try to make a nice family dinner. Our grocery bill is half the reason I work. All boys, remember!

Doing social media for ministries means that people are often writing about their problems. And I care about that. Sometimes they ask me for prayer. This is my job, but I would do it for free; it's part of my mission. I did social media for a bank one time and hated it. I can't do things in life that I don't believe in.

Trump was my favorite from the beginning. This is a true story: I had just ordered Trump's books and started reading them because I felt like we weren't doing this real estate thing right. We did pretty good but were missing something. The real estate was to be our retirement; we purchased a bundle of eight properties. It was a big deal. We had gone to some of these *Rich Dad, Poor Dad* seminars and thought this was what we could do to put the kids through college. (Because we're your typical middle-class, a lot of our money goes to taxes. We make pretty good money, but it's going a lot of places.) Anyway, I had just purchased Trump's real estate books, and I was literally sitting on the couch reading his book when Trump came on and announced. I put my book down and said, "He speaks to the heart of the people. He's going to be our next president." I don't know how to explain it, I just knew.

We've had enough insincerity. I despise insincerity in anybody, in a politician, in a salesman, in a friend. I would rather a person tell me, "You look horrible today, are you okay?" Because then I feel like they care! I like truth even if it hurts. Trump spoke to that. He was telling America what we needed to hear, not what we wanted to hear. I used to watch *The Apprentice* because I thought it was funny, but I didn't really respect the man. Now, I'm just astounded by him. When I hear him speak, I hear a patriot.

I knew from the beginning that Trump would have a backlash because he's so – I don't want to say polarizing because that has a negative connotation – but because he is so very black and white. You don't usually have to guess what he means. I thought, "I don't think he's doing this for himself." I never believed he joined the race for personal gain, because he could be making a lot more money and not have to deal with the backlash. I knew his safety would be threatened. So why is he doing this? From the minute I heard him speak, I thought, "He's doing this because he cares." I heard sincerity in his voice. Passion can't be feigned. So, I was sold from day one. My husband wasn't.

We have lost our way in America, as far as understanding who we are. It's an intricate situation because we are a melting pot. I, having a heart for missions, absolutely love people from other countries. When I went to Bible college, it was a very mixed pot of people from all over the world. I embrace that, and yet I picture America as a house without doors and walls. When we are undefined we can't really answer, "Who are our people?"

Here's an analogy: my kids have teenage friends who often fight with their parents and come to stay at our house when that happens. Teenage years? It's a very volatile time. So I tell these kids, "Our home can be a safe place for you, as long as your parents know where you are." But this one time, I knew the child had a drug issue. My heart bled for him, but I couldn't let him come. I have to protect my family first, and that's what I see in Trump.

Is the wall the best way? I don't know. But the message conveyed, "I will protect my people." That spoke to me. Like a father saying, "I care about everyone in this world, but my family first." I don't think our leaders have represented Americans for a long time.

I had never worked for a campaign before, but I'm currently on the Republican platform committee; I'm a delegate, and I'm also the chairwoman of my precinct. Trump pulled me into all of this. But the moment that they get political and play games, I'm out, because I don't feel Trump plays games. I feel he means what he says and he says what he means. He knows there's going to be retaliation, and he still does it. I respect that immensely.

I volunteered at Trump headquarters in Tulsa, which is across the hall from the GOP. It was not incredibly friendly. That made me see that Trump did not even have *Republicans* behind him. I'm still not sure Paul Ryan is on board! I watch him and I see a snake. I just see Paul Ryan saying, "I'll slither away from what the people want." I don't like that. That's why I have never liked politics. Paul Ryan makes you wonder what he's doing in the background. It's creepy.

When Trump came to Tulsa, I hired a babysitter. It was thirty degrees. I took my twelve-year-old with me and let him miss school. We stood in line for over three hours. I was not properly dressed, and it was so cold. People were buying me hot chocolate and stuff, but it was miserable. I just wanted to be there. And let me tell you, the energy in the room was electric. I walked in and said, "These people are on fire!" He had captured their hearts. You could just feel it. There were some protesters there, but I didn't feel like anybody was mean. Sometimes passion has two sides.

I was pretty far in the back of the line even though I waited over three hours. I thought I'd be in nosebleed territory, but when I walked in a security guard grabbed my arm and said, "Go down there." I said, "Yes, sir" and we ended up eight or nine rows from the front.

I was very impressed with how many college and high school students were there at the rally. It struck me that they cared, because we're always told millennials don't care. It's not true. They were so hyper.

Trump was over an hour late. We'd been out in the cold for three hours and now I'm standing on this floor for over an hour. My son couldn't see over the crowd, so a lady grabbed his hand and started pulling him toward the front. I'm trying to stay with him, and the next thing you know, everyone is helping us get to the very front. We were packed in like sardines, but they're pushing the children to the front. Ordinarily, people would be pushing to get in front of me, but here they are giving children the front so they can see and breathe. I was impressed with that; I was impressed with the whole crowd.

Trump's speech had no placating or pandering. I listened with my heart open, and I was just so impressed. Afterwards, he came down to the front row to sign things. He caught my eye and said, "Thank you for coming. Did you have a good time?" And it just stunned me. I didn't even know what to say. I felt like he actually cared whether I had a good time, and really? You know what I mean. He wanted to make sure, if I invested the time to be there, that I got something out of it. He cared.

He said to me, "Is that your sister?" There was a lady next to me that I'd been speaking with. I said, "No. She's just a friend." He said, "Oh. You two sort of look alike and have similar faces." This girl next to me was actually really attractive, so my twelve-year-old son's takeaway was, "Donald Trump thinks my mom is pretty!" That made him feel good.

This Russia stuff? I will preface my comments with, "I love truth more than Trump." So if I ever thought he was just a total put-on, he would lose my support. But I think this Russia thing is bogus. I'm not a conspiracy theorist, I'm not. But I feel like the media very much doesn't like him. I feel like they're trying to undermine him any way they can, and Russian ties is just one of the ways. I won't watch CNN anymore. What Trump stands for and what he speaks to in the American people is bigger than any bombshell they could uncover.

I went into the post office with my three-year-old son. The lady behind the counter engages with him a lot, so while I was buying some stamps she says to my son, "What is that?" A picture of the American flag was on the stamps. He goes, "They're stickers." She goes, "What is that on the sticker? What is that?" He said, "Well, that's Donald Trump's flag." There was about six people behind me in line and they all started cracking up! When he sees the American flag, he thinks Donald Trump. The movement is bigger than the person, but Trump captured the heart of the movement. He didn't even create the movement, he just awakened it.

The amount of people on welfare under our last administration just went through the roof. I have a firm belief: if my children are going to drive a car, they're going to pay for the repairs and they're going to pay for the gas. You pay your own way. I don't mind helping people that need help, but you don't help them by giving them entitlements. Entitlements never brought anybody to their highest level of excellence. Human beings lose respect for themselves when everything is just given to them without having to put forth any effort. It's very wrong for us to be taking from the middle class, who are out there working sometimes two and three jobs, in order to give to people who refuse to work. The Bible says, "If a man doesn't work, he shouldn't eat." Most people would be very motivated to go get a job if they were hungry.

When I believe in something, I can't be silent.

CHAPTER FIFTEEN
The State Lobbyist

March 30th, 2017
Indianapolis, Indiana

In my last meeting, Heather appeared with poise and grace in the opulent Mayo Hotel, then spoke with poise and grace about her adoration of Donald Trump. Were I forced to label the feelings she presented, I might have to collectively call them "hero worship." It's an utter, perhaps wide-eyed fascination with the man. Now that I've moved on to Indianapolis, I'm encountering a bit of the same.

Tony is a state lobbyist who invites me to spend an afternoon with him in the Indiana Statehouse while Senate is in session. He'll introduce me around to state reps, tour me around the historic capitol building, and sit with me in the chambers to chat. The local GOP office tells me that Tony worked directly with Trump on the Indiana campaign, and – being the realm of Governor Mike Pence – I know this should offer powerful insight.

Tony and I speak for hours about politics, family, and lobbying in general. But the most striking thing for me is his own version of hero worship. Perhaps I'm exaggerating, and I'll have to let his words speak for themselves, but this thing I'm calling hero worship a recurring theme; I'm seeing Trump's celebrity status has a definite, tangible impact on voter support. The lock-screen image on Tony's iPhone is his family posing with the president. So, Tony is an accomplished political operative who carries this personal picture of Trump in his coat pocket every minute of every day. He's very proud.

Tony was witness to an accidental meeting between President Trump and Mike Pence during the campaign. It was this meeting that apparently sealed the deal on Pence's becoming the VP nominee, and the Statehouse is close to where it happened. An accidental meeting that produced the VP? I'm anxious to hear the story.

###

TONY: I'm of Pakistani and Indian heritage, though I was born in Manchester, England. I've been twenty-five years in and out of this building, most recently with my own lobbying firm. I've been up front on the Trump perspective from day one, and I've been appearing on the local Fox affiliate's Sunday morning talk show to help people understand the great stuff Trump's been doing. We'll get to that, but first some background on who I am and how I got here.

I'll be fifty-one on Saturday, but I came to America when I was three. My parents moved us to Indianapolis because my mother's family had immigrated here. Keeping the family together was important to them, and it's hugely important to me. There was a lot of love growing up, and my kids are everything now.

Did my college here at Indiana University, graduated from the School of Public and Environmental Affairs. My concentration was financial administration, so it sounds like I was smart. I wasn't! I just fell into that. At the time, I didn't know I'd be getting involved in politics and government. After graduation, I went into a Blockbuster store just to practice my interviewing skills. I didn't expect to have a job with them, but it was offered and I didn't feel like looking around, so I took it. I got promoted after only five months. I was on my way to being a district manager and would've had a career in retail, but I knew I couldn't stay in that kind of field. It was seventy, eighty hours a week, which is fine if it's something you love and want to do the rest your life, but it wasn't for me. I put in those hours *now* with my lobbying firm, but retail wasn't my passion.

All this time, the one interest I really had was politics. I just didn't know how to get started. I was drawn to politics because I wanted to help. I wanted to do something noble. Even today, I try to work only on important issues that are doing real good for people and industries.

When I was younger, I probably could have been a Democrat or Republican. I didn't consider the issues much until Reagan got me. It boiled down to wanting a stronger country, stronger defense, and stronger military. I was realizing what could happen with war – we were seeing it on the news – and I respect those dangers. Reagan was a defense leader; he was like a cowboy.

I didn't consider the social issues too much back then. I really could have turned out pro-choice or pro-life, either way. But now I'm definitely pro-life, and I'll tell you what solidified it for me. When my wife was pregnant with our first, our daughter, at five or six weeks she had some issues. There was some spotting. She had just told me that she was pregnant, and we really thought we were going to lose our baby. We went in, they did an ultrasound, and they said, "You see that light? That's the baby." And I don't care if you call that a fetus or what, but it was tiny and it was ours and there was this flashing. They said, "That flashing? That's the heartbeat. Everything's ok." And that got me. I'll never forget that. It really solidified my views.

How to get started in politics seemed like a mystery, so one day I just cold-called the Republican party and asked them who I could volunteer for. This is January of '92 and the primary is coming up. I volunteered in the communications office for one of the campaigns, and after three weeks they hired me on full-time. Here's the crazy part: for some reason I can't remember, the press secretary quit. Being a campaign that was trying to save money, and with only a few months before the election, they let me take on the title of press secretary! That was my lucky break, and I continued many years working in state-level communications offices.

I was actually a little bit lazy about looking for jobs, but I've always had things happening at the right time in the right place. When you work hard and develop a good reputation, that can work.

I got a wild idea once and decided to run for Congress myself. I lost in the primaries; he got about eleven thousand and I got about eight thousand votes. I raised more money than he did, but it wasn't enough money to get me on TV. And I didn't like raising that money. You're asking your friends and family for donations, then you're asking people you don't know, and you're so focused on having fundraisers and putting out mail pieces asking for cash. That's the one part of politics that I don't love.

My lobbying career started as a fluke. A friend of mine on the Democratic side asked me to join the governmental affairs team at Comcast to lobby for them. This Democratic friend realized I had good relationships with Republicans in this building, so I started my own business and Comcast became my first client.

Folks ask, "What does a lobbyist do, exactly?" Here's the deal: when you need help in the legal system you hire an attorney, when you need help on the government side you hire a lobbyist. You need somebody that understands the process, understands the people, and understands how a bill becomes a law. Lobbyists get a bad rap, but most folks can't work with government on their own because they don't have a good enough knowledge of how committees work.

I think lobbying is an honorable profession even though, like in any profession, there are bad actors. Mostly those bad actors are on the federal side, not at this state level. I've never taken a client that I was morally or ethically opposed to, but I've questioned it periodically. Actually, my biggest client now is one I questioned: Reynolds Tobacco. Republicans were about to take control of the Indiana House again, and Reynolds realized they should hire a Republican lobbyist. They had a Democrat already. Now, I've never smoked, but their issues concerned taxes and regulation. Tobacco is a legal product, and this company is the leader in tobacco harm reduction. There are folks that can't or won't or don't want to give up tobacco. But Reynolds is the leader in creating products that are non-combustible. They don't have the smoke. I honestly think that the harmful effects of combustible cigarettes are a huge concern, and this company is trying to move away from that, creating products that are less harmful by removing the smoke. The FDA in Washington, however, has been blocking Reynolds' innovation, so we've got lobbyists working in D.C. on that. It's taxes that are the big problem here on the state side. It's a legal product and, like any business, Reynolds wants to keep taxes light for their consumers. That's what I lobby on. Reynolds doesn't even bother fighting the smoking bans anymore.

So, that's my background. I tend to be long-winded about it.

With Trump, I was a fan from all the way back. I went to Trump Tower in New York and bought a hat that said, "You're fired." I remember seeing him being interviewed in the eighties on Oprah, and *The Art of the Deal* and all that. He was very well known and well regarded. Obviously, he was a great business leader, entrepreneur, and builder. All that was always impressive.

Getting closer to the election I was actually thinking I'd vote for Jeb Bush. My wife and I both were fans of George W. and his dad. But then I saw Jeb Bush stumbling all the time. I kept saying, "Well, that's not good, Jeb. That's not good." And here was Trump coming down the escalator and right away I was fascinated. Every time he says something controversial and I think it's going to be bad, he manages it! He has great control. I wanted to get involved with his campaign, but again I didn't know how. Here's how it finally happened: I was talking to a client about the race and I said, "I'm a pretty big Trump fan." She goes, "I just met with his team this morning." She's working for a company that does digital advertising, and she says, "Do you want me to introduce you to someone?" I get sent up to a guy who is political director of the Trump campaign. (He's still with the campaign, actually, and is in charge of the re-election effort for 2020.) I had a twenty-minute phone conversation with him and find out the Indiana state chairman of the campaign is a guy named Rex Hurley. He's eighty-two years old, and we know each other. Now I get to work.

It's a month sprint to the primary, and we're very busy. I'm the one talking to the media and that kind of thing. See, we had a lot of Republicans here in Indiana that weren't for Trump, Republicans who thought he'd lose in the primary. We had to take on those pre-conceptions, because our goal was to win all nine congressional districts and all 57 delegates in the state. Guess what? We did!

We had *thousands* of volunteers all over the state, real help with yard signs and things from all kinds of folks that love Trump. What we saw at that time was an absolute groundswell of support. The rallies were incredible.

Here's a fun story: I'd come up with an idea for candidate Trump to come into Indiana and talk to our Republican state committee. They meet one Wednesday a month. We were having trouble from people in the party saying they were going to support Cruz or Kasich and I wanted Trump to come in and meet these guys in person. We'd do a rally and they'd see the base of support. So this one day, I'm sitting at my desk at home and Trump calls! This is April 12th, and I had been hoping for the visit to be the next day. I remember those dates. The phone rings and he says, "Tony, this is Donald Trump." I thought, "No, this is a joke."

Playing it carefully though, I said, "Well, hello. How are you?" Then he starts talking and says, "Tony, I hear you've got an idea, and I've heard good things about you, so I wanted to talk to you about what we need." After a minute or so, I blurted out, "Oh my God, it's really you!" I wish I hadn't said that.

We talked for almost eight minutes and I tell him my idea. The main thing was to get him to Indiana as soon as possible. Here's why: on Tuesday April 5th, Trump lost Wisconsin to Cruz. Then, on April 6th, the press was all about, "Trump's on his way down, Cruz is going to keep moving up." They were already projecting Trump's demise. We said to them, "There's not another primary for two weeks, and it's New York, where of course Trump will do well." We knew that, coming out of New York, he'd have momentum. Then a week later there would be five mid-Atlantic states – Maryland, Delaware, Connecticut, whatever the others – and that was also kind of his neck of the woods. So, by the time we get to our primary in Indiana, the momentum will have really shifted. We told all the TV and radio people that. And we were right!

Trump came to Indianapolis, and I set up a meeting with Governor Pence's guy. There were rumors at the time that Pence might be endorsing Cruz, so we got the Trump meeting set up at the governor's residence. They hit it off right away.

Then Trump had his first Indiana rally at the State Fairgrounds, and it was great, great media coverage. The five mid-Atlantic states hit, so we had the momentum we'd predicted for our May 3rd primary. Mike Pence, in the meantime, went ahead and endorsed Cruz. We thought he wasn't going to. But we *won*, and we won big. Cruz saw that and dropped out that night. Pence then did the smartest thing he's ever done. (He's a smart guy, but this was the absolute smartest thing he's ever done.) Pence turned around and endorsed Trump right then and there.

All these other Republicans around the country were staying out of it. If they had a chance to knock Trump, they would. But Pence was saying yes. Mike Pence and I are friends. I could tell how sincere he was about Trump and believing in his vision.

After the primary, we weren't as busy. We planned a fundraiser for Trump to come back here, and speculation was starting about Pence becoming the VP. It certainly wasn't set in stone, though, because there were many others: Jeff Sessions, Chris Christie, and more. So, Trump comes and does the fundraiser, and afterwards there was this rally about forty-five minutes north. Trump was going to fly back east, but most working on the campaign were going to the rally. I declined, because I had a dinner appointment. That was a serendipitous decision.

I'm walking to my car and I get a text: "Trump's staying at the Conrad tonight because his plane has a flat tire and brake problems."

I get in the car and I drive over to the hotel to see what I could see. There are some folks there that I know, including one that works for Pence. We're hanging out, and over by us there's Donald Trump, Eric Trump, Governor Pence and his wife Karen having a private dinner. It's that dinner, I think, that really secured Pence's VP nomination. And the dinner wasn't supposed to happen! Trump was supposed to fly out of here, but the flat tire and brake problems made them have to wait for a whole new plane. Trump had to stay overnight and opted for dinner with Pence and his wife. That dinner went on a long time, and the next day they followed up with a breakfast meeting. This was all a big turn of events! Trump wasn't supposed to spend that much time with Pence at all. It was damn luck that the day of our fundraiser was the day the plane got a flat tire.

I was a delegate, and I took my wife and kids to the state convention. That was really cool. I have this picture of us with the kids are wearing hats that say *Trump's Kids*. They're not campaign hats; they are from his hotel! We stayed at his Chicago property three years ago. It's an amazing hotel, a bar on the 16th floor facing the lake, and all kinds of games and stuff for the kids. We did the family package there and the hats came with it. Trump has such great attention to detail! The family package had these little cakes when we walked in the room, and the cakes had the kids' names on them. There was popcorn. There was candy. There was soda. There was a movie for them to watch already playing.

So we had these *Trump's Kids* hats, and we took Sharpies with us to meet Trump. He talked to us for a long time, but I choked and didn't ask him to sign the hats. He was so great with the kids, but after we said goodbye my son was just standing there looking at him. I said, "Why are you just staring?" He goes, "We were supposed to get our hats signed." Oh, I felt bad. I'm a dad; I had to fix the situation.

So that Friday morning, I find out Trump's doing a thank you event for staff. I got in there, close to the podium, and I brought the hats. Trump went down the row shaking hands, but he didn't see me. Folks were kind of pushing to get close, holding their phones, and just not getting out of the way. But Pence was trailing next to Trump and I said, "Governor." Pence takes the hat and starts signing one of them himself and I say, "No!" He goes, "Oh, sorry about that! Donald, you've got to sign this for my friend, Tony." Trump looks at me and says, "I know Tony." And he signed both hats. That was really cool.

The Trump campaign officially hired me as communications director here soon afterwards. I was on the payroll from August 1st to the election. They hire eighteen state communications directors, one for each of the battleground states. Indiana wasn't usually a battleground except for the fact that we had a big Senate race going on at the same time. I was in on all the national campaign strategies, but they weren't working well here. The media wasn't paying as much attention to the Trump campaign because of all these important local races. So we decided to do our own thing: we traveled around the state to campaign in person, and we got to over half of our counties. Doing that, we saw people come out who hadn't participated in politics before. They'd tell me that they either never voted or maybe hadn't voted for twenty or thirty years. And now they were coming out for Trump. One guy I remember specifically saying, "I've been waiting for a guy like this. I don't trust Washington. I've never trusted the process. I've been waiting for this kind of guy." That's how I knew we were going to win.

I predicted we'd win by twenty. The polls were showing anywhere from four to twelve here. Folks thought that Hillary had a chance. Some folks in our local media, just like nationally, didn't believe there was a real movement for Trump. I knew we'd win, but the morning of the election, I went on the radio and said we'd win *big* by twenty. They thought I was crazy. But guess what? It was twenty.

What we saw here, we heard about in other states. People were just ready for someone from outside of the system. They'd been let down over and over again, and they believed in Trump as someone who meant what he said. When I say they, I mean *me*, too. We believed in Trump as a man of action.

You don't have to be in politics to run for office. But you have to have accomplished something. Trump built a worldwide, successful company. I've been in his hotels and in his buildings. I've seen the attention to every detail. This is a man who cares about doing things right. Even though I'm part of what you might call "the establishment," and even though I'm non-white, I've seen the downside of the establishment from within. I've always thought things could be done better. Politics sometimes plays too big a role in decision-making, and Trump can clean that up. Right now, you see it again in D.C. where they've pulled the bill to repeal Obamacare. These guys could not get their act together! Democrats wouldn't participate. Republicans didn't handle it the right way if they wanted Democrats to participate. They've had seven years of complaining and they had time to get a plan together, but they didn't. I honestly think that Trump wants to do what's best for all Americans. I'm sure he's let down by this healthcare thing. You'll see Republicans reaching across the aisle more now, I'm sure of it. The failed Obamacare repeal was a good learning lesson for them.

Some people are opposed to Trump because he's a billionaire. They don't trust that. But when you go back and find these old interviews on YouTube, videos of him talking to Oprah back many years ago, he was already talking about what's broken in our country. He would always mention bad trade deals hurting the American worker. He was asked long ago, "Are you thinking of running?" He said, "No, I love what I'm doing. In business everything's doing well. But if I ever thought things had gotten so bad and there wasn't anybody that could get it fixed, then I would step up." That's what's played out here. Things have gotten bad, so Trump is stepping up.

As we travel around Indiana, we see a lot of people out of work, a lot of people that are on support because they lost their job. Factories here have closed down, and all these small towns down in southern Indiana have people on falling into addictive drugs and all that stuff. We're slipping. I know it's a slogan, "Make America Great Again," but I do think we need action there. People around me are turning to drugs, and the drugs are so prevalent; there's definitely something wrong.

We all have to worry about security. I worry about taking my kids to a show or to a football game because what if there's a bombing? What if somebody crazy, a terrorist or somebody who thinks they're a terrorist, wants to hurt us? It just wasn't like that when we were growing up, and it's getting worse. I remember everything about 9/11. I remember everything about that day. Kids that were young back then are facing a new reality today. Fifteen years from now, I don't want my kids having to worry about it anymore.

Trump's message gets drowned out a lot. I'll give you an example by just picking the most controversial one: the border wall. See, he's not really talking about Mexicans. He didn't mean Mexicans. Instead, he meant illegal immigrants. And he said illegal immigrants. But the media, first gradually then just flat-out, and would just say "immigrants" or "Mexicans." That's not fair to him. I'm an immigrant! Trump's wife is an immigrant! My family are immigrants. Trump wasn't talking about me or my family, he was talking about *illegal* immigrants. They're coming in the country by not going through the process, by not waiting in line, by not taking the test, by not proving that they should be citizens. And a lot of them are criminals. A lot of them are gang members. The media got Trump's message on illegal immigration so twisted. Maybe he could have said it better. Yeah, he really could have said it better. But that's also part of his appeal to folks here; he says it like the guy in Bedford, Indiana might have said it! That's how he relates.

There was a really disturbing story recently of a guy in Avon, Indiana, a suburb, that was arrested for running a drug ring. He was bringing in drugs from Mexico, bringing them across the border. This suburb was the central hub, and then the drugs were going to all kinds of places: Oregon, East Coast, small towns, bigger towns. The guy got arrested, but there was also this element of violence; some other gang had killed somebody in his ring, right over in Avon, Indiana! This was a real story right in our backyard. So when Trump talks about building a wall, he's talking about keeping real people safe, even in Indiana. He's not talking about preventing diversity.

Here's one thing that I've never said to anybody: there's all these little things that I like about Trump, too. Where I grew up, we're all huge fans of the Jackson Five and Michael Jackson. I saw the Jacksons in concert in '79, '81, '84, the Victory Tour. Saw Michael Jackson here in Indiana from the third row, once in Cleveland, once in Hawaii in '97. I'm just a huge fan. I knew Trump and Michael Jackson were friends and all that, but with Anderson Cooper on CNN, during the primaries, Trump was asked who he likes in music. He talked about Michael Jackson! What other candidate would have said that, knowing that there was controversy with Michael Jackson and it might turn people off? Trump has that loyalty.

There's so much division right now, and so much misinterpretation of what Trump says and what he's trying to do. We're getting to a point in the country where, no matter what, certain elements of the Democratic party are opposed to *everything* he says. They started talking impeachment right off the bat, and that's making it harder for anyone who is actually trying to work with him. I don't know how you change that vocal minority of Democrats, but somebody's got to reach across the aisle. From both sides. And everybody's got to tone it down. On both sides.

Remember, if half the country thinks just the way I do about Trump, we can't all be wrong. The other side has got to give us a chance.

CHAPTER SIXTEEN
The Bankrupt Cashier

March 31st, 2017
St. Louis, Missouri

Tony drove me over to a museum when we were through speaking at the Statehouse in Indianapolis, saving me dollars I would have spent on an Uber. It was in those last few moments riding together that he spoke aloud a goodbye message that has stuck with me all the way here to St. Louis: "If half the country thinks just the way I do about Trump, we can't all be wrong. The other side has got to give us a chance." I'll re-read Tony's comments a few times, because I do owe him that chance. He's a talker though, and a convincer, so I'll have to keep my defenses up. As a professional lobbyist, talking and convincing is what he does best. How else can he work so committedly for Big Tobacco?

I admit it, the tobacco industry lingers right up there with the gun industry in my liberal distaste. (Or perhaps it's my liberal distrust?) The two industries strike me emotionally to the core; I sincerely view them as enemies to our country's well-being. But that's pretty leftist of me, isn't it? Tony's centrist view is that he is supporting the tobacco industry's right to create reasonable, safer versions of products that people want to buy. Widening out to compare that lobbying viewpoint to his views on Donald Trump, I can understand that he also sees Trump as a product that Americans wanted to buy, and now we should all help create reasonable, safer versions of the policies that come with the purchase. Tony says, "People want him. So let's find ways to compromise with him." That's not a bold statement.

###

DEBBY: I voted for Reagan both times, but then I remember my step-father telling me that the Democrats were for the poor and the Republicans were for the rich. I was definitely poor, so I started voting Democrat. I had humble beginnings, and a very difficult childhood. There was violence and a little bit of foster care, and then I got into a marriage that was abusive. I guess I was a little more susceptible to something like that, with my childhood background. I was going to school to be a paralegal assistant, but my husband didn't let me finish. He was worried about me being able to take care of myself. But I weathered that storm and raised four children by myself, so I've mostly been a single mother with not a lot of income. Always had a lot of financial hardship, actually. But you know what? It's made me stronger and more appreciative.

We didn't need a lot of income while I was growing up. Maybe your car would break down and your neighbors would just come and help because they wanted to help. Now, you're afraid to help anybody. All this stuff in Ferguson, in Chicago, in New York; there's just a lot of violence nowadays.

When my children were raised and I came back into the workforce full-time, the economy had changed a whole lot. It became more and more difficult for me financially, but I was still of the mindset that Democrats were for the poor. That stayed with me for a long time, right up until this election.

I loved the enthusiasm of Mr. Trump, and I was a fan of his before. It was very refreshing to me to hear him speak the truth, for the most part. Maybe he did get a little bit rough around the edges. He was rougher than the average politician, but I started to see there's more to it than that. Maybe Republicans are for the rich, maybe

Democrats are for the poor, but Trump is just for all Americans. Trump brings hope for a brighter future.

Where was the money going for our country? Why were Americans being pushed backwards? Why was the government out of session a lot the time and politicians making so much money while we're in poverty? I think the hope is that we can stand looking over the fence talking to our neighbors without worrying we might be losing our homes. I think the hope is that our jobs can give us something reliable again.

I am losing my house. I'm going through bankruptcy right now. Hopefully, that will bring me a fresh start, a new beginning. I've got four young grandchildren. I want things to be right for them.

Tell you what, I'm really worried about illegals coming in. Some immigrants are probably great people, but Sharia law is something I'm genuinely fearful of. I worry about my daughter being able to walk down the street feeling free and not be forced to cover her head. I'm a Christian and I don't want to be forced into anything else; I don't want to be beheaded. You see these people being stoned, women being stoned. It can happen here. Sharia law can happen here. You see it in Europe already.[48]

You're seeing illegals walking up to people and just hitting them, trying to rape women. I've heard a lot about that. Trump is the guy that can fix this, because he's honest and he is patriotic. The way he's gone about things has been a little rough around the edges, but I think that most Americans get it. "We, the people," finally! He is the first president in a long time that is for *us* and actually wants to see us triumph. He's not even taking a salary, probably doesn't need one.

I think that Trump hears us loud and clear and speaks for us. I do believe he's been called by God. I do believe that he's just a vessel, but can be used mightily to turn this around, to make America great, to make us less fearful. To make us Kumbaya again. To make us feel we can overcome the adversity and the evil that's out there. He's not going to do it all, obviously, but I just feel so hopeful.

I've always loved that Trump faced a little bit of adversity himself, having to file bankruptcy. But I also thought that he had a winning smile, so to speak. A winning attitude. He wasn't going to let anything stop him, and certainly not bankruptcy. He's unstoppable! He didn't care what people thought. He did what he had to do, faced

---

[48] There is no Sharia law in Europe, though many conservatives believe there to be. This rumor began with gusto when correspondent Steve Emerson made the claim on FOX News. He has since fully retracted his words and apologized.

his financial troubles, said, "Okay, this is what I have to do," and started again.

I voted for Obama. Both times. The second time I was a little bit apprehensive, but the first time I was all-in. I really thought that he had a good spiel and that hope and change was really important. Sadly, it's gotten worse under his administration, in my opinion. A lot of people have that opinion.[49] But if Trump can change the economy, give people a living wage, then we could take a breath.

And there's another thing: Veterans are homeless while immigrants are coming in and taking over what we're supposed to have. Ha-ha! That's the way I feel. We're supposed to have those jobs, especially those jobs that pay well enough to support a family. I am a cashier; that is what I do. I still have my daughter and granddaughter living with me, but I just felt defeated at every turn. I haven't really been able to make ends meet. I got a couple evictions. A lot of people around here have a similar situation.

There's lot of heroin use here in St. Louis. I know it's everywhere in the country, but it's particularly bad, extremely bad, where I am. And addicts are just stealing from people like me who work hard.

If we had elected Hillary or anyone else, I think it would have been more of the same. We would be stuck in that same pattern. The last twenty years have gotten more difficult around here. Now, the Macy's is closing, the K-Mart is closing, the Sears is closing. Everything's just going out of business. The car plant, that's gone. It went overseas. So this thing Trump talks about with companies leaving the United States? It's not just speculation, it's definitely happening here.

I'm living in a more impoverished area. You go over a county or two, it's a little bit better. I hope to do that for us, because I'm starting to make a little more money and my bankruptcy will give me a fresh start. I was making $7.50 an hour, and they were giving me only about twenty hours per week. People can't live off that. I've earned my way up to $10.00 an hour now. I'm making it work, but just barely.

---

[49] Did things really get worse under Obama's administration? The NY Times says unemployment dropped drastically, the number of illegal immigrants convicted of crimes and deported doubled, the number of Mexicans living in the U.S. illegally decreased, and violent crime continued to decrease. The national debt, however, nearly doubled.

I'm not old, certainly, but I do think to myself, "I'm successful as a human being, but what did I do? What do I leave my kids?" My kids are doing better than I am.

I don't have any health insurance. I haven't had it in years. I had Medicaid for many, many years, but not anymore. I didn't qualify when I started making $7.65 an hour; they cut me off. Didn't make any sense. Then you see all these people coming in with $500, $600 of food stamps and nicer cars than I do, and they're not even from America. That's a tragedy, my opinion. I had an emergency appendectomy without insurance about three years ago. They took care of me, but now I'm sorry to say I've had to put those bills on my bankruptcy. People like me just don't have anything set aside for emergencies like that. There's no extra money. It makes you feel hopeless. I can't even get a teeth cleaning.

The Trump campaign got me on board through Facebook and Fox. I used to watch CNN and all of that, but I thought a lot of that seemed fake. My neighbors, real good friends of mine, were Democrats, too. For years. Then they switched over to Trump. We all just needed something different, because we are impoverished, and it is absolutely overwhelming. Poverty just overtakes you. You don't feel you can take another step. I've always been optimistic and faithful, but I'm often on the verge of losing that.

I want life to be the way people always dream it to be. We only have one life to live, and so we need to live it right. But we're always a work in progress. I'm always a work in progress.

CHAPTER SEVENTEEN
The Southern Northerner

April 7th, 2017
Norfolk, Virginia

Debby in St. Louis presented the most concise, if disappointing, argument for Trump I've heard so far: Things haven't been going well, so let's vote for something absolutely different. Her first vote for Obama was for the same reason. She's not a traditional liberal or conservative; she just embraces a clean slate when she might benefit from it. She wants change when our larger government isn't having a perceptible impact on her life. She wants to take a risk on something different because the thing that's the same hasn't changed anything for her. Who am I to blame Debby for wanting the latest "change candidate?" And an empathy reminder: Debby is working hard every single day, willing and wanting to work even more, but still she is "impoverished, and it is absolutely overwhelming. Poverty just overtakes you." My heart must take that in.

But then again...

Debby did say she believes Sharia law could come to the United States. She is fearful of being beheaded for her Christian beliefs. She did comment that illegal immigrants are randomly hitting people and sometimes trying to rape them. None of this seems rational. While I can respect Debby's vote for change, I also believe she is being irresponsible in researching the issues she claims to care about.

Time to leave the Midwest and fly east. On the military coast of Virginia, Norfolk is a city of contradictions; conservative due to its nearby naval base and requisite traditions, and liberal due to its nearby political centers and spring-break destinations. There's a tornado warning today, and I'm to meet Dave outside. It's blustery. No, it's a full-blown gall wrapping around this part of town. Dave and I meet in an open park because I prefer to walk-and-talk, but it quickly becomes obvious that this is not a sustainable environment for conversation. I suggest we move to a nearby McDonalds's. It's loud in here. It's busy in here. The place is absolutely full to the brim and it's pretty clear this crowd spends a lot of time within these walls. They all seem to know each other. They come into McDonald's to talk. They come into McDonald's to rest.

There's a housing project across the street, lots of cinder block buildings in tan colors. I admit a probable conclusion: most people spending time in this McDonald's are probably neighborhood locals, residents of the housing project across the street. So who is to blame them for nearly overtaking a public place when it's available? For relief from the blustery weather? For variety? But do they have to take up nearly every table?

Wait. Am I being too judgy? Yes, I guess they are allowed to be in here. But do they have to commandeer the space for so long? Dave and I spend two hours talking. Nobody around us moves to leave or to buy food during that time. This is a living room. McDonald's is their living room. Dave and I are just their guests.

While I check my attitude and my privilege, let's hear from Dave. Who is he?

###

DAVE: Who am I? I'm a southerner who was accidentally born in the north. I was born in Queens, in New York City. But the South feels more like home.

I had a traditional, probably upper middle-class life. I was painfully shy as a young person, didn't date or have girlfriends in high school. Not that I didn't want to, but I just couldn't figure out how! I immersed myself instead in sports and music. One thing I noticed in junior high was this list of awards that were given out in high school. One was the *Long Island Press* Athlete-Scholar Medal, given to the combination of top athlete and scholar in the senior class of the high school. I made it my mission to win that medal. I was up against the captain of the football team and a wrestler. I was a soccer player and a golfer, but I ended up being captain of both sports and did well enough academically to win, so that was my big accomplishment in high school.

East Carolina University kind of fit. I wanted a school that was big enough to have a lot of things, but not so big I was gonna get lost like you do in New York. Plus, it's warmer down in these parts. (I was the only son in the family, so the snow shovel was attached to my hands for about three months every year.) The South sounded right for me. Turned out to be the luckiest and greatest decision of my life.

After college, I was recruited by the United States General Accounting Office, the audit agency of Congress. That's when I came to work here in Norfolk. Got my first exposure to the Federal Government and its rules, regulations, and red tape. I had some frustration with that. And the travel had a negative effect on my marriage, which ended up not working out. Next week, though, I celebrate my thirtieth anniversary with wife number two, so that's awesome.

Through being involved with the East Carolina alumni association, I met a distributor of floor covering products. He needed a controller and was very persuasive. He convinced me to leave my slightly higher salary and cushy federal benefits for a future opportunity that could possibly pay off more. For the most part, I guess it did. We worked really hard, but there was less of that, "You have to do it this way or you're going to violate some rule or regulation." Not that we didn't have rules or regulations, but they were more normal than the government's.

One of my main responsibilities was credit management, which is something I had never done before. I was responsible for investigating new customers and deciding how much credit they should get. Once they started with us, I was monitoring how they did, going to visit them, and putting the hammer down if they didn't pay up. I was meeting lots of really nice people, primarily small business people, who often had just mom and pop type operations. We also dealt with the larger businesses, national chains even, but the meat of our business was the smaller type company. I liked interacting with businesses that were smaller because you get to know the people better. It just was more comfortable and enjoyable; I don't know how else to say it.

What do I like about Donald Trump? I like that he's not a politician. I was frustrated for many, many years working for the Federal Government. Our agency worked for a Congress that was, in theory, keeping track of the executive branch and making everything run right, but we were all supposed to work together. In our work, we were investigating for weaknesses and fraud and abuse and things like that. There's plenty of it out there. There's plenty of money rolling where it probably doesn't need to roll. When you're a federal auditor, you note it and write a report that gets sent to Congress, and then you hope they do something. But they never do.

As far as Trump's specific angle, I'm a total term limits proponent. Any congressman after probably about twelve years has done his fair share to help America, and I think it's then time for somebody else to get their shot. These guys and gals who build up thirty years of power? I don't think that's in our best interest.

My personal values seem to align with Donald Trump: honesty, family, strong leadership, willingness to help those who need help. I'm somebody who was very liberal in college. I was a supporter of George McGovern. I voted for Jimmy Carter. But right at about that point, something changed for me. I was Reagan, Bush, Bush – not Clinton. That change to being conservative began because of money. After leaving the federal government, I began to really feel the impact of working every day in the private sector where your paycheck doesn't depend on the government printing a check. It depends on your business being able to generate cash. In the early eighties, interest rates were like 12, 14, 16%. The company I worked for was borrowing hundreds of thousands of dollars. Not a lot of money in the big scheme of things, but for our company it was huge. We had a million-dollar credit line at the bank, and we had to make that interest payment every month. At the beginning, I thought, "What the world am I getting myself into?" It was a lot easier in government, where I didn't have to worry about the realities of where money would come from.

Ultimately, it was fun and exciting to work together and push through that uncertainty, devising strategies to sell more and collect more and keep on rolling as the economy recovered. It gave me real pride. That pride was a transition from liberal to conservative. I felt the pride of success out in the real word instead of just the government world. And I saw so many people in our customer base working their tails off, employing other people, and being what I perceive to be the backbone of our country. They did hard, prideful work.

A lot of my Democratic liberal friends have government jobs. There is some thought in my mind that they lean that way to help protect the lifestyle they live. Our Federal deficit under Obama's eight years was equivalent to the deficit of our entire country's history before he took office.[50] I don't think that's a good thing.

My parents were conservative, financially. We lived a very nice life, I think. We went on our one week of vacation to the Poconos every year and that was pretty much it for fun time. Nowadays, there's a growing force giving our government the responsibility for taking care of more and more in the world, and there's less self-responsibility and self-reliance. Self-responsibility and self-reliance is what my parents had while giving us a great life, and I think it is a better thing for people to have in general. The statistics on food stamps, on Federal disability, are just going up, up, up.

I saw an article a couple of weeks ago: like 50% of our people, if they had to raise $1,000, couldn't do it. That just blows my mind, and it's heartbreaking. It's terrible. That's not how it should be. And here we are, in beautiful downtown Norfolk, and we could throw a rock over there and hit the federal housing projects where people live in row after row of awful buildings. We can see it right there.

My wife and I took several driving trips last fall. We drove from here to Blacksburg, Virginia, which is about five hours away. We drove from here to Ohio, to Michigan, back to Ohio, and back home. I will tell you that in all of that driving around, we saw maybe five Hillary Clinton yard signs and five hundred Donald Trump yard signs. That told me something. That told me that even if he didn't win, there's something resonating out there.

My cousin lives in Hickory, North Carolina, in the western part of the state. The number of factories or warehouses that are empty in her town is in the dozens. We have other friends who live up in Erie, Pennsylvania, but are selling their beautiful home because Erie, Pennsylvania is dead. There's empty factories, empty warehouses all over. They had to sell what they thought was a $600,000 house for about $300,000.

Our tax system drives me absolutely crazy. I'm a CPA, but I hate doing tax returns. I pay somebody to do my tax return. Last year, my wife worked part-time for the school system, and she has her state pension. We both have our 401(k) and some IRAs. We took a little money out of that to survive through the year, because neither of us are on social security yet. I'm sixty-three, she's sixty-one. We have some charitable deductions and some tax deductions and whatever. All of that feels pretty normal, but my tax return is still thirty-three

---

50 Shoot. I guess that's pretty much true.

freaking pages long! That's ridiculous. I'm an accountant saying we need to totally redo the whole tax system and put half the accountants and half the lawyers living off the crazy system out of work. We should make them find a productive job, because what they're doing now is just spinning wheels in a crazy system that is not working.

Tax cuts for the wealthy? You tell me, what should the tax rate be for a wealthy person? Is giving up half of what you're making enough? I think they're doing that already. That seems pretty generous. We've got people who don't pay any taxes who get money *because* they don't pay any taxes. We've got too many social welfare programs when what we need to focus on are the underlying causes, like the terrible problems we have in our inner cities. We have crime. We have violence. We have families breaking up. We have drugs and alcohol problems. These are keeping people from rising up out of their situation.

My wife intentionally chose to work in the inner city. She is an uncommonly great teacher and wanted to make a bit of a difference. On balance though, it's been really a mixed bag. She's been recognized as the top teacher in the City of Norfolk, three times the top teacher at her school. She received the Presidential Award for being the top math teacher in the State of Virginia. She's all into education, but she has taken physical and emotional abuse being a teacher in Norfolk. She's taught for principals that were racist. She's taught in classrooms that are like trying to teach in this crowded McDonald's. The leadership is not willing to confront bad behavior. Two years before she retired, she was physically assaulted in her classroom. A student who was suspended came back at the end of the day, picked up a chair in the classroom, hit her over the head with it, knocked her to the ground, and then hit her twice more. So that's been a tough heal. But she still believes in public education. More than I do. I'd rather try other options. Let's give parents some flexibility with vouchers, like Trump says. That DeVos though? My wife thinks she's terrible.

Right after I retired, my church got involved in a project to offer volunteers to our local elementary school. Being newly retired and the husband of a teacher, I thought, "Let me just stick my nose in a school and see what's going on there." Let me tell you, it is just mind-blowing, the wide disparity in abilities of first graders. There are four or five kids in this class who, I have no doubt, could go on to an Ivy League college. These are Black, Hispanic, white, all different colors. And there are some kids in there who can barely read, can barely count. Some of them are in great family environments and get supported and read to and get help, and there are other kids who are in broken families who are starting so far behind that I can't imagine how they're ever going to catch up. I try to help best I can, and volunteering in school is literally my favorite part of the week, but the disparity is crushing. The half a day I'm in Mrs. Williams' first grade class at Taylor Street Elementary School and I walk in and they go, "Mr. Dave. Mr. Dave..." I just love it. So what's my point? Our education system needs a re-boot, and some families need to take more responsibility for their young children.

We need, as a country, to get more people involved in their community, and I think it can happen in two ways. First, everyone getting out of high school should be required to serve their community, their state, or their country for one year, doing something paid for by the government. That would help young people focus on good values and being good citizens. Second, we need to marshal our retired assets into volunteer work. I'm just one person doing very little, but I'm looking for *more* to do. I can't play golf every day. We've got all these retired people that could really do good things and wouldn't cost us anything.

You know what? I'll go there. I think everyone would benefit if we promote a society that focuses a little bit more on religion than it does now. Religion has been a fairly positive force in society, but the trend in my lifetime has been down, down, down. I am a Christian, born and raised Roman Catholic.

My mom made sure I got my First Communion and Confirmation, but then we stopped going to church. She had done her duty. That was confusing to me. I really didn't go to church in my twenties, but when I met my second wife, she was going to a Lutheran church here in Norfolk. Of course, after dating for a while, she said, "Ok, it's time for you to go to church with me." I wasn't really excited about it, but I went. And I thoroughly enjoyed it! It made sense to me. It wasn't as scary as I remembered. Catholicism had the big priests who talked in Latin and the mean nuns with the clickers. Here was a minister who had a wife and a family, lived in the real world with the rest of us, and had a very biblically-based religion. Been going there for thirty-two years now. They made me the treasurer.

I think our country has lost a little bit of its moral compass, and part of that is related to the decline in people being interested in religion.

Can we be Christ-like by supporting entitlement programs? If there is a true need, then I say, "Amen." I think the $64,000 question is, "What is the true need?" We have to balance filling the needs of the truly needy with helping too much. If you don't have to keep your family together, if you don't have to raise your children properly, if you don't have to avoid abusing drugs and alcohol, and you'll *still* get everything you need from the government... well, I'm just not sure that's good for society. Jesus obviously helped the worst of the worst, the lepers and the blind, but there has to be some kind of limit or the system will come crashing down. No one will go to work if you have to give all your money back to the government to take care of people who are challenged, hurting, or unwilling. We've gone further than we should, and we have to keep the needle balanced. That's the attitude I hope I'm seeing in the Trump presidency.

The news starts for me every day with *The Virginian-Pilot*. I'm one of those crazy people who reads the newspaper in print from front to back. So I get my news from that very liberal paper. The headlines, the stories selected, and the editorials are primarily liberal, so that's frustrating. But I take that in and that's how I start the day. Beyond that, you can imagine I do enjoy watching some Fox News.

One of the things that I like about Donald Trump is that, unlike the previous administration, he's willing to recognize there's an evil force in this world called radical Islam. We saw that in New York on 9/11, and we see it around the world all the time. Yes, it's a very small percentage of the Muslim population, but a small percentage of the Muslim population is a whole lot of people. It's my firm belief that there's a Jihad in progress that wants to take over the world and make it all Islam. It may not happen for fifty or a hundred years, but I think that's what they have in mind. We need to confront that.

Trump blew up some of Assad's aircraft, and Assad's a big ally of Russia, right? Doesn't that fly in the face of Trump supposedly loving Russia so much? He wouldn't do that to one of Russia's allies. Would he?

This Russia thing is funny because we had a prior administration that shrank and handcuffed our military. Here comes Trump, saying, "I want to build up the military. I want to let our military do what they can do." The theory is that Russia wanted Trump and not Hillary. But Trump wants to build up our military! Wouldn't they prefer a president who would continue hamstringing the military? Doesn't make sense.

I don't usually talk this much. I have no plans for the evening, other than to rest my throat. But it's very interesting to find somebody like you out in the world that is curious about what's happening in our country and wants to shed some light on it. Thanks for that.

CHAPTER EIGHTEEN
The Military Teen

April 12th, 2017
Dayton, Ohio

Is it just me, or didn't Dave back in Norfolk seem completely befuddled by his own support for Donald Trump? I mean, it's endearing, and it makes me like him a whole lot, but still... Dave wants to support entitlement programs for those with true need, and so do liberals. Dave believes in being fiscally conservative, and so does Hillary. (Yes, she is fiscally conservative! I believe that.) Dave believes the tax code is in dire need of repair and equity, and so do both parties. So why can't Dave come over to our side? The tipping point for him seems to be the acknowledgement Trump has given to Dave's real fear of radical Islam. I happen to think Dave's fear is unfounded, but I've spoken to enough people now to know that Dave is definitely not alone. Donald Trump named a fear that real Americans hold. Who is wrong? The Americans who voted with real fear in mind, or the man who named it to grab those votes?

Landing in Ohio, I enjoy the potential see-saw of being in a solid swing state. Here in Dayton, I find myself willing to speak with someone a lot younger than usual. Still in high school, Collin is articulate and secure in his views, and ready to debate me on any issue I choose to invite. Smartly, Collin always has a story. He knows that debates are won more easily when you have emotion attached to them. We are in a generic hotel lobby, hidden away by the second-floor ballroom so as not to invite onlookers, and Collin launches into his perfectly prepared speech...

###

COLLIN: I'm from Dayton and my passion for politics started when I was really little. Since I was six or seven, I was always with my dad in the basement watching Fox News. That really influenced me. He called it brainwashing! It wasn't. My grandparents are very liberal and always saw me as "Republican just like his dad, because his dad's making him that way." But no! I had a genuine interest at a very young age in listening to different opinions. Obviously, I couldn't understand it all. But seeing this war on terror, seeing these children be killed, seeing these lives that were lost abroad, I was very interested. My dad would say, "You need to listen to what the commentator's insight is, both sides." I started actually debating politics aloud in fifth grade. I spoke against my best friend, supporting McCain against his Obama.

My father is military. My grandfather is military. It's something I have a vivid family background in, but it's not a family heirloom thing. This is really something that I came to myself: The military is the best next step for me after I graduate high school in a few weeks. It's April now, so I guess I'll be joining up soon. I really want to make a difference in the world. That's what I'm all about. I love the United States of America.

I am Catholic. Not very devout, not really practicing, but I am a Catholic. And I'm definitely upper middle class and in the suburbs. Always went to Catholic school until after my freshman year of high school when I decided to make a jump over to public school because, in all honesty, I felt like a lot of the kids who go to private schools are raised to be very egotistical. A lot of them were very stuck up, cocky. I'm not like that, even though I am like a lot of them in that my parents are able to afford me a lot. My parents are very good and caring people and have done a lot for me. But I just don't buy into that whole uppity, preppy stereotype. This whole thing that, "We're better than you because we go to this school. Our parents are this way. Our parents have this job." I've always felt as if everything should be earned. Just because your parents have these accomplishments doesn't give you anything. You're not owed anything by anyone, and you need to be your own person – a humble person – and accomplish things on your own.

I'm not really concerned too much about religion. I don't really care about why we're here. I just know that we *are* here and you only get one chance at this life. Whatever it is that you want to do, just do something you're passionate about because this is your one shot. We can figure out whatever it is that put us on Earth later, maybe after we die. But for right now, this is the only time I'm ever going to be Collin Miller. I want to make the best.

I'd love for the military to be my career because it's something that I'm extremely passionate about. But even if it doesn't ultimately become my life, it's something that can afford me many opportunities as a civilian. I can go to school for free. A lot of people my age are going to be in student debt, and college doesn't guarantee them a job. That's a common misconception with people my age, but then they wake up to the real world and realize there are many other people out there with the same qualifications. You've got to bust your butt to compete, but a lot of people don't want that; they just expect things to be handed to them after graduation.

If you go back to our inception, to what made America come about, you see we were founded by men that were fleeing an oppressive government. They came up with these ideals on their own: life, liberty, the pursuit of happiness. They decided the Constitution was the best way to do things. And it's the greatest document ever written, even greater than the Magna Carta. Greater than other documents that have tried to ensure liberty, but haven't succeeded. Today, a lot of people like to complain that they aren't being treated equally. There are problems that we need to fix, just like any country. Like with the police versus society matter, the people aren't wrong in that police reform should be made, but also the police work a very tough job – I'm going a little off track here. Basically, the point I'm trying to make is that this country ensures liberty for everyone: any race, any ethnicity, any gender. That's why you have so many people trying to get here, because they want to be a part of the greatest power ever in the history of the world.

President Obama's point of view was that he wanted to do a little bit more for refugees, and President Trump is the exact opposite. He says, "We need to cut this off until we can get a better grip on the problems that we have in our country." That's a great dilemma. I have a soft spot in my heart, a very soft spot in my heart, for helping other people. But when you're governing a country as vast as ours, as powerful as ours, you've got to make tough decisions that are going to benefit our country first. You've got to say, "Hey, I'm the President of the United States. What can I do that is going to keep our people safe, that is going to benefit our citizens first?" After that, you can worry about maybe bringing people in that are Syrian refugees.

Who are these refugees affiliated with? What are their beliefs? Do they want to buy into our culture? Do they want to better

American society? Do they want to come over here to be free, or do they want to endanger us? Do they want to cause death and destruction to us and use what the book of Mohammed says... Wait. Sorry, that's not Syria. That's the radical interpretation of the Islamic faith. But there are people *in* Syria, and other countries, that generally adhere to that form of extremism.

Trump says right away, "Obama is trying to let in ten thousand refugees. We can't do that." Because it's also a technique that ISIS can use to infiltrate our country. They're going to take advantage of weakness. What does any villain, any bad guy do? They prey off of weakness. If you let your guard down, you're going to let in some people that we shouldn't be letting in. For all the good people that we're letting into this country, there might be one or two that can cause death to hundreds of Americans. To me, one American life is not worth letting people in that could endanger our lives. There's things that we can do instead to help them over there where they live.

I was a traditional Republican and was charmed by Trump, even more so because I was very disheartened by the candidates the Republicans were putting forward. None of them were exciting. But I guess it wasn't really about excitement, it was more about somebody that could capture the imaginations and the hearts of what Trump called "the forgotten American." That's us, and it felt like for so long we had just been brushed aside.

The forgotten Americans are people that feel left behind by our stagnant economy; they are losing jobs, or jobs are fleeing the country. They are people who were told, "Listen, everything's fine. We're creating jobs. Everything's fine." With the Obama administration, these jobs reports were coming out looking good, but it was mostly part-time jobs being created. Not working for GM, not working for manufacturers. They were just part-time jobs, like maybe Dollar General. Not necessarily Dollar General; that's just a term that I like to use. None of these were full time, good paying, middle class jobs that people could actually thrive from. The elite were telling the forgotten Americans to be quiet because everything's fine. It wasn't fine.

To an extent, these policies did benefit people at the very, very bottom, but it didn't benefit people in the middle class and top because Obama's America brought people from the top down to the middle. His vision put a ceiling on success. Obama didn't want people to become too rich, too wealthy, too powerful. He also didn't want people to be too poor. That's not the American philosophy. That's not the American ideal. It didn't foster an atmosphere of hard work. It didn't foster an atmosphere of self-empowerment, self-independence.

Tax reform would be a huge, huge move toward encouraging people to move upwards in society and making something of themselves despite where they may have come from. A major tax overhaul would benefit people in the middle class and at the top, but also it take the training wheels off of the lower class. It says, "Listen, here are the tools to be what you want to be, but you've got to do it. You've got to do it for yourself." We may help you from going under, that's fine. We don't want anyone to go dying on the streets. But people have to do it for themselves. We're not going to help them do it. That's the American way.

The media propaganda says Obama was doing a great job, when really he wasn't. CNN liked to talk up Obama accomplishments that weren't really accomplishments. They liked to gloss over the actual reality that a lot of Americans are destitute. There were a lot of people who needed help. We needed somebody to come forth that represents the American, the everyday forgotten American. I told my dad, "It's got to be an outsider." It was like a prophecy.

I knew Donald Trump the billionaire, but when I saw his first debate, I was just blown away. Everything that he said, literally everything that he said, I totally agreed with 100%. I said, "This is the guy." This is when he's still maybe 1% in the polls. I said, "This is the guy I was talking about." I felt like Donald Trump was going to win and was really going to shock everyone. If I had said that too loudly back then, I would have been laughed at just as many, many other right-wingers were laughed at and pushed aside. It was like, "Stay over there. This is the big boys' area; you don't need to state your opinions at all." And that's just another problem that we have in this country. People don't like to listen to other thoughts or ideas or really engage in debate. They just like to stereotype people as old white republicans. Or in my case, a privileged white republican. In doing so, they're really not listening. And I guess that exists on both sides. We conservatives, I guess, need to listen to the snowflakes![51]

I'm very pro-life. I really believe it. It's not a deal breaker for me, though, being pro-choice or pro-life. It's just something that I believe in. But I can get past the fact that Donald Trump is more moderate on social issues. I appreciate that he's open for debate,

---

[51] Aww. That's really sweet.

thought, and discussion. What most people don't realize is he has very, very moderate stances. He's flipped flopped on pro-life and pro-choice, and other things like transgender bathrooms, same-sex marriage. These issues are things that Donald Trump has said he doesn't really have a stance on. He wants to send these things back to the state, which is how the Constitution works. He allows states to decide, "Do you want transgender bathrooms or do you not?" President Obama said, "The Federal Government is going to decide for all the states." That is governing based off of emotion and your own political agenda.

To some people from the left-wing I may sound a little bit cold in saying this, but we still have to determine if these transgender people are really what they say they are. Are they actually transgender or is it a different psychological thing that's making them think, "Really, I'm a girl," you know what I mean? We still don't know if maybe they're B.S. or not, you know? I don't know, maybe they just want attention. No one had ever heard of transgenders twenty years ago. It's a new thing, and maybe it's part of our generation feeling entitled, feeling fostered, feeling that you can have everything handed to you. It's our generation saying no one can offend you, no one can talk to you about anything you disagree with. You're going to have everything, and God forbid if anyone offends you! I'm really torn on the transgender issue, but at least the states decide on it.

America, for so long, has been weak. Obama drew that red line, then took no action. Assad used chemical weapons under President Trump's administration, and Trump said he'd deal with it very severely. The next day, he blew Assad's airfield into the next century. That's what we've been lacking for so long in leadership.

As for Russia... Has something come out yet? I haven't heard anything. Nothing's come out and it's been eight months. If something came out, if something magically just appeared from the ashes about how Trump is tied to Russia and he's Putin's puppet, then maybe I'll be a little bit affected by it. But where's the evidence? Can liberals actually bring us cold hard evidence? Or can they only keep talking-talking-talking? They're playing politics. This isn't a story, it's a witch-hunt. The investigation in the Senate is good, we need to give it due process, but I view it as a witch-hunt because there are no facts to back it up. Can we just move forward?

Democrats would rather see the president fail for four years, then get a Democrat back in power. How is that good for the

American people? That is Democrats serving themselves, rather than serving the people.

A bit more about me? Well, this is my senior year in high school, and I admit I haven't been the best at getting up for school every day. I'm not Mr. Perfect Attendance, but I do go to school. Due to the fact that I'm going into the military, I just need to get passing grades this year.

I love playing disc golf. And football. I wasn't a football star or anything, but I enjoyed it. I loved the people. I also play golf and basketball, but most of my evenings are spent working at Chili's. I close there a lot.

At Chili's, I work my butt off because that's my conviction. I don't always agree with our management, but I've got to listen so one day I'll be the one that's giving orders. Everybody has their place in the world, everybody's at different stages, but it's all about working hard so that one day you'll have people working hard for you.

Morally, I'll never smoke, I'll never use cigarettes, marijuana. I'll never do drugs. I'll never partake in anything of that nature; that's also part of my conviction. I have a mission-driven life. Every human life has a purpose, and you just need to take action and follow it.

If you're okay with living a destitute lifestyle in government housing, I'm sorry to tell you that you're not going to be able to take advantage of taxpayer money forever. You've actually got to work. I'm sorry if you're upset by that, but a greater amount of people will hopefully be okay with it, and that's my goal: to make a difference for the greatest amount of people.

CHAPTER NINETEEN
The Red Cross Fundraiser

April 21ˢᵗ, 2017
Detroit, Michigan

"To make a difference for the greatest amount of people." That's an admirable quality. And that's what Collin back in Dayton wants. "Obama drew that red line, then took no action." I agree with that, even though I try to be a pacifist. Then, "The forgotten Americans are people that feel left behind by our stagnant economy; they are losing jobs, or jobs are fleeing the country." That too makes some sense to me these days. I won't say Trump has the best answer to these economic issues, but I will say that he is so extremely vocal about them that he presents as the leading spokesman. Let me say this clearly: Trump spoke more inspirationally to the unemployed American than Hillary ever did. Trump pretended to feel pain. Trump pretended to have empathy. Hillary offered to fix problems with logic and policy, Trump just complained loudly and often until people that were struggling began to think he was the only one communicating with them at all. I still feel that Hillary's method of reasoning is far better than appealing to raw emotion, but I have only one vote.

With my one vote — a vote unwavering but ever more understanding — I move on to Detroit. This is still a struggling town. I gawk at the burnt-out ends of the city with fascination, sadly but honestly admitting that exploring urban decay can be a guilty pleasure. (I don't like this about myself, though I'm sure I'm not alone.) But there's art and music out here too, and the far-reaches of Detroit offer the greatest blues clubs a late-night crawler could ask for. In fact, last night's adventure to one of Detroit's best old-school clubs, the Raven Lounge, has left me still recovering

###

TREY: I brought in my first $5,000 today, which is great after only one month. I work for the American Red Cross as a major gift officer, which is basically raising funds. I actually don't have a background in fundraising, but they wanted to get more salespeople in the door. They feel that we're more aggressive and we hustle to get the money in. So that's what I did today. Kudos to me; pat on my back!

Sales is a love-hate relationship; what can I say? It's not what I want to do, but I'm good at it. Fundraising is just a different kind of sales game. It's longer and more drawn out and more relationship-building. I'm learning a lot. I don't know everything I need to know yet. My degree is actually in communication. The Red Cross mission does appeal to me, but honestly I jumped at this job because I was sick of retail and needed to find the next gig.

I grew up in upper-middle class America. My mom was a teacher, my dad is still working as a sales professional in the printing industry. We weren't rich, but money was not an issue. We took four vacations a year. We weren't living extravagantly, but money wasn't tight either. The older I get, the more realize how blessed I am. The general public would say, "You're super wealthy." Maybe I am, but I'm definitely acknowledging that I had a really great upbringing. I'm thirty-three. I've been on visits to homes that have burned down, seeing really impoverished people who really need help from an organization like the American Red Cross.

I'll take you back: Growing up, they used to do those fundraisers at school where you sell stupid stuff for the holidays. I was always really good at it, getting all the neighbors to buy stuff. I've just always been very people-oriented and aggressive in whatever I do. Sales comes pretty easy to me.

I grew up just outside of Detroit in a suburb called Troy. It's fairly affluent. Actually, Detroit would have been the richest city in the United States had the riots not happened, and had we not had all of the race relations problems, which was horrible. All the wealth moved out of the city to the suburbs.

I get asked a lot, "Why would you vote for him?" I am not necessarily Republican, but I do lean more conservative. I'm definitely not a Democrat. Definitely! The Democratic Party is not the same party that it was growing up. My mom is still a Democrat, though. She's fiscally conservative but defines herself as a Democrat. My dad is more Republican.

Growing up, everybody loved Bill Clinton. Everybody had money. People were successful. The United States was on the up and up, so there wasn't a whole lot of complaining. I was young and I didn't really know politics, but the Democrats always said they were a party of the working class and inclusion. I just don't believe it anymore. Even though there's a lot of different colors and backgrounds and orientations in the Democratic Party, I feel it's a front to get support and votes. I know that's horrible; I just really feel that way. So, not to disclose any personal information about myself, I just don't feel like they truly care about the people they say they are reaching out to. Like me.

A real-world example: here in Michigan there was the horrible water crisis in Flint. The Democratic Party has run that city for many, many years. The council was all Democratic. When this water crisis happened – and I'm not saying that they're the sole people to blame – it made us question, "If Democrats are in power and this horrible lead poisoning can happen just to save a couple of dollars, why should we trust the Democrats to actually have people's interests at heart?" They hurt poor people in Flint and said the EPA is to blame, or the Republican governor is to blame. The Democrats washed their hands of it. Sure, the EPA and the governor knew what was going on, so it's a collective fault, but why do people vote blindly without getting into the nitty-gritty of the issues? Democrats could have prevented the tragedy in Flint if they had the people's interests at heart.

I became a Trump fan at first due to his sense of humor. He's very funny! I don't agree with all of his crazy statements, but he was charismatic from the very beginning. He talks just how we're talking. He doesn't have to make a big grand speech to talk to the common folk. I'm not saying that he's the answer to the world's problems – he's not and he doesn't know everything – but I feel that he talks to me personally in a way that I can understand and I can respect.

He's brought strength back to the United States. "We'll always be number one. We're not going to be pushed around. We're not going to deal with Iran being crazy. We're not going to tolerate North Korea trying to threaten us." You win with strength and you win with power. We've spent too long apologizing to people, and that's the weakness of Obama's presidency. The first year that he was in office, he did that speech in Egypt apologizing to a bunch of Muslim people. And that theme played throughout Obama's presidency. There's a shooting: "Well, the white people are at fault." Always blaming the police. Always commenting on the Trayvon Martin shooting. I mean, it's horrible. Loss of life is bad; doesn't matter what color they are. But making comments on criminal cases that have nothing to do with national security, nothing to do with Washington?

Some might argue, on the other side, that it's a cultural thing and America is still racist. Racism still exists, but I don't think it's as widespread now as it was during the eight years of Obama. We were taught to *think* that it was. The last eight years divided our country horribly between classes and races. Talking about cases like Trayvon Martin from the White House caused more racism, more of a split. You know why? Because Obama, out of his own mouth, was like, "Trayvon Martin could have been my son." To me – and maybe it's just how I was raised – you don't go around wearing all black, a black hoodie, walking around at whatever time it was in the middle of the night.[52] I'm not saying that it's his fault he got shot; I'm not saying that. I'm just saying that it does look suspicious. We'll never know what happened. I'm not defending whatever-his-name-is. I'm not defending him. It's a tragedy all around. I just don't think the President of the United States should have injected his beliefs into a case that we know nothing about.

Even though I didn't vote for Obama, I actually thought it was awesome that we had a Black president. But when he started fueling the fire, pulling the Band-Aid off of old wounds, he was just stirring things up. I thought it was so cool that he was elected. I thought he would bring people together, but I've only seen the opposite of that.

I voted for Trump mostly for economic reasons. He has a lot of successful businesses. People always point out his failures, but he's obviously doing something right because he has a very successful company and books.

---

[52] Where I'm from, you don't shoot somebody at 7:17 p.m. because of their fashion choices. It is very, very hard to listen to Trey's commentary without judgement.

But also, Trump calls terrorism what it is. He doesn't sugarcoat it, like, "It's a hate crime or it's this or that." I just feel that Obama danced around it, even though everybody was thinking the same thing. Even some of my liberal friends agree; Obama didn't talk about terrorism because he didn't want to call attention to it. But that made me uneasy.

I don't think Trump has all the answers; no president has all the answers. There are some things that he, as we all know, has changed his mind about. But I don't look at it as flip-flopping, I look at it as "working through it." He's getting other people's opinions and advice. For example, he said China was manipulating currency but after he met with the President of China or the Republic or whatever they call it, he backed down and switched course. Immediately after, we saw China taking coal back from North Korea. That's a great thing. I think people don't give him enough credit just for changing his mind.

Here in Detroit, we have the largest Arab population in the United States. (Just for historical reference.) I also found out through the Red Cross that we're the second largest place to bring in refugees. I'd be lying to you if I said it doesn't make me think about our safety. People might call it xenophobic or whatever. I'm definitely not xenophobic, but it does cross my mind, "Who is this person? Are they going to go crazy and shoot up the place or something?" It's not something I think about every day, but it has crossed my mind. The reason I bring it up is that there's a really popular mall in our community that's very wealthy, and I do see a lot more Muslim people there. Not that I think they're planning something, but it just makes you think about it a little bit.

I'm a born-again Christian. I found this faith in 2010 after going through a bit of a struggle. At that point, I found myself going to a religious service like five nights a week; I was psycho! Lately, I've come to believe that you don't have to go to a building to pray. I'm not as fanatical now, but I do pray twice a day. I know, from my experience in 2010, that there is a higher power.

Muslims? I'm fearful of what they believe. This is not a blanket statement for all Muslim people, because obviously that would be stupid, but the people that are radicalized literally take stuff word-for-word in the Quran, which is why they carry out these attacks. The Bible is very bloody and it's a very crazy book, but the main goal of the Christian faith is, "Love our enemy and love our neighbor." It's just gentler. "If they hit you, just turn your cheek and get hit again."

With the Quran, I can't say that. Maybe I need to study it more. (But I really don't want to study it more, because I really don't care.) What I've seen is, "Kill in the name of your God, and everybody should be converting."

I have Muslim friends. I have talked to some of them about this. But I'm not afraid of them when I see them. Why? Because I've gotten to know them and I understand where they're coming from. I'm mainly talking about people who are radicalized. People who look online and think Sharia law should be everywhere and women have no rights, gays are thrown off buildings, the no-go zones in France. What?! No-go zones, to me, are crazy.[53]

Supporting Trump, I've been called every name in the book. Crazy Democratic people throw horrible names at me when I'm just supporting my candidate. I've been called racist — I don't look at them as Black friends or white friends, but it was one of my Black friends — and I'm like, "You know me. I've done philanthropy work with you. And you're calling me racist? If I'm so racist, why would I be working with you on stuff?"

Just because I express my opinion doesn't mean I agree with everything Trump has said word for word. He has said crazy stuff. "Locker room talk." I've said worse things to my friends about inappropriate stuff. When did everything become so offensive?

Did Trump get loud and in your face at the debates? Yes! I loved the debates! They were entertaining, because these politicians that don't deal with real, everyday people were thrown.

I went to a Mike Pence rally and shouted, "Build that wall!" and "Lock her up!" and I thought it was fun. CNN paints us all as devil worshipers. I just laugh at it because it's a pep rally; who cares what we say?[54] Give me a break. Do I think that she's going to go to jail or be locked up? No, probably not. Trump would be stupid for doing that. Do I care if the wall is built? Not really.

I think that gay marriage should be passed or should continue. Everybody is entitled to marriage. Now, what I don't agree with is churches being forced to marry gay people if that's not what they believe, or the whole bakery issue. It's like, "Why are you harassing these people? Just let them bake for who they want to bake. If they feel that it's imposing on their religious views, why destroy their business that they worked really hard for?" It's a fine line that I walk.

---

[53] We all agree that no-go zones would be crazy. But many of us also know that no-go zones don't exist.
[54] I care what you say. Hitler had pep rallies, too. Maybe that's an unfair comparison, but slogans do matter.

I am pro-life. I don't think it affected my vote like some of the other issues, though. I was pro-choice at one time, but then I switched my view. So did Trump. I participated in this thing at church and it just opened my eyes to the abortion procedure; I guess you could say it was a rally, but that sounds cheesy. It was a church service about abortion. We don't have to go there now, let's not talk about it. It wasn't a huge thing; don't make me look bad now!

What I would like to say is that we're not bad people, we conservatives. We are just like every other American. We want the best for our country, for our neighbors, for everyone. To be labeled as evil people makes us feel that we that we have to hide. Democrats are not including us in their narrative; I think that's why they lost.[55]

---

[55] Van Jones, CNN commentator, agrees: "When you're so passionate about including the traditionally marginalized, you sometimes forget to include the newly marginalized folk. And they've got pain, too. I didn't show up when those factories closed. The NAACP didn't go. The big environmental groups didn't go. You know who went? Donald Trump went. And that says something."

CHAPTER TWENTY
The Military Contractor

April 24th, 2017
Detroit, Michigan

Back on the other side of Detroit, Trey explained that he is a born-again Christian and fervently pro-life. That strong pro-life stance is a recurring theme; so many people with whom I speak see abortion rights as the most important dividing line between Democrats and Republicans. Trey showed his cards when he tried to avoid further discussion of the issue, pleading, "Don't make me look bad now." He is passionate about abortion rights, but not ready to speak too publicly on it. Instinctually, I would like to box Trey up as a one-issue voter (who doesn't want to talk openly about that one issue), though he spoke at length on other conservative ideas, too. Trey is skeptical of Islam and believes the Democratic leadership doesn't care as much as they say they do about people of different "colors and backgrounds and orientations." He believes the Dems use a leftist front to garner votes. I'm not convinced of any of these things.

One common thread here in Detroit is the blaming of Democrats for the Flint water crisis. With a Republican governor, I find it hard to get behind this line of thinking. That said, these Detroiters have inspired me to read a whole bunch about Flint blame, and I can't honestly put it on the Republicans either. Seems like a cross-party disaster to me.

In any case, I'm darting to the other side of town where Gloria is making time for me while attending her daughter's track meet. The thing that catches my attention? She is a bit sarcastic in her support for President Trump. We are fast approaching

###

GLORIA: I am a female veteran, having served in the Army doing communication for Black Hawks, Apaches, and Humvees. I grew up in Midwestern Ohio, and I landed here in Detroit. Now I work for the Army as a contractor.

See, the economy in Detroit fell kind of apart in the mid-2000s and there weren't a lot of opportunities. I decided to go into the military because it was an appropriate time for me, not only to help my family – I am the mother of four children – but to support my country. Some people join the military for true patriotism, other people because they want a career. I did both at the same time.

I am very patriotic. I love our country. At forty-six now, it's obvious I joined the military a little bit later than most do. I had absolutely no IT experience whatsoever prior to joining, but they trained me up. The military provided very definite career paths for many of us in Detroit where it was really needed.

I think we need a complete overhaul in our government. We're moving to bigger and bigger government, and there's just too much overhead. There's so much bureaucracy that I thought maybe a businessman could bring a new perspective. Trump could clean house. With this huge deficit, maybe he could take the burden off the taxpayers?

I experience a lot of that bureaucracy in my work. I see it every day. Older people are just sitting in these desks. They've been working for the government for thirty-plus years; they're no longer effective at their jobs. That's where change needs to be made. One guy I know makes probably $180,000 dollars a year but he can't even operate a printer. He has people that work for him write his emails. Why is he allowed to sit there?! He's several years past retirement, getting this huge paycheck, and he's not even effective at what he's doing! We could get someone else in there that's younger, has the same education, and is more technically savvy. In my opinion, "draining the swamp" is getting rid of people like him.

I'm not happy with Hillary Clinton at all. I don't trust her as a human, let alone a politician. I think her family is just very shady and underhanded with the whole Clinton Foundation thing. I was not comfortable with anyone from that family being a leader of our country; that's just a personal feeling.

If the right woman were to come along, I would vote for her in a heartbeat. It's just that Hillary Clinton wasn't good, with the criminal background and activity in that family. I just cannot, in good conscience, vote for them. I have a hard time trusting her to take the country in the right direction, because you just never know who's in the back pocket.

I get cyber security training annually. For Hillary Clinton to say she didn't know her server wasn't allowed? It's just, "No." She knew she was breaking the rules. I have secret government clearance. And I have civil responsibilities in order to keep my clearance with the government. Part of that is not to violate any of the rules. Her clearance is "top secret" and probably above that. For her to just disregard the rules? How could she be an effective leader when she couldn't even follow the rules *before* she became president?

My main concern for Trump's presidency, now that we're a few months in, revolves around a lot of his campaign promises. Now he's saying, "We'll have to come back to that," or "We'll have to look at that later." I understand it's only been a hundred days, but you need to give us something a little more than that.[56]

We should all come together and support the office of the president. We may not agree with the president himself, but we should always support the office. I did not agree with a lot of the things that Obama was doing, but I always supported him. As Americans, we have to want our president to succeed, regardless of who he is.

In the next hundred days, you know what I'm hoping for? That Trump stops making golf trips to Florida!

---

[56] Gloria is the first Trump voter to whom I've spoken who is *disappointed* in his first hundred days.

CHAPTER TWENTY-ONE
The Sausage Factory Wall-Funder

April 28th, 2017
Detroit, Michigan

Gloria wanted the swamp drained, and she's not seeing that happen. She is frustrated with stifling bureaucracy in government, a dysfunctional system she sees daily in her work as a military contractor, and Gloria believed Trump when he said he would come in to streamline and get rid of those that are underperforming. This is a logical reason to vote for a leader; I get it. But what made her believe Trump was the guy who would actually do it? Sure, he fires people on television, but Gloria must know the difficulty attached to changing entire systems of federal employment on a whim. Her reasoning is good. I agree with her. I think Trump's message of streamlining regulations, establishing term limits, and breaking up unfairness in the system is a great message! It's a message that puts me more in line with traditional Republicans. But Trump is certainly no traditional Republican.

I don't remember any Democrat with a clear message about streamlining government. Trump is the poster boy for that message. And Gloria responded, even if she feels his follow-through is weak.

Here in the Eastern Market area downtown, I see that there's at least one factory doing well here in Detroit. They make sausages. And they've been doing it for almost a century. I'm set to meet one of the guys who runs the plant, and he tells me he's been praying for a leader to come along and save our country from liars and schemers.

###

WILLIAM: I was raised in a conservative family. I'm a deeply-rooted Christian. I'm sixty years old and, aside from politics, my faith is most important to me. I run a sausage manufacturing company. Been doing that for thirty-seven years. Not many people have careers that long with one company anymore.

Prior to Donald Trump announcing that he was actually going to run, a group of my close friends and I prayed fervently that God would deliver us a holy man, a godly man. Now I'm not necessarily saying that Donald Trump is or was a godly man, but he had all of the boxes checked for what we were looking for.

I think I could certainly trust him more than candidates the Democrats were putting in; I didn't trust any of *them*. I am prejudiced against Democrats, of course, because I was raised in a Republican household and those views have never waivered. John F. Kennedy was the only Democrat I even considered voting for.

Obama and his administration sold out America. They hurt us in many ways, not just with the immigration. It was like they stole America's light. Particularly Hillary Clinton, because I don't know how people could possibly accept a person that has that much lying, cheating, and scheming in her past.

When Obama was elected the first term, I was not happy but I certainly didn't go out and riot and beat up people who voted for him. That's where the two parties differ tremendously. The Republican Party works and the other people don't; they want what we have without having to work for it.

We have more than three thousand members in my church and we have a Bible study on Wednesday nights. We prayed for President Obama because the scripture tells us to pray for all our leaders. But we prayed *more* that God would show his hand in this election and allow Donald Trump to be elected. And I think that God really did have an influence. This election showed me again that God really is in control.

Specifically, we prayed that God would deliver to us a man that would be of faith. Now, I'm not sure that Donald Trump really is a man of faith. I can't judge that, but he represents that he has the potential to be a man of faith. We asked for God to deliver to us a person that would put America first, put our values first, so we could actually be proud to say that we are American and that this person represents us. I haven't been able to say that in a long time. Even Bush's second term, he didn't represent us. I think he sold us out before Obama did.

Trump does a fine job. He's passionate about his position. I just applaud any man or woman willing to make the sacrifices that Trump has been willing to make. Incidentally, I do think we will see a woman elected president in my lifetime.

I truly expect that Trump will improve the health care system. At sixty years of age, it doesn't really bother me that much; I'm not as concerned for me as I am for my children. I would like to see better coverage, equal coverage, and affordable coverage. Obamacare was not affordable. My daughter doesn't work. I support her, so I had to go out and buy her health insurance and it was not cheap! $571 a month, I think. That's not affordable. I'm already burdened supporting my family, but I'm blessed that God's given me the ability to have a good job. And my daughter actually used the health insurance. I thank God that we had it for her because she had an epileptic seizure and cracked her head open; she had severe head trauma and, had she not been in insured, I'm afraid we would not have gotten that same type of care that we got.

I am privileged to be in a position to pay for insurance, so I choose to pay. Certainly, my daughter would have been taken care of if she was uninsured, but I think that is a typical left-wing attitude... the haves vs. the have-nots. The have-nots want what we have, but they don't want to earn it or work to get it. That just stresses me out and annoys me. I'm constantly dealing with people who come up to me at work and say, "I need five bucks. I need this, I need that." Whatever. I do not take it as personally as I used to.

One thing in my life that I do on a daily basis is help a person that's not expecting it. And that's not to pat myself on the back, it's just what my faith has taught me to do. I'll give you an example: I was at the gas station and a woman came in who was clearly not dressed properly. She put down $6.71 in change and wanted gas; that was not going to last her very long. When she walked out the door, I gave the attendant $20 for her, and the attendant says, "You'll have to go out and tell her to keep the pump going." I went outside, but I said, "The guy inside said to go ahead and toss in an extra $20." I didn't tell her I did it. I truly believe that what comes around goes around, and that you need to give to get back. I may not get back in this lifetime, but I will when I see my Lord up in heaven. I hope it doesn't disturb you that I talk like that.

For the past two weeks, I've been setting up a GoFundMe page titled "Build That Wall." My goal is for every person that voted for Donald Trump to donate $10. My wife and I prayed about this and feel it is something we can do to help our president and help America. I don't do it for any praise or glory; the glory is from within and it always has been. I'll tell you though, if it goes well I'd really like to be able to meet Donald Trump because of it.

There is nothing wrong with immigration; it's what founded America. But there is something wrong with *illegal* immigration. I don't think that this wall will stop the drug trade as much as President Trump wants it to, but if it will cut illegal immigration in half, then whatever we pay for that wall will come back double for America. I truly believe that and I hope I'm not wrong.

I encounter a lot illegal immigrants in my line of work. A lot of them. Mostly Hispanics. I have a very good friend – she's worked for the company for twenty years and has never made an attempt to get citizenship. She once offered an American $10,000 dollars to marry her, but has never actually just tried to be legal about it all. Do I think what she is doing is wrong? Yes, I do. Would I turn her in? No, I wouldn't. But I don't like the fact that the company knowingly employees these people. Of course, they don't personally employ them; they go through a staffing company. Most of these immigrants have illegal documentation that they bought from somebody else, and the staffing companies turn a blind eye and plead ignorance.

Do I expect that President Trump will deliver on every promise? No, but I think that he is already trying his best to have an impact on what he considers to be his priorities. And I've allowed myself and our prayer group to accept his priorities as our own.

CHAPTER TWENTY-TWO
The Keystone Oilman

May 4th, 2017
Grand Rapids, Michigan

Ok, ok. I thought William back in Detroit was nuts because his prayer group saw the presidential election as a direct sign of God's hand. I'm an atheist. I think anyone who believes in an active, living god is nuts; it's not just William. But if I can get past that one point, then I must allow myself to acknowledge one of William's more logical arguments: staffing companies hire illegal immigrants en masse, and factories contract these staffing companies to fill positions. This is a workaround to avoid hiring legal and/or union workers, and to dealing with unions in general. With "temporary employees," major companies are unethically saving tons of money in employee benefits and union wages. In this way, I can get on board with the "illegal immigrant problem," but I see it as more of an "unethical American staffing company" problem. William introduced me to that issue, and I appreciate the contribution. Interesting, right? William responded to Trump's message against illegal immigration by placing blame specifically on staffing companies. These companies are an interesting and different antagonist than I've heard mentioned before.

In the meantime, I was able to celebrate Donald Trump's 100th day in office, April 29th, by attending the Detroit Climate March. This was a nice capper to my time in Detroit before I move westward across the state. The keynote speaker at this event had a simple message: make our mission louder. In her view — it's becoming my view, too — attacking Trump is not an effective strategy for liberals or Democrats. Rather, if we believe our mission is righteous, then our voices must be louder than his. He can make his voice pretty damn loud, though, when celebrating the "mother of all bombs!" But we must be louder, the speaker says. And we must be less destructive, I say. That bomb he dropped on Afghanistan still bugs my pacifist heart.

Trump held a rally of his own on his 100th day. Those gatherings he hosts are so much more visceral, so much more emotive, than anything I've ever seen! My thought of the day: Wouldn't it be great if a more intelligent, centrist politician could create this kind of event? Trump rally attendees are loving them! Trump's in-person gatherings continue to have an impact, I'm sure of it. There are so many people that reference the rallies as thrilling, once-in-a-lifetime events. Liberals need somebody that can create that same enthusiasm, that same rally. (Insert your Bernie comments here: _________.)

There's a controversy in Detroit: Marathon Oil is buying houses from people in an area they polluted, but are they only buying houses in the white neighborhoods while ignoring Black communities that were impacted equally? That's the debate here at this local climate march, but I guess that debate is for another book; Trump hasn't weighed in on it.

With climate change on my mind, I'm heading west to Grand Rapids to meet an oil guy. Truth: I recently had dinner with Bill Nye the Science Guy. I respect Bill Nye the Science Guy. And Bill Nye the Science Guy insists wholeheartedly that there is a reasonable plan already in place for the United States to become renewable-energy independent if we only choose to be so. That plan can be found at TheSolutionsProject.org. I'm here in Grand Rapids to speak with Roger at a convention center. I am ready to disagree with him already.

###

ROGER: I live in Grand Rapids, but I've worked all over. I am sixty-five years old and I've been in the oil and gas industry my entire life, working on some of the biggest projects in the United States, including the Keystone Line. Also, I'm a member of the unions. I believe in the unions.

I used to vote Democratic. That's when the party was more or less for the working person. Now, it seems like they're only for themselves. I guess I'm confused about everything with the Democratic Party right now and not sure who they're supposed to represent. In the last eight or nine years, I didn't see any real growth, just corruption. We don't need any more of that corruption.

Don't get me wrong, Republicans aren't perfect. Not one politician is perfect. But politicians can get everybody excited about something. Like, all we working people have done is pay through the nose for healthcare, taxes, and everything for so long. That has to change, and maybe it's why Trump is in office; he got people excited about changing that!

I believe that we're all pawns. We've been sold. Everything we've been told the last several years has been lies, like saving on your healthcare. Mine went up 1000%. No joke. You wonder why people are pissed off? We've been lied to about keeping our doctor under Obamacare. We've been lied to about the insurance actually being better under Obamacare. That's why everybody is upset. We were supposed to have an open and accessible government. After eight years, it's just turned into a completely corrupted ball of crap.

The Keystone XL Pipeline Project, of course, never got finished. But forget about your liberal politics for a minute and let me just tell you that the project itself was corrupt. I was in Calgary when the notification came across that it was shutting down. Keystone XL was shutting down, and instead they got a deal with Warren Buffett to ship the oil from Canada to the Midwest U.S. on trains. Buffet made two billion, and what kind of deal was that for the American taxpayers or for the environment? There have been more train accidents in the last eight years than have ever happened on the pipelines.[57]

Not to say pipelines don't need to be replaced, because they're like roads in America today. If you're from New York, you know what I'm talking about. The roads turn around and, after a time, they need to be replaced! That's the same reason these oil and gas lines have to be replaced. The ones that are in service now have been there for fifty or sixty years. All these people protesting the pipelines because of environmental concerns have no idea what they're protesting about. They should be protesting for us to go out and build new pipeline, because *that* will make the lines safer!

One of the things I'm really disappointed about is that we used to have protection – as Americans – from the Department of Transportation. When Bill Clinton was president, he laid off five thousand workers who were there to protect you and me from the gas and oil companies; they were the oversight for the industry. Clinton's

---

[57] On the exact day I was editing this conversation, November 16th, 2017, the Keystone Pipeline leaked more than two hundred thousand gallons of oil in South Dakota. I write this footnote in disbelief of the coincidence.

last comment on it was, "Let's just let the oil and gas companies police themselves." Let me tell you something: I've been a witness to how they police themselves, and they don't do it very well. It's always based on whatever is cheapest, not on what's right. See, each pipeline project has a set of specifications. They're required by law to follow those specs, but they all do things backwards and not up to code when they can get away with it. If they don't have anybody watching them – and they don't – then things are going to go wrong. That's what we should be protesting. The Democratic Party took away the oversight, and I'm very disappointed that they betrayed us all.

You remember the Whistleblower Act? The reason for that law was a pipeline project in Alaska. Richard, the guy who testified in front of Congress about the project, only did it because company had murdered his best friend. Well, guess what? Richard used to work for me, and he showed me all his paperwork. It was unbelievable, the stuff companies thought they could get away with. He was on the cover of *Time Magazine*, but then this guy couldn't beg, borrow, or buy a job. He didn't work in the oil and gas industry for eleven years. It destroyed his life.

From personal experience, not more than ten years ago: I worked as a construction manager for Enbridge as their number one construction manager on all projects in the United States. I'm the one who hired the inspectors. I tried to make sure the contractors did what they said they were going to, that we built to specs. All of a sudden, they hired a new engineer from Texas who became my new *boss*. For some reason, he couldn't stand the fact that I was trying to do it right. There was this billion-dollar deal on a pipeline from Wisconsin to Illinois. It was forty-two inch pipe. They wanted me to find out all the problems, so I dug just fifteen holes and found *eight* cracks in the wells, everywhere they did a directional drill across the river using what they call a transition sleeve. The specs say that whenever you go from a standard size to a larger diameter pipe, you're supposed to install a transition sleeve. That's what their own spec said. But instead, what they did was just grind it out and weld it together. After they welded it, it had cracks in the pipe. I sent an email to the head engineer and the next morning I got a reply that said, "No more written communication with welding." Three days later, they fired me. I didn't say a word, because I remember what happened to Richard, my friend who stood up and testified before Congress.

Two weeks later, I was working for another company, BP Pipelines. I was given this position to watch all the pipes from Iowa to Pennsylvania, from Michigan to Kentucky, Tennessee border, all the way down there. I was to make sure they were repaired and right. I had inspectors. Every time we found an anomaly, they were working to repair it. I have to say this: BP bent over backwards to try to do everything right. They really did.

I worked for BP for about a year before they had that spill in the Gulf Coast. Remember that? The head of BP told Obama, "We're going to fix this, but it's going to take us six or eight months to do it." He found the problem, and he did exactly what he said he was going to do. It wasn't more than three months later that Enbridge – who had fired me for calling them out on their mistakes – had a blowout in the Kalamazoo River using a pipeline more than thirty years old. They dumped huge amounts of oil into the Kalamazoo River, ten times more than they predicted was possible. You know what happened? They called me three days after it happened and said, "Hey Roger, what are you doing?" I hung the phone; I cannot work for somebody who is dishonest.

When Bill Clinton was president, do you remember who the Attorney General was? It was Janet Reno. At that time, Iroquois Gas was under investigation from the FBI. They raided the corporate headquarters, and it cost them $21 million in lawyers, lawsuits, and all this other stuff. The reason they were persecuted was because some inspector got caught being bribed by a contractor. The inspector got fired, but he went to the FBI and started lying, telling them they had rocks on the pipe, that the company was doing everything wrong underground. Well, I'm here to tell you: the Iroquois pipeline, built by TransCanada to supply New York City during the Iran-Iraq War, was the best pipeline I've ever seen built in the United States. They did everything according to the spec. Doing everything right, they still got persecuted by the FBI and by Janet Reno. So much so, in fact, that Reno had ninety FBI agents dig up a loaded pipeline! The only thing they found was some rocks pointed at the pipe. No rocks *on* the pipe, like other companies have. No, TransCanada built the pipe with concrete coating. They bent over backwards doing everything better than a lot of companies do in America. And *this* is the company they shut down on the Keystone project?!

Those agents that Janet Reno sent down knew nothing about loaded gas lines. They knew nothing about digging around it. They *scratched* the pipeline while digging ninety holes. When they couldn't find anything wrong, they just filled in the holes. But what people don't understand is that if you scratch it, you damage the protection on the pipe. There's an electrical charge on that pipe, and all the rust goes right to that scratch spot. It may not look bad today, but ten years from now it will develop a rust spot and blow up. When Janet Reno dug those holes, she jeopardized everybody along the pipeline.

That's one of the reasons why I'm very against the Democratic Party at this point in my life. Republicans have a more favorable and more responsible view of the oil and gas industry. When Trump approved the Keystone Pipeline, he said, "You're okay to build it, but you've got to build it with American products." I'm 100% behind him for that. It puts people to work in America and provides better quality to the pipe itself. It's about time somebody had the set of balls to do that.

Do I agree with everything that Trump does? No. But he's got ten times more integrity than Obama before him. How would you feel if you had health insurance that went up as much as mine did? You'd feel betrayed. I know young married couples whose insurance went from $300 a month to $1200 a month. How do you think they feel? They're mad as hell. I don't blame anybody for that. That reason alone is good enough to get rid of the Democrats. But that's not the only reason; there are thousands of reasons.

My health insurance went from $389 to $1789. Who in their right mind thinks anyone can pay that each month? My wife doesn't work. It used to be, you could work in America and your wife wouldn't have to work. In the last eight years, it's come to the point where couples can't survive unless both of them go to work. Then they're both so frustrated because they *only* work and have no life. It's sad to say, but that's why people are mad. Actually, that's why people are furious.

I have to work, so I'm back in the gas industry with a fabrication shop that I started, doing gas metering and stuff like that. I'm trying to do it the right way, and I'm getting rewarded. It's not that I've got a *lot* of work; it's just that I've got some *good* work. I don't mind working with people who want to do things right.

I was brought up in a small Dutch community. My grandfather was a carpenter and he said, "If you don't do it right, it's not worth doing." I believe that's the way it is. If you're doing oil, gas, carpentry, or whatever, just to do it right. Because, believe me, there are plenty of companies who try to do it wrong.

Then, on top of that, we had a president that was elected because of his color. I'm not a racist person; I've got a lot of friends that are colored, I don't care. But Obama was elected *because* of his color, and that's not right.

Excuse me now, I'm taking my wife out for a lunch.

CHAPTER TWENTY-THREE
The Hispanic Nurse

May 9th, 2017
Kalamazoo, Michigan

Roger the oilman took an issue that we liberals usually feel pretty strongly about and gave me new perspective: what if blocking the Keystone project really was a bum deal for the local environment (because trains were going to carry the energy products anyway), and a bum deal for the economics of our nation (because we had to hire an expensive, Warren Buffet-owned railroad)? Or is Roger's entire argument negated by those comments about Obama at the end? That's the challenge of this book project, and I suppose a great challenge of our divided era.

Before leaving Grand Rapids, I attend the 2017 Conservative/Progressive Summit, hosted by the Hauenstein Center at Grand Valley State University. The mission of this gathering is to bring red and blue thinkers together and highlight the smart stuff — not the extremist stuff — that both sides have to say. The best part of the experience is that I'm never quite sure which speaker is the liberal and which is the conservative; all parties speak with moderation and intelligence. I hear Vincent Phillip Munoz of Notre Dame preach my current philosophy when he says, "I think it's critically important that students with opposite viewpoints read each other's arguments, and then talk to one another." I learn that there is real debate as to whether religious freedom is guaranteed under the Constitution, for that founding document only forbids Congress from enacting laws around religion, leaving individual states to their own devices. I learn of the Fairness Doctrine, created by the FCC, that required even-handed reporting on our limited airwaves; then I learn how the Fairness Doctrine was abolished in 1987, launching the separation of liberal and conservative media. I learn how Spiro Agnew railed against the instant analysis of political speeches in live media, arguing that these were just the improvisational opinions of a closed, elitist fraternity of men. I learn that some argue reporting should avoid exclusive objectivity, including instead a heavy dose of heart. I learn that conservative leaders often argue that general ideology is more important than accurate facts. Finally, in the most eye-opening session for me, Nicole Hemmer from Vox.com encourages media commentators not to focus on facts, but on emotional honesty. She encourages us to expose our politics up front, and let our commentary be viewed through a truthful, political lens. She argues that the era of balanced journalism fell apart because "liberal vs. conservative" was polarizing, actually leaving out an enormous population of those who didn't fall squarely on one side or the other.

So, it is with a new dose of political honesty that I say: I am still a leftist, but I'm seeing how blind I've been to many conservative arguments. Were there some kind of re-do, I'd still vote for Clinton, but I would be less inclined to automatically dismiss Trump's supporters. I admit that I'm succeeding in my project goal: I'm actually learning from smart people with whom I disagree.

With this attitude, I move on to Kalamazoo and agree to meet Jacquiline on the campus of the University of Western Michigan. She works full-time and has four kids at home, but she feels absolutely compelled to share her story. Ok, Jacquiline, I'm listening.

###

JACQUILINE: I am a Latina woman, and I moved here twelve years ago from Puerto Rico. I consider myself conservative; young, but still conservative. I have my religious beliefs and my values, and I have always voted Republican. I had my mind set on Ben Carson, but when he decided to leave I had no choice but to support Donald Trump.

I'm a working mother – single mother – with four children at thirty-six years old. I'm a registered nurse here in Michigan, and I came here due to the financial crisis in Puerto Rico. America saved me. In 2006, I could not find a job in Puerto Rico that would pay enough to support my children, so I decided to move here. The nursing profession in the United States is very valued and compensated; not so in Puerto Rico. The wages there are really low. You can have a bachelor's degree there and make $12 an hour, but as a nurse here you can make $20, $30, even $40 if you certify in a specific area. That was very tempting.

I was working as a sales rep for RadioShack in Puerto Rico, so I just transferred my job to the U.S. while waiting to take the boards and get my nursing license. Once registered, I found it quite easy to find work. My mom kept my kids with her for three months while I got settled, but when they arrived we settled in Kalamazoo.

I'm kind of a super success story. It's great. I have a support system: my mother and my faith. I really give honor to God. I believe that he aligned my life in a way that has let me be successful. I have tried to stay away from trouble, and it's easy to get in trouble when you're a single mom trying to make money to support your children. You can easily make a bad choice, but I've made good choices because I have the knowledge of God's word, and that's what my foundation is. How could I deny that God is real?

That's what actually made me successful. I said, "You have the tools to achieve prosperity like people have in the United States; if you don't use those tools, they're useless." We have so many tools here, but sometimes all I hear about is being the victim. Well, I'm a victim! I have had it hard in life. I have abuse in my family. We were financially oppressed. But here, we have opportunity! We are not victims; we are blessed.

I've lived in Mexico, too. I married a Mexican. I lived there for two years, so I can compare. Puerto Ricans are lucky, and the way people live in Mexico was difficult to witness. People are living on the ground and in cardboard houses. I lived in a desert in the state of Sonora. We were not well off, though we were lucky compared to many others. I had not completed my education and I was not a nurse. I found jobs to do there, but nothing like the profession I wanted. And I was allowed to be there! It was important to me to be completely legal. I got my papers, my visa, my passport, and I even brought them today because I wanted to show you. This is the Mexican permit to work, this is a letter from the Mexican Consulate stating my status, and this is my American passport.[58] I chose to do things the right way; why do so many people want a free pass?

People are like, "Oh, we should not call people illegal." But that's what you are! You're illegal in a country, and you're working? You're saying you're paying taxes, but when the tax return comes

---

[58] This is the most attractive passport photo I've ever seen. Some effort (some pride?) was put into preparing for this picture.

you're getting quite a good lump sum refund. So you're not actually paying taxes. See, these illegal immigrants claim to be supporting children in Mexico and get credit for that. I know how it works because I know people who do it.[59]

I don't buy the argument that sometimes you have to make a choice between providing for your family in some desperate way or living your life in Mexico. When I went to the U.S. consulate to register my son who was born there – my son Benjamin was born in Mexico – there were lines of people waiting outside to get an interview to come to the United States. They have the ability to apply, and they allow a certain amount of immigrants to come. But they go there and lie! They claim they have never been to the United States, when actually they have a record of being deported. People who go there and lie to the system are setting themselves up for failure.

Immigration was my top issue in this last election, but almost as important is having a pro-life candidate. I've been very religious since I was young. Protestant. In Puerto Rico we're all Catholics, but I started studying the Bible and seeing things a little differently than the Catholics. Some people simply can't vote for a candidate that is pro-choice, but I actually feel that everybody has their freedom to choose already. You can have an abortion if you want to, but tax money should not be paying for that abortion. I feel that's their choice, and I'm not going to be judging; I'm not someone to be judging people. Some people say putting Trump in office means he could put in a Supreme Court Justice who could turn over Roe v. Wade, but it's not going to happen. The Justices have minds of their own; they're not going to be influenced by politics. But to be clear, I don't think federal money should be given to any type of institution that supports abortion. That's *my* money. I'm a citizen. I'm paying into the pot. I don't want the government to have any say in that type of activity.

Trump has a lot of advisors. He's not closed-minded. I believe, even though people might disagree, that he's a smart man. He's not going to be a dictator; I don't see him as a dictator. I don't think he's politically correct and I don't he says the right things at the right time, but I feel like he has the common sense to see that, in order to get a good deal, you have to have balance. You have to be able to work with everybody. And because of that background he has as a

---

[59] I must admit I was surprised to learn that unauthorized immigrants would be filing tax returns at all. About half of them do, according to the Pew Research Center and the IRS. One of their incentives is to have a paper trail of tax payments in case the law allows them to apply for legal status one day.

businessman, I think he is used to getting opinions from everybody to gather data and *then* making a decision. He doesn't go on feeling; he gathers data and makes a call.

Cruz was just too much for me. He didn't have leniency like Trump does. Trump is flexible. He was pro-choice in the past, so that's some flexibility right there! I have to be real; I don't think he was the perfect candidate. But he is studying and trying to fulfill all the promises he made. It came down to me saying, "Let's get some fresh blood in here; I'm going to try Trump!"

As for Hillary, I just couldn't vote for someone who was with her husband for so long while he had so many unfaithful relationships. I mean, if it's an open marriage, why don't you just go and say it? "This is an open marriage, and I can let him do whatever he wants." But she was not that way. She was calling herself religious and painting a picture that it was a happy marriage, and I think that was not true.

I work in the health care industry, and I think health care should be available for everybody. But people have to understand that the state shouldn't pay for your health care. If I want to have a good quality of life for my children and me, I have to have a job. I have to work. And that job provides health care.[60] I will invest myself in this company if this company is going to give me something back.

The same goes with my type of work and my pay. I know how much I'm valued. I know how much my work is valued. So I'm going to apply for jobs that are up to my level. If I don't feel satisfied, I will pursue education. I will go and get myself trained, and I will get a *better* job. People want to work in the fast-food industry and expect a good paycheck?! What are you doing to improve your life? You expect people to pay you $15 an hour without any kind of education? Paramedics don't get $15 an hour. And they're saving lives.

Health care should be available for everybody in an open market where you can select the company you want to cover you. You should have alternatives and options to choose from. But the government should not be paying for it. The people who come to my hospital often don't have insurance, and they have very poor outcomes. They're smokers, they're homeless, they're drinkers, they use street drugs. Or they're obese, or the place they live is compromised. I'm not judging them, I'm just saying that this is the type of patient that comes without insurance. That says something.

---

[60] Must be nice.

We have to reach out to those who are struggling and not deny care, and we have to offer alternatives. But I don't think that making the working-class pay for their health care is the right alternative.

My friend is a nurse and a part-time professor. She doesn't qualify for insurance from work, so she went to Obamacare. She's paying $800 a month, and the insurance won't kick in until she pays her $6,000 deductible. So she says, "I'm voting for Trump because I can't afford this anymore." But then people making only $12,000 a year will pay $100 a month with the subsidies?! That's not right.

The working class are getting frustrated. For example, my children don't qualify for free meals at school because I make more than $60,000 a year. I'm a single mom with four kids, and $2.15 per child per day is actually hard for me. I say to the school, "Hey, I know my kids owe $40, but please give them something to eat. I'll pay when I get my check." I look forward to those months where I get a fifth check, so I can catch up. I thank God for that fifth payday.

We want to be treated equally, right? We want everybody to enjoy this country. Well, what education is available for everybody? Trump wants to use vouchers to give kids from the inner city the choice to go to a nicer school. Those parents are struggling. They're saying, "Man, my kid has potential, but look at the school that they are supposed to attend. It's in the inner city where there's drug dealers, shootings on the corners, two liquor stores on the block." You can roll around Kalamazoo and see what I'm talking about.

I hope people have the wisdom to work with our president, no matter their opinion of him so far. If we work together, we're going to make this country a better country. I thought the same about Obama, but then he started doing all these deals with other countries and I lost my hope. I'm like, "Iran?! Why are you giving them money? Those people say 'kill America.' Why would you do the business with them?"[61]

I'm Puerto Rican, but I was raised singing the United States national anthem. You go to Puerto Rico, and they have *both* flags waving. I want everybody to love America.

---

[61] Yes, I can see how the timing of our cash settlement with Iran had particularly bad timing. Both sides of this issue are interesting, should the reader care to follow up.

CHAPTER TWENTY-FOUR
The Medicare Recipient

May 10th, 2017
Kalamazoo, Michigan

She's Latina. She was born in Puerto Rico. She lived in Mexico. And she supports Donald Trump with passion! Oh, Jacquiline, I have a hard time understanding. Here's why: as a single mother of four who studied nursing while working at Radio Shack, Jacquiline is an absolute economic success story. She's the American Dream, rising above personal hardship and succeeding. She didn't want handouts, she says. But she moved here into a social-service system created by presidential centrists (Bill Clinton and both Bushs), and the system worked as intended. She succeeded in centrist America, not in far-right America.

And she is so honest! Jacquiline applied for free or reduced-cost school lunch for her kids, reporting her accurate and honest income information. Doesn't she know that there's a trend to misrepresent one's income in order to qualify for free lunch? Doesn't she know that it can help the school get funding? (Wait. Is that just in New York, where the liberals live?) I admire Jacquiline so very much. I want her on our team. She sounds like a Democrat, except for that pro-life thing. And that pro-life thing is a real trend in conservative voters, isn't it? Would Jacquiline have voted for the Republican candidate just to diminish abortion rights? She never clarified that for me. It makes me wonder if her support of Trump is less important than the pro-life stance of the Republican party in general. But Jacquiline speaks like a centrist, I swear. She even pointed up Trump's willingness to change his mind, a trait I support in all centrists.

I'm sticking around Kalamazoo a little longer and am now off to meet Gary. He's warned me that our fountain-side meeting spot is bit far from his car and he may be late. He walks slowly and gets pretty winded, he says. I'm not sure what his medical issue is, but it's health care that I want to talk about. Gary's on Medicare — which I view from the outside as a terrific program — but he doesn't want it. He doesn't really need it, he says, as he pants up the walkway.

###

GARY: I have no energy. For me to walk from my car to here just about killed me. Plus, you can tell my voice is a little weak. I'd rather be all excited and energized, but it just don't happen anymore. It's out of my control. I can't work because of it.

Right after I quit working, I had no insurance. With my heart attack, I paid cash. It was just about twelve grand. I just took it out of my savings, I didn't call somebody. Everybody's always taking up hospital emergency rooms with just a sniffle. Jesus, what a waste of time and money for everybody.

The State of Michigan put me on Medicaid for three months, then Medicare. I never use it. Why is the government involved in medical anyway? It's $138 a month plus my deductible, which is $3,000-4,000, I think. That's a reasonable price.[62]

Kids going to college here at this University, how many of them want to spend money for health insurance? I have four kids, but I'm by myself now. My kids, they're all young and in good health. Why would they want to spend money for insurance? They'd be better off putting in the bank or investing it. Wait until you need some procedure, then you already have the extra money to pay for it. I was smart, I saved money.

I'm sixty-five years old, and I'd love to work again. I was in the automotive business for myself for forty-four years and had ten locations. Never been into politics until this year. Never paid any attention to it, and never had a party. Now I'm caught up every day watching politics. It's all I do: I turn on the TV in the morning when I get up and keep it on until about eleven o'clock at night to watch the news. I change channels, watch all the different variations. It's amazing how many different sides there are to each story. You can definitely see the spin. When you're watching Fox, and then you go to

---

[62] Keeping it a reasonable price is precisely why the government is "involved in medical."

MSNBC or CNN, it's like a whole different world, even though they're talking about the same thing.

I grew up Saginaw, Michigan. It's beautiful there. Business brought me here to Kalamazoo, and I'll stay here because I'm tired of moving. I used to move a lot. I'd just sell everything I owned and then buy new; they delivered the new stuff in a day. Except for books. I had tons of books. Tons of books. 1911 encyclopedias, original, thick. I moved them around for a long time.

When I saw the candidates available this year, I knew that I sure as hell wasn't going to vote for Hillary. I didn't trust her for a minute. I wasn't thrilled about Trump either, honestly. But then again, he sold his shit pretty good. He really did. And he's been trying to stick to his word the best he can; I'm pleased with that.

I'm sick of this Russia crap. Just so sick of it. After what, nine months now? What are they looking for?! They ain't found nothing. They keep looking and looking and looking for something, but everybody so far has said nothing's there and they just keep doing it.

The only guy I've ever contributed to was Ben Carson. I sent him money four times. He never got elected, but Trump was smart enough to put him in office. Carson is smart, has a good temperament. (Hold on a minute. There's a spider on me. That's what we get for talking outside. Though I get spiders in my bed sometimes, too.)

So, Ben Carson. Sent him money four times. The only problem with sending candidates money is that you always get asked for more. Is this March of Dimes or what? But I liked him.

I expect the FBI director to indict Hillary Clinton, to actually do an investigation and indict her. Because when Comey had a press conference, he basically laid out what she's guilty of. I thought for sure he was going to indict her right then and there. Then he turned around and said he wouldn't touch her. What do you mean? You just told us all the guilty shit she did! That got me pissed off more than anything. I started getting behind Trump even more.

National defense is my number one concern. We ain't got nothing otherwise. We need to have a country that is protected and can defend itself. I've watched as budgets for the military have gone down every year for the last eight years. Our military is devastated and now Trump is bringing it back, which I really appreciate. I signed up to go into the Air Force "early entry" back about 1970. But I had medical issues, thyroid or something, and they wouldn't take me. That's fine. Vietnam was going on and I didn't really want to die. A bunch of us guys from high school had just gone down there to do early entry because we wanted to show our support. One of those guys just retired from the Airborne. He'd been there since that day.

Our country is in danger because of that little midget. I'm talking about North Korea, of course. That scares me a little bit. You don't know what's going to happen one day to the next. Plus, we have thirty thousand guys over on that border and they've got about a hundred thousand guns pointed at us. That could be a bad situation. I like to think that our new president's just calling the midget's bluff.

And that MOAB bomb, the Mother of All Bombs? I wondered why they didn't use that a couple of years ago, because I knew we had it and it was made for these cave areas. Finally, Trump took the advice of some general and just went ahead and used it. Cost us about $100,000 per guy that died, but it sent a message. We needed leadership again. Obama was always apologizing. For what? We're America. We're not supposed to have to apologize to anybody for anything. If we did something wrong, fine. Let's apologize. But we haven't done things wrong overseas. He's wasn't giving us any credit. It's time we stood back up.

Ok, maybe we have to apologize for the Vietnam War. I don't agree with how that went; I think our generals fucked us. Excuse my language. A lot of politicians weren't telling the truth, and a lot of guys died. Other than that, I don't think we have anything to apologize for.

I'm really glad that they're doing something about all these business regulations. I had a place in Florida ready to open up and I was waiting, waiting, and waiting for the approvals. Finally, I called up the mayor. It was in Fort Lauderdale. He actually called me back and says, "Why in the hell are you waiting? This place should have been open a week ago!" He understood. Sure as hell, the next day, my place was open. I couldn't believe it. But why did it take calling the mayor? We spent thousands of dollars on permits. I'm sure some of that's for a good reason, but some of it's stupid. Just plain stupid.

I totally agree with what Trump is doing on immigration, simple as that. Why in the hell should we let everybody in? If you want to be here, learn the language, fit in. You've got to be a productive person. There's nothing worse than somebody that's here who don't want to work. And I've hired guys from Mexico before, but I hired ones who worked their assess off. I was pleased with them. I hated to see them go, but eventually they went back to Mexico. They were good guys.

I'm not a staunch Republican by any means. I'm the common sense guy. That's all I want, common sense. That's why I like Trump; the guy uses common sense and says what's on his mind. He may be lying, I don't know. I appreciate the boldness. He's a good bullshitter. And he is an outsider. You know what? I think when the country was founded, these guys didn't spend their life in Washington. They got in, got out. Nowadays, it's a lifestyle; they're there forever. Trump went in there as a citizen politician which, somehow, I think is a bright light for our future.

I wish they'd give him a chance. Since he got into the office, everybody's coming at him from every direction. They don't want him to succeed. You got these people like Pelosi, saying, "Impeach him." For what? Because you don't like him? Okay, I don't like you either, but...

I own my house and everything else outright. But I still appreciate the way the stock market is going since Trump's been in office. It makes my bottom line happy. I'm collecting about 6% interest on my investments right now, which ain't bad. Now, this market could crash any day, but I have few bills. I live cheap, I tell you. I've always tried to be independent, and that's a big deal, man. The car I'm driving right now is this big old Cadillac that I paid cash for.

I used to drive an '84 Corvette. It's an ideal car, except for tickets. I'd get a ticket doing more than a hundred miles an hour in a fifty-five. This one time, a guy who used to train for me was in the passenger seat. It was five in the morning, brand new blacktop, and we were just buzzing. So fast, it was like I was starting to fly. I was just starting to let off the gas on one of the hills when I spotted a state cop in the distance. I just pulled over. I just waited. My employee opens his door, takes off his shoes, and relaxes. Sure enough, I'm seeing smoke from the squad car's tire and I'm just waiting for him to come. You know what the cop tells me? He just wanted to look at the car! Well, and he wanted $200 cash. He needed the money before I left the county, or else I was going to jail. My employee's sitting there with toes sticking out of his socks, but he pulls two new hundred dollar bills out of his pocket. I've still got the ticket; I had the cop sign it.

I've had a good life. Fun. I played guitar for a bit. Just rhythm. I wouldn't know how to do it now. Our band was *The Cherry Slush*. We had one record. It probably made Top Fifteen in Saginaw, Michigan!

It's amazing how fast life goes by. The last twenty years feels like yesterday. What would I do different? Get laid more often, I guess. I don't know.

CHAPTER TWENTY-FIVE
The Immigrant Fan

May 18th, 2017
Syracuse, New York

Gary in Kalamazoo paid cash when he had a heart attack. He owned automotive shops across the country. He owns his house outright, and his Cadillac, too. Can we agree that Gary is an extremely successful man, financially? Well then here's a trend that isn't so new: many people who profess to have earned their way to the top seem to be distrusting of social-welfare programs. Gary is on Medicare, but he doesn't quite call that an entitlement and definitely claims not to need it. But Gary is also adamant that Washington needs an outsider. That's a new trend. It started with Obama, an outsider candidate I loved. Is it possible to win a presidential election anymore if you are viewed as an insider?

I'm cutting north to Syracuse now. Anthony and his fiancé will be meeting me in an urban park downtown. (He hasn't told me his future wife's name, referring to her only as his fiancé. Repeatedly.) Syracuse has always been a cold town to me, but I've never visited in summer. The month of May brings industrial warmth to the town, though the storefronts are largely bare. It's not rundown (yet?), but also not populated or bustling. Most people here in the park are just sitting. Ah, a realization: most people here in this park are homeless.

Anthony says he wants to talk immigration. He's bold, loud, and a proud Italian.

###

ANTHONY: I'm from upstate New York, and my family are all legal immigrants. My fiancé came here from Bosnia, legally. My mom came here from Italy, legally. They did things the way you're supposed to do things. I voted for Trump and I believe he's going to handle our immigration problem the right way. If you are an illegal immigrant and you've committed a crime, then you've got to go! But if you're an illegal immigrant and you've been here working for ten, eleven years... well, I think Trump is going to find a way to let those people stay. I really believe that's his intent.[63]

I raised my two brothers by myself when mom died. I found us an apartment. I got one brother into college and the other one into the Army; I'm proud of that. I'm also the first one in my entire family to graduate high school, the first one to graduate college. My fiancé and I each have three kids from previous marriages, and they're all doing great.

Thomas Jefferson predicted what's happening right now in America. Look it up. Jefferson said that someday the country might start moving in a bad, bad direction, but that we shouldn't worry about it. He said that when the country gets that bad, the people will take it back. "We the people" have just taken back our country! Republicans control the House, the Senate, and the presidency. And getting a conservative onto the Supreme Court? This is us taking back our country from the devastation of the past eight, ten, even twenty years. The eighties were the last time this country was great. But we've taken it back.

Look, unemployment numbers are way higher than they're reported them to be. With African-Americans, unemployment is up to 56%! That's crazy, and it's got to stop. Trump will get jobs back into downtown cities like Syracuse, and give these people hope.

I've been a production manager for thirty-two years, currently in the uniform service industry dealing with garments, shirts, pants, and towels for nursing homes and hospitals. I've had to manage people all my life. That's where my strengths are. I think I'm a natural leader; I know how to be in charge, and be kind while I'm in charge. I haven't had one union grievance in my company; not one, ever. I think Trump leads the same way. Direct, in control, but kind and reasonable.

What really got me engaged in this election was that I don't like the direction of our country. Donald Trump ran as a Republican,

---

[63] Hmm.

but I don't believe he's actually a Republican. What I do believe is that Trump really cares about America and the American people. He doesn't have any ties to anybody, he doesn't have any lobbyists to cater to.

Regardless of whether or not he's a real Republican, Trump is doing a great conservative job with the Supreme Court. He nominated Neil Gorsuch, a principled conservative who goes by the Constitution in a no-nonsense way. What the law says is what he enforces. Donald Trump is learning as he goes, but all he has to do in most people's eyes is get someone like Gorsuch on the Court, and he's winning!

I like that in these first hundred days, Trump has already been lifting regulations to give businesses more opportunities to create jobs. He freed up the Keystone pipeline, which will create a lot of jobs, and he's freed up private land to start drilling so we can be energy independent and not have to rely on places like Saudi Arabia. Saudi Arabia's in cahoots with half our government anyway.[64]

Our foreign policies have been literally laughed at and mocked for eight years. The President of the United States is the leader of the free world and should be setting a tone of respect. We are a peaceful nation who provides for the goods, services, and needs for a big part of the world. We give a lot of money out every month to countries that don't even like us. NATO is supposed to pay their fair share to help keep all these nations safe, and they are not paying anything. Trump's just making them pay their fair share. He is being open minded, watching, and making sure that we're respected and have strong allies.

Trump inherited a mess. We pulled out of Iraq in 2012, which was a huge mistake. We've opened up a lot of space now for ISIS. Mubarak in Egypt kept that region safe for over forty years, but Obama got rid of him. That nuclear deal with Iran, come on. Assad in Syria was murdering his own people and the leader of the free world should not allow that to happen. And Obama supported the Muslim Brotherhood and no one wants to say a word about it.[65] Trump's got to deal with all of that.

---

[64] According to the U.S. Energy Information Administration, our net import of petroleum is around 25%. The largest foreign provider, by far, is Canada.

[65] Indeed, many debated the U.S. position on the Muslim Brotherhood in Egypt. Roger Cohen wrote in the New York Times, "What is the alternative to supporting Morsi and the Brotherhood and urging them to be inclusive in the new Egypt? Well, the United States could cut them off and hope they fail – but I can think of no surer way to guarantee radicalization and aggravate the very tendencies the West

All this stuff coming out about Russia? Come on. If they had something about Trump and Russia, they would have found it by now, believe me. Russia hates Donald Trump. But Trump could cure cancer and the Democrats would find a problem with it. It's frustrating, because without California and New York City, Donald Trump had a landslide victory. He destroyed Hillary Clinton, destroyed her!

Democrats have seen over a thousand seats changing places since Barack Obama took office; that's the anger in our country showing its face. I'm not a racist, but all the Democrats want to do is play the race card. They can't run on their policies. They can't run on what they've accomplished. I think the American people have a movement that is above race, above the Democrats, and way above and beyond the Tea Party.

I think you're going to see a lot of politicians ousted this year because Donald Trump has an agenda. He's already done a lot for this country and people don't even know it. Well, some people like me know it. They want to us to lie and say that he hasn't passed anything legislative through the Congress. He's passed twenty-eight bills! Look it up.[66] These are facts.

Just like with Obamacare, you have the right to go ahead and read the facts. Obamacare is in black and white. Read it. They're not going to lie about what they've got in black and white. But the Democrats passed Obamacare at three o'clock in the morning?! And Nancy Pelosi says, "If you want to see what's in the bill, you've got to pass it first." Really? Okay.[67]

Barack Obama said, "If you want your doctor, you can keep your doctor. And I guarantee everybody's plans are going to go down $2,500." Everybody's health care is skyrocketing. You got major companies that are pulling out. In the state of Iowa, there's only one insurer left. Go to the state of Virginia, only two insurers left. People are losing insurance left and right. With Republicans in charge, we have to repeal and replace Obamacare.

---

wants to avoid as a poverty-stricken Egypt goes into an economic tailspin." My translation: supporting the Brotherhood appeared to be the lesser of two evils.

[66] I looked it up. It's true. One might argue that these bills are largely insignificant, but they have been signed into law.

[67] The full text of the Affordable Care Act had been publicly available for months when Nancy Pelosi spoke these words, so she was certainly not intending to pass it in secret. The context of her speech matters here. According to Snopes, "It appears that the sense of Pelosi's remarks was that the benefits (in her view) of the bill – rather than the contents of the bill – would only be fully revealed to the public after it was passed and implemented."

We put Donald Trump in there because he's an outsider, he's a businessman, he's got no ties to anybody, and he's got no lobbyists. He says he's going to shake it up and mix it up and he's certainly doing that, isn't he? We got chaos right now in Washington, D.C.

You know, I'm not exactly sure why I'm so passionate about things like the unemployment rate for other people. I've done well for myself, but I still know things need to be done for other people. The current system just hasn't been working for them. God gave me the ability to be a leader, to be outspoken, to defend people, to help people. This is just the way I've been all my life. I'm very passionate about doing the right thing and taking care of people. Remember, not one grievance has ever been filed against me at work in thirty-two years, because I believe people need to be treated properly.

People want to come to the U.S. because it's a land of opportunity. My grandparents told me how hard it was, how they had to struggle. They came here with no money, with maybe five dollars in their pocket. But hard work, dedication, getting a good reputation, and surrounding yourself with good people will make good things happen.

My hope for immigration reform is that we put a limit on the number of people we allow in the country, but we also acknowledge the illegal aliens who have been here working and being good people. They should be issued proper green cards and be eligible to become United States citizens. I don't see how it would even be possible to just rip up eleven million people and throw them out of the country. I think that would be insane and I don't think that's Trump's intention at all.[68] But if we got people that are breaking laws, we throw them out. We had that beautiful girl in California that was killed by an illegal immigrant who had been allowed to come back into this country seven times. Seven times; are you kidding me? That's ridiculous.

Trump wants to do some great things with taxes. He wants to take the corporate tax level from 35% to 15%, make it so anyone making $25,000 or less pays no taxes, let married couples making $50,000 and under a year pay no taxes, and make there be only three

---

[68] President Trump has actually said very clearly that he would like to round up eleven million undocumented people and send them out of the United States, though he leaves room for the idea that they can come back. His words: "We have at least eleven million people in this country that came in illegally. They will go out. They will come back – some will come back, the best, through a process. They have to come back legally. They have to come back through a process, and it may not be a very quick process, but I think that's very fair, and very fine. They're going to get in line with other people." Actually, Anthony's stance on immigration sounds more similar to Obama's than Trump's.

other tax brackets overall.[69] These are major tax breaks that we need. We haven't had these kind of breaks since Reagan.

Our corporate tax is highest in the world. We get killed on trade. Too many countries like China have been taking advantage of us. We don't win nothing anymore, but Trump will change that with his business mind.

America was on the road to becoming a third world country. You travel a lot; you know. Our cities are terrible. Our infrastructure is terrible. This is the United States of America, and it's an absolute joke. Our bridges are in terrible shape, our roads have potholes all over them. But I'll tell you what, neither he nor God can fix this mess in four years or even eight years. This is going to be hard.

---

[69] This does appear to be President Trump's hope.

CHAPTER TWENTY-SIX
The Health Care Italian

Up in Syracuse, Anthony spoke so proudly of his family's classic Italian immigration success story, and his fiancé's more modern Bosnian immigration success, that he caused me to notice a trend in the Trump supporters I interview. The trend is for established, legal immigrants who navigated the system successfully – or know people who did – to find truth and connection to the way Trump speaks about immigration policies. To paraphrase many with whom I've spoken, "I worked my way through legally, so why can't they?" Our president touched a nerve when he brought this issue to the forefront.

Anthony values the outsider quality of Donald Trump; that's another obvious trend. He also believes America is on its way to becoming a third-world country and that Trump is the solution; that's not as much of a trend.

Oh, and I've just noticed a personal trend! I find myself sympathizing with the people I'm meeting and enjoying them very much... until they say one crazy thing. Anthony, for example, was an extremely likable guy with some debatable-but-not-awful things to say, until his last comment about America being a third world country and Trump being the solution. That seems extremist, and it makes me question some of the other, more logical arguments he made. Many Trump supporters seem say one crazy thing if I sit with them long enough.

And now I'm connecting with Rhode Island, and with another self-defined proud Italian. This is my home state, and home to the only conversation in this book that I actively sought out in advance. You know how we all have that one Facebook friend who is always posting inflammatory comments that are the opposite of what we personally believe? For me, that's Victor. We went to high school together. We weren't really friends then, nor have we kept in touch in our adult lives. But he is the guy in my feed that always has something to say, something deliberately confrontational to those on the left side of the spectrum, and Facebook's algorithm always shows it to me.

We're from the same area. We're the same demographic. And yet our views are decidedly different. Why?

I contact Victor. He is ready — really, really ready — to talk.

VICTOR: My father had his own Italian restaurant here in Rhode Island. Having that place was always his dream, and he worked so hard to make it happen. See, he was born into poverty in Southern Italy, where it was just him and his mother. He had no male figure in his life and lived in complete poverty. His goal was to come to the United States and build a future here. When he was a teenager, he took a seventeen-day boat ride across the Atlantic — people sick, people dying, no food. Then he worked and saved for three years to be able to bring his mother over. He has the classic Italian immigrant story.

Later, he joined the United States Army. In his own words, "I had to give back to the country that allowed me to come here." Listen, I know that this book is not supposed to be about my father, but he is probably the most influential person in my life. It's important that I tell you a little bit about him because it's a lot of what formed my views.

When my father got here, he didn't speak a word of English. He got a job as a chef, and the person who owned the restaurant was kind enough to put signs on all the different things. He learned what a pot was because there was a sign in English that said "pot" hanging off of it.

My father poured his blood, sweat, and tears into opening his own restaurant. It was successful for a long time but, during my senior year of high school, he was forced to close the doors because of the recession. I felt what it was like to have a big house, a beautiful Cadillac, a pool, to attend a private school... and then lose it all in a moment. We lost everything. We went to live in a two-bedroom condo near the Army base. My parents were sick with embarrassment over it.

The economy just turned on them, and my father did not have a chance to plan properly. He had just reinvested in the business. He had pride in his food, he had a great reputation, but he couldn't sustain that downturn in the economy. I was brought up with comfortableness, then I'm a senior in high school and I'm buying groceries for my family. My parents reacted to those groceries the first time like I was bringing home a child I was adopting. They gave me the most amazing stare; they couldn't believe what I had done. That triggered something in my brain, made me and my brother realize that we actually had to take care of our parents. In order to do that, we needed to be able to amass wealth. We needed to be able to work hard so that they wouldn't have to keep working. My father had gone from working sixty hours a week in his own restaurant to mopping the floors of someone else's for $10 an hour. That made me hungry. It made me aggressive to be successful.

I live in Warwick, Rhode Island. I went to the University of Massachusetts for a short period of time, but the tuition was so high that I had to drop out. I saved money for a couple of years, then went back to the New England Institute of Technology to finish my bachelor's degree in telecommunications with the belief that I was going to do something with television. However, I found out during an internship that I was working with guys that didn't even go to college and were shoving cameras in the bottom of a mobile television truck at 1:00 in the morning after a Celtics game, then driving home to their families that late at night. Sure, they were making a thousand dollars a day, but they were 1099. There was no security; if they didn't get the phone call, they didn't get the gig. I needed something more guaranteed, so I went into sales.

I enjoy meeting new people. I can get along with anyone, regardless of how strong my views may be. I can talk to people. My aspiration was to be in medical sales, but I started off doing copy machines because that's what people say to do to get experience. They're very difficult to sell. They say if you're successful there, you'll be successful anywhere.

Fast forward, I've been in laboratory sales for the last sixteen years. We concentrate on urine drug screening for providers that are prescribing controlled substances to their patients. My job, primarily, is to go around and get these providers to understand that they need to be drug screening their patients. We actually have the science to tell the provider if the patient is taking the meds as prescribed. In this division that I head, I've had a number of providers tell me that not only have I changed the way they treat medicine, but that we've saved a number of people's lives who were abusing narcotics. They've come clean with their doctors, they've entered rehab. It's turned their lives around.

I have a vending machine business that I operate on the side, a network marketing business that I operate on the side, and I own five properties with my brother that have rental units in them. I'm pretty busy. Trying to amass wealth, you know?

I was brought up a Democrat. My family were Democrats. My uncle, who was a very successful businessman, picked up John F. Kennedy at the airport once; they were personal friends. I come from a very strong, liberal background. I voted for Obama first-term. I was not always the conservative that people see me to be. I am a victim of having gotten sick of the liberal mindset. I'll really dumb it down: If you're making money and doing well, you'll never feel like the liberals or the Democrats have your best interests in mind. Income taxes go up, property taxes go up. I live in the second most liberal state in the country; Massachusetts is number one, Rhode Island's number two. We're taxed to death by liberal leadership.

Obamacare needs to go away. I know it's helped some people, but it's also hurt the health care industry. Obamacare drove reimbursement down. It actually put providers and people that deal insurance in a position where they started making far less money. My insurance deductibles have gone way up over the last four years, when they hadn't risen a dime over the previous fifteen. That's because of policies put in place to pay for this Obamacare. In my industry, we took a 45% pay cut in reimbursements for the same tests.

Imagine you're a business, and you're cruising along and it's going well. We get paid on the gross revenue, so imagine I bring in a hundred samples in 2010. A hundred samples that I bring in equates to $50,000 worth of revenue. If I'm going to get 8% of that, I'm looking at a $4,000 commission check. Now imagine a 45% cut from that! I'm bringing in the same hundred samples, and instead of making $4,000, I'm making $2,300 dollars. At the same time, the company is making less so they start doing layoffs. My territory went from Rhode Island and Massachusetts, to Rhode Island,

Massachusetts, Connecticut, and Long Island. I'm doing more work, covering more territory, for less money. I have more time away from my family.

From an industry standpoint, the only way Obamacare was helpful was that my competition went out of business. That's helpful. There used to be a very competitive marketplace, but not every company could stay afloat.

I'm not going to lie to you and say Trump is the most amazing president we've ever had. Sometimes he does things and I'm like, "Oh, my God." I'm not an idiot. But I never once said, "I'd rather have Hillary." Not yet.

I'll tell you this, I don't care about Trump's stance on abortion. I don't care about some of the greenhouse issues. For me, it was all about making America great.

Some people seem to feel entitled to handouts, entitled to things that us hardworking people don't take. I hate to say that all liberals don't work because obviously that's not the case, but I want to imply that the Democratic mindset is to take care of and fund those programs and those people. That's what started to turn it a little bit for me. I would say that pride in our country was lost during Obama's second term. I felt like he went on an apology tour. So the nationalism that Trump brought to the table, the "Make America Great Again" campaign, really resonated with me. With Trump I was like, "You know what? It's time to do that again."

American pride and immigration is huge, especially in my family. My father, who struggled to get my grandmother here, went through all the processes America asked of him, then decided he had to give back. He was concerned about learning English. Why do we accommodate people that don't want to conform to the way this country is? In other countries, they don't do that. My mother worked at the Cranston police station doing the tickets. She would collect tickets from people who came in to pay. It was only a few hours a week, but they wouldn't let her go full-time because they needed to hire a Spanish-speaking person. She always had more seniority, but she'd be skipped over because the Spanish-speakers could cater to those who came in to pay. How is that fair? Cranston is a relatively white, upper-middle-class city. But the ticket window was, and this is coming from my mother, a revolving door of illegal immigrants.

My father is as old-school an Italian-American as you can find, but to this day he will tell you – when we're building a project like this big garden area where he cans his own vegetables, the area where he cures meat, or the area where he makes his own wine – he will always say, "If you're going to do it the right way, you do it the American way." He always references America as the greatest country in the world; they do everything the right way. Everyone's who's here is lucky to be here because the opportunities are endless if you're willing to work hard. That nationalism and pride runs so deep.

Whether to deport illegals is probably the most difficult argument. I own a property – you're going to like this one – where I'm sure I have tenants that are not legal to the United States. I know this because I had a tenant who got a DUI and was deported back to Guatemala. I don't know want to be the person that's like, "Everyone should be deported." We need a moral decision there, some fair play. I don't think we should start rounding people up unless they have a criminal record. I think that they should be allowed to stay here if they are functioning, upstanding members of society. But they should be given an even shorter leash than someone that was born here.

I'll give you an example. If I came to your house and kicked over a glass of water, you'd probably be like, "What the heck did you do that for?" and question me about it. Whereas, if maybe your wife did it, you would just think nothing of it and clean it up. She's your wife. She lives there with you. If she does it, it's not a big deal. When a guest comes in and disrespects your living space, you would have a shorter fuse. I should have to be held to a higher standard because it's not my house. I should have respect for you in your home.

Obama's path to citizenship included too broad a population, and there was no proper enforcement around having it done. I think even Trump has realized that we can't deport everybody; we need a balanced solution.

"We don't have enough time to be politically correct anymore. We need action." When Trump says that, it hits me right in the gut. Makes me feel like this guy is for real. This guy doesn't want any bullshit to keep going on. See, people in our country who decide not to work to pull themselves out of poverty are entitled to a free ride. I have a tenant that has been on Medicaid and government assistance since I bought my first home in 2002. She's always lived downstairs, getting a check from the government every single month. Her rent is paid for by the City of Cranston Housing Authority. She's had a kidney transplant, all her medications are free, she smokes cigarettes, and she goes to the casino every chance she gets. My mother and father cannot afford their medications. Now, I don't think that one side is 100% right, but something isn't fair there.

Liberals seem to look as us conservatives as having no feelings, as wanting other people to suffer. Even yesterday, I was debating with a liberal friend from North Carolina. It got a little heated and he apologized. I said, "I don't need an apology. I'm fine." He's like, "Well, I know you're fine. You're a conservative; you have no feelings." Of course he was joking, but there are just so many times when I've been made to feel like I'm dumb or unintelligent, like I don't care for people. The very reason Trump was elected is because conservatives are sick of being told we are less-than. I think that's what put him there.

CHAPTER TWENTY-SEVEN
The No-Muslim Conservative

June 12th, 2017
Bethlehem, Pennsylvania

My high school classmate back in Rhode Island seems absolutely concerned about payments and incentives for the health care industry. His words: "Obamacare helped people, but hurt the industry." My either/or mind wants to say to Victor, "You've chosen industry over people, but I choose people over industry." My more mature mind knows it's not that simple; real people are employed by that industry, after all. And Victor's tenant on Medicaid that smokes and gambles? Doesn't seem right, but maybe that's just a sign of the system being broken. Democrats want the system fixed as much as Trump does, don't we? But we're not as loud about it. Victor also mentioned that liberals "look at conservatives as having no feelings, as wanting other people to suffer." Frankly, Victor is correct. He's correct about me anyway. I thought people who voted for Donald Trump were heartless, and it's taking this entire book project to open my eyes to another point of view. I've broadened my outlook since November of 2016. Still nagging at me, though, is the fact that the people I'm meeting always tend to say something crazy. Here comes a good example...

I'm in Bethlehem, Pennsylvania, near Allentown. Bill Joel rings in my head. And Thomas' aggressive stance on Muslims has me cringing already.

THOMAS: The immigration policies in this country are outrageous. I don't feel we should let any Muslims in at all, none.

I'm from well-to-do Pennsylvania. My father owned companies. He was a wealthy man. My father invited me to work with him, of course. I'll have to say, I didn't take advantage. I had all the opportunity presented to me, but I didn't really take it. I could've done better, but that's another story.

I really never understood what politics my parents were into, but I suspect they were Republican. My father always kept it a secret for some reason.

I've had a pretty very nice life. I went to Alaska for thirteen years, commercial fishing in Kodiak. I've been everywhere, but I'm retired now at sixty years old. I'm on SSD. I'm old. I have very limited income. I done it. I'm done. Now I just fight politics on Facebook all day. I have a beautiful little apartment, and I'm a single man at the moment.

Listen, what the Muslims are doing to Western Europe is outrageous. No-go zones? The Muslims have been doing this for fourteen hundred years. It's 20% religion, 80% invasion and take over. It's a way of life. It's the Sharia law. It's a form of government. This is not like anything we've seen before. They are not going to assimilate. This is not their point.

I feel that there is a large war coming in the Middle East. I feel that. The shit is going to hit the fan in the Middle East like we have never seen. And Democrats are ridiculous not to see it coming. These people don't have a brain in their head. They're embarrassing. They're embarrassing to the country. They're embarrassing to everybody, even to their own party.

I've seen groups of Muslims congregating together here in Bethlehem, Pennsylvania. Never with others, just with themselves. There are places in the world already drastically affected by this. Not so much in America, but in Britain they're twenty years ahead of us. Sharia law is not the norm for American Muslims yet, but I don't want to have to tell the difference between what different Muslims are thinking. I don't want to have to put a meter on it. They haven't built that kind of meter yet.

You can't say this is a free country for American Muslims. Their extremist brothers have ruined this for all of them. Trump has some strong views on this, too. He'll handle it.

I go to church. I believe in God. I'm as religious as anybody usually is in the later part of their life. And I'm involved in my church. I do my best.

You know, Trump has got to handle the EPA, too. Regulations from the EPA have gotten out of control. Everything is regulated, just everything. We all want clean water. We all want clean air. But at some point it becomes ridiculous. In Kodiak, we had regulations on commercial fishing, but that was a must. You have to regulate fishing.

Changes are coming to Kodiak these days. It was still the Wild West when I was there, and just ending when I left. You could live there and never take the keys out of your car. No one had a lock on their front door. You could leave money in your car, go fishing for two weeks, come back and still have the money to drive into summer, you know what I mean? Of course, everybody had a gun. Everybody had a gun up there, everybody. Mom in the supermarket, two kids, shopping, and the mom's packing.

I have to be able to carry a gun, but I think there needs to be a background check with the craziness of today. You have to be careful who you give guns to. Increasing background checks? Sure, there has to be some control.[70]

You hear about these no-go zones in France, in Sweden, where there are areas police cannot go into? Areas where police will be physically chased out by Muslims? This is happening.[71]

The police are on edge. And the police force in *this* town will shoot you. The police are being more and more militarized. They are definitely militarized in Pennsylvania. I can just see that their tactics are military. But they have to be, I guess. There can't be any other way. You have people that are just plain crazy people. It's not like what it used to be. Now, there's some really violent, evil people out there. Real animals.

I was raised in a country club setting. I did well up until around age fifty-seven when, for health reasons, things fell apart a little bit. But I believed in work. You went to work. You worked. You worked. I think that when you allow people to have children – just unwed mothers and we're paying them to have children – this is a problem. You get people on welfare and then they have no

---

[70] Well, yes. We agree.
[71] No, it's not.

alternatives. I don't think welfare was ever meant to take care of as many people as it does.

Then you have immigration and the free handouts the second they come here? You're asking for trouble. I think you're asking for trouble.

I was on board with Trump very, very early. You remember those speeches? They were very good. And trust me, the concept of Donald Trump as president was as crazy to me as it is to everybody else. But now, I couldn't see it any other way. He was the only one that made any sense. He's the only one that wasn't like the rest of them. And we're extremely lucky to have that whole family.

I swear it's all one party there in Washington. It's almost a red flag swaying for just one party. Even though we call it two parties, it's one large machine working for its own self-interest. Trump is the first one to come from outside of that and actually get something done. He's refreshing. Every day on the news, you actually see what you're part of, what's going on. Unlike any other politician, you feel like you have some connection with Trump. You feel that somebody in Washington actually gives a damn about what's going on.

Yesterday, another appeals court turned down Trump's travel ban. How can they do that? The President of the United States just has a right to do this. He has control over immigration 100% and doesn't have to answer to anybody. Why do the courts come into it? This is in the law, clearly stated.

If the Muslim population in the United States were to get up to 8%, 10% of the population, then we're done. We lose the country. I am pro-immigration. I find it unfortunate that we have to build a wall. I think that a two-thousand-mile wall at $11 billion is just a damn shame. It means everything else failed; all kinds of policies and control of the population all failed, so you've got to build a wall. And we've got to just stop issuing visas to anyone who self-declares they're Muslim. The travel ban would probably cut out 90% of the problem, though. I'm glad Trump is still trying for that. That kind of law would cut the Muslim population down to the point of tolerance.

CHAPTER TWENTY-EIGHT
The Chinese Scientist

June 12th, 2017
Philadelphia, Pennsylvania

I didn't care for Thomas' stance on almost anything. But this time there was a reverse, a moment when I found just one thing to agree with in the string of crazy things. Here it is: "I don't think welfare was ever meant to take care of as many people as it does." I agree, Thomas. I agree that the welfare system can be viewed as too expansive or somewhat dysfunctional. Ok, you all convinced me! But Trump isn't the one fixing it, he's only the one speaking loudest about it. Perhaps the Democrats could speak more loudly on reform for the system? There are so many that believe it needs reforming. Not elimination. Oh god, not elimination. Just gentle, reasonable reforming.

Off to the big town now, Philadelphia. Qirong, a scientist, has an organization that raised money for Trump. They raised so much money, in fact, that they started turning away donations. (First time I've heard of that, for sure.) They hired planes. They rented billboards. They are the "Pennsylvania Chinese-Americans for Trump."

###

QIRONG: First, you've got to keep my last name confidential. Please just mention my first name, so it's indicating my Asian heritage. I'm concerned because the company I'm working for is a globalization company. They don't care about "America first." They care about the company first, the profit first. Google, Amazon, they're all the same. They obviously don't care about America; they care about profits and their money.

And big companies don't care where the money *sits*. For them, the money can sit anywhere in the world. Right now, most of the money in my company is in Europe. It's an American health care company – the number one health care business in the world, and with the most profitable drug – but their money sits overseas. The manufacturing is overseas. The new employees are overseas. Why? Corporate tax.

One country we partner with has a 15% corporate tax rate, another one 12%. That's versus 35% in U.S.! No question, all the money's moving overseas because the tax rates are so much better there. The CEOs or big board members don't care, because all their money's sitting in Europe, too. I can speak for majority of our American employees when I say we have to change this, but we are scared to talk about it at work because we may lose the job. Our company presents as very liberal, and we have a teamwork culture. We have European colleagues, Chinese colleagues, Indian colleagues; and our collective goal is to make money for the company, wherever that money sits.

What do you do? You have to bury all those not-happy feelings underneath. All our jobs are being outsourced to Europe, to China, to India. And whenever there is layoff, the number one person to be laid off is a U.S. employee, not a European employee. If we speak out about that fact, we are basically disrespecting our European or Chinese colleagues. But get this: of our top ten most profitable drugs, not one of them is manufactured in the U.S..

When Trump first mentioned changing the corporate tax rate, I was shocked. I said, "Man, this has been an issue for twenty or thirty years. No one's dared to talk about it until now." Finally, a person stand up and say, "U.S. has been taken advantage for so many years. It stops now." That's the main reason pushing me to really support Trump and help Trump to win. I realize not a lot of people are focused on corporate tax law, but it's so important. And lots of people just don't know.

I'm a legal employee, a legal immigrant. I immigrated to U.S. roughly twenty years ago. I spent ten years in order to get my green card. The reason why is, like Trump said, immigration is a privilege, not a human right. It's not. It is not. I fully agree. I have to prove to Immigration Department that I'm a valuable asset to U.S. through publications, patents, an academic degree. On top of all those achievements, I have to have ten reference letter from well-known scientists or engineers. In order to get my green card, I have two feet high documents I have submitted for the proof. Ten years it took me! When I hear Trump talking about illegal immigrants, it totally echoed in my heart. We both want illegal immigrants to go back home, then come back again as legal immigrants. The only difference between legals and illegals is that *we* chose to follow the law.

Sometimes, people are saying, "Oh man, my family is in U.S. I want family reunion." Come on. I have family in U.S. and I have family in China. They could become illegal immigrants in order to come here. But no! I tell them no. All of us choose to follow the law. We choose to obey the law.

Do you think illegal immigrants getting all those benefits is fair? Lots of my family in China are thinking, "Why we have to follow the law? Illegal immigrants getting so many benefits, and the U.S. doesn't do anything to stop them. They climb the wall. They come to the U.S. land and taking all the benefits. Why you ask me to follow the law?" This is our choice. The U.S. is encouraging that, encouraging immigrants to break the law. The liberals are encouraging that.

I'm an oncology scientist. Chemist. I'm working with drug discovery for a cancer cure and cardiovascular disease. This is my career. I have a PhD and a master's degree. I'm well-educated, and my degrees are from the U.S. I know U.S. tax law probably way better than lots of people who were born here. Obviously, I'm not easy to be brainwashed. Liberals, they're all just talking about love and it's total bullshit. It's bogus – sorry – because so much of it is not making sense. If refugees come in and only 1% of them are bad, that 1% kills thousands of Americans. I go to Europe a lot for business, and they all wanted Hillary on board. You know why? It's very simple. They told me very strictly to my face: if Hillary's on board, they can export all the refugees to U.S. You talk to every taxpaying EU person, they will tell you they don't like refugees.

My European co-worker's neighbors are refugees. They don't work. Muslims, they don't speak English and they don't work. They take benefits every year. Every month over there they will get, I think, €5000 for the family. Then his wife – he has two or three wives, all paid by the government – starts a business to bring in even more money. What kind of business does she do? You can't imagine. The business is that his wife becomes a prostitute. Actually, my co-worker is very happy because of that, because at least they are not terrorists.

I have a friend in Florida who is dealing with all the refugee benefits. He told me clearly it's a $2,000 monthly payment under Obama's policy. $2,000 per refugee per month. Who's paying that? You and me. In Belgium, 85% of the Muslims are using benefits, taking social benefits. They are not working, including very young, strong Muslims. This is the reality. Europe is gone. In the U.S., we still have a chance. But if Hillary was elected, yes, we'd be gone. The U.S. would become a third world country. We'd go broke, fully broke. And we'll be full of terrorists.

The Democratic Party has been hijacked, I think. Back in nineties, blocking refugees had bipartisan support. Because this is so obvious. America first, this is so obvious. Now in this era, we can't get that support anymore. If it's not American first, who is the first? Tell me. I don't know. China first? Muslim first? This is totally nonsense. I just can't stand their logic right now. Anyway, that's why we support Trump.

When Trump started campaigning, we started doing lots of education for Chinese-Americans through social media. When he became the candidate, we decided to step out of social media to do real things. From July to November of 2016, we went out every day to knock on doors in Pennsylvania, because we knew we were a key battle state. We knocked on hundreds and hundreds of doors. Every day after work, I was out there until dark. (My husband had to pick up the kids.) And we saw so much enthusiasm! Immigrants like us who came here to pursue the American dream were applauding us because they saw their dream country going to hell!

We printed fifty thousand fliers outlining Trump's policies in an easy-to-understand way. We took in donations and in two days our team got $30,000. I had to stop accepting money because we had enough and didn't know what to do with it all! Some people wanted to give $10,000 right away, but I wanted more real people to feel a part of it all, so I set the individual limit at $200. We flew six planes across Pennsylvania that had Trump banners flying behind them. We took out newspaper ads for six weeks just to publish Trump's policy. We put up six or seven billboards. We had such passion from Chinese-Americans!

There were people that didn't react well to us, for sure. Some people hit me, many said f-words to me. We just stood still and said, "Here are some simple reasons we'd like you to vote for Trump." I went to canvass a neighborhood outside of Philadelphia wearing a Trump shirt and had a gun pointed at me, so I took off that shirt and continued canvassing!

I knew one thing very clearly: if Trump was not elected, I would leave this country. This was the last fight, and I was doing it mostly for my kids. I'm forty and I have a family. My husband and I are legal immigrants; we applied using the category of exceptional scientists. We are both well educated, have very decent pay, have two kids born in the U.S., and are a very traditional U.S. family. We ask nothing in return for our donations, our taxes, and our devotion to the country. We maxed out our donations to Trump at the $5,600 limit. I didn't have one day of vacation last year because I used up all my time canvassing for Trump. Every day I worked until midnight for the Trump campaign, and I had no complaints.

We never got to meet Trump, but it didn't matter. The only thing we got was a thank you letter from the Trump campaign! For us, as long as he was elected, we knew America will be a nice land in which to live. Americans will have jobs, and that's what we want. Nothing in return. We wanted to dissolve our local organization, *PA Chinese-Americans for Trump*, because Trump was elected, but now we see him under so much attack that we'll continue trying to say what we can to help him. The thing we stick with is this: we only support Trump. We don't support Republicans, we support Trump.

CHAPTER TWENTY-NINE
The Multi-Marriage Independent

June 22nd, 2017
Little Rock, Arkansas

The Pennsylvania Chinese-Americans for Trump campaign is still well-funded. There's more work for them to do as Trump prepares to release his tax plan. Is lowering the corporate tax rate something Americans will support, or even really care about? It's certainly a good talking point for Trump supporters, and I think I'm seeing their point. I'll be curious to follow how involved in corporate tax our regular citizens will care to be. In the meantime, I'm going to Clinton territory.

Here in Little Rock, the Clintons are imprinted on walls and ingrained in minds. Due to their local presence through the seventies, eighties, and nineties, it seems like everyone I've been in touch with here has a personal Clinton story to share. Brenda is one of them.

We meet along the River Market downtown. I suggest going for a beer in a funky, colorful music joint, though we're the only ones in the large performance room at this time in the afternoon. Tropical Storm Cindy has pushed rain up and into Arkansas and there's a torrential downpour outside. It's humid in the bar, and Brenda cools herself with a giant, pink fan. Welcome to Little Rock, the only place more Clinton-centric than D.C.

###

BRENDA: I'm in my fifties now, and I've always thought of myself as pretty conservative. I take my fifteen-year-old daughter to a non-denominational Christian church every week because I think she needs that in her life. I'm against abortion, for sure. But on the other hand, I care about specific candidates, so I've actually voted for Democrats and Independents from time to time when they appeal to me. I consider all options.

It was Trump who decided this election for me. When I saw him speak for the first time, I knew he didn't take any crap from anyone. He was not beholden to anyone. And the Clintons? I mean, they're from here in Little Rock, but the people here know what the Clintons are really like. Because we know, a lot of us don't support them.

Here's a story about how I got some insider info about the Clintons: when I was in my thirties and working for the *Democrat* newspaper right down the street from here, I was followed to my car by one of those transients. He tried to rape and kidnap me, but I got away by rolling under another car. This was one of the episodes that led to my PTSD. The whole thing happened right by the Capitol building, so the first responders were some of the government security guys, like Secret Service. After the trial, one of Bill Clinton's security guys took me to lunch. He told me all about how they used to bring women in for Hillary, and other women in for Bill. He turned me on to all the government contracts that Bill was giving away here in Arkansas. We know what they were like here in Little Rock; that's why we don't vote for them.

I've had five husbands. Two of those ex-husbands are in jail now, and one of them passed away. One of my kids was sexually abused by her father. I've lived some life, you know? But I'm independent and strong, just like Trump. Our president has nobody padding his pocket. I admire his strength in the face of so many hating on him. I like strong leadership; it's part of my upbringing.

My father was a self-proclaimed minister. And he was a snake handler. Really! That was his brand of old-fashioned religion. He never attended any educational facilities like a seminary or anything, he just always preached. He believed God made men superior to women. He believed his wife should give him lots of children, even to the point of endangering her health. (My mother secretly took birth control because the doctor told her she could die if she had more kids.) He believed he was a prophet of God, and if you were chosen by God no evil could come against you. So he handled venomous snakes. And when we were sick, he believed God would heal us; we were never taken to the doctor or dentist in our childhood. When I was about eight years old, I remember being very ill from jellyfish bites. Looking back, I think I came close to dying. My entire body was puffed up and very red, and I was very sick for several days. My mother begged him to take me to the doctor then, but he refused.

My father believed in "spare the rod, spoil the child" to the extent of real physical and emotional abuse. He was extremely strict and harsh in his discipline. He beat one of my brothers with an extension cord until he passed out. He would whip us with wire coat hangers, switches, and belts. I believe strongly that he was mentally ill. He never once told any of his seven children, "I love you," or showed us any form of affection.

Liberals are kind of difficult for me to understand most of the time. Here in Little Rock, Black people are more prejudiced than white people. For example, I work with a Black lady who thought I hung the moon, she loved me so much... until she found out I voted for Trump. Now she now rants about how Black people are mistreated and white people have always suppressed Black people. She makes comments at work that she is "just a slave on the white man's plantation." I've had Black people that I've greeted at the store just turn their heads as if they are too good to be spoken to by a white person, totally ignoring that I spoke to them.

Trump is probably slightly racist, but I don't care. When it comes to political correctness, it's just time somebody like Trump said some of these things out loud. Things about deporting illegal Hispanics, Muslim extremists, and refugees from Syria. We need that wall to close our borders, and immigrants wanting to enter the U.S. need to be able to financially support themselves and not rely on government aid. The majority of illegal immigrants are criminals!

We need to bring companies back to America to provide more jobs. We need to put God back in the White House, drain the swamp, and set term limits. All these things, Trump has said and I agree with. He says, "Americans come first." He is against abortion and he is defunding Planned Parenthood. Our previous presidents never stood up so boldly for these issues!

I've worked very hard supporting my family by working full time since age twelve, and even did those fourteen years at the *Democrat* newspaper! I grew up in a very poor family. When I went to work, it was at a family owned restaurant. I started out bussing tables and washing dishes, then became a cook, and then a hostess and waitress. I worked twelve hours every Saturday and Sunday and made over $100 each day in tips. This was a lot forty-five years ago. I work on military contracts now.

The harder I worked and the more I learned, the more money I made. This is how America should be. I have always been a very hard worker; I think you should be punctual and, unless you are deathly ill, you go to work. I've successfully instilled this same work ethic in my two adult daughters. They are both very hard workers and have been very successful with promotions and raises in their jobs. Younger people joining the workforce feel "entitled." They feel they can do very little work but be paid high wages! If they are thirty or forty minutes late for work, no problem.

Trump will fix all the problems I've mentioned, I know it! God bless you, God bless the U.S.A., and of course, God bless President Trump. Ha! I just had to throw that in there.

CHAPTER THIRTY
The Natural Gas Rep

June 23rd, 2017
Little Rock, Arkansas

I learned nothing from my conversation with Brenda down at Little Rock's River Market, save for the fact that a person is willing to vote for a president they admit is "probably slightly racist." Brenda was a very nice conversationalist, and I'm sympathetic to all the hardships she has experienced: abusive father, five husbands (including two now in jail and one now deceased), PTSD from an attempted rape. However, in my quest to more deeply understand the motivations of devoted Trump supporters, my empathy does not overpower the fact that she whispered, "Here, Black people are more prejudiced toward white people," and followed shortly thereafter with, "It's just time somebody like Trump said some of these things out loud." If that explains her vote, I'm just not interested in learning from her.

But then, does it actually explain her vote? Or was she just riffing? It would be easier for me to understand an explanation revolving around the fact that Brenda grew up in an ultra-religious household and remains steadfastly pro-life, but Brenda insists she has voted for Democrats many times. Her first point about Trump was that he impressed her by "not taking any crap from anyone." She likes the front of strength that he demonstrated early in his campaign. She likes the image of a loud man leading a proud country. I guess I just don't. I always prefer compromise and, after months of Trump being in office, I haven't seen any real benefits from his brash style. That's a key revelation for me: no matter how much I am beginning to understand some of the financial reasons behind a vote for Trump,

I still see nothing better in his style than a more nuanced, traditional, diplomatic leader.

It's still really humid in Little Rock as I walk the edge of downtown to a giant office tower. I'm to speak with Vickie, long time resident of Arkansas and one who has spent her entire career in the natural gas industry.

###

VICKIE: I've lived in Arkansas all my life. I was born here in Little Rock, was married thirty-seven years, have children and grandchildren. I consider myself a stable, probably middle-class person.

Natural gas distribution has been my business for thirty-five years. This whole building is a natural gas company. I am a business rep here on the sixth floor. I started when they had payment offices, but I've been in a couple of different positions since then. Planning to retire next June. I've got thirty-five years out of thirty-seven, but I have two they are going to restore. The restore thing is an interesting benefit. Here's how it works: when I had my son, I left the company, but I would come back and fill in periodically. I ended up filling in enough days that they're giving me that time of service back for retirement. I guess that's pretty lucky. This is a good company.

My dad worked Reynolds Metals Company, and we were probably middle-class most of the time. We vacationed, we had a boat and a camper. But almost everybody has boats down here. There's lots of really nice lakes. If you've never been to Hot Springs, you should really go.

I would say that I'm pretty conservative now, and I would say my parents were always conservative. I can remember my dad saying, "Don't you vote for that man," talking about Bill Clinton. So I didn't the first time... but I did the second time. Truthfully, my vote for Bill was actually a vote for Hillary. I wanted her to have some power, and I knew she'd be the brains behind their operation. I've since changed my mind about Hillary.

Hillary Clinton screwed up everything Bill gave her to do. I don't trust the Clintons anymore. This is my personal opinion, but I believe they had something to do with the death of Vince Foster.

There were a lot of things they did here in Arkansas that were shady. I really don't trust them; you'll hear that a lot here in Arkansas.[72]

Have you ever heard of the "boys on the tracks?" There is a book about them; it is two boys that were killed and laid on railroad tracks, and they think it's because of drugs and stuff that they saw. People were saying that the Clintons were heavily involved in drugs coming through the airfield in Maumelle, Arkansas. It seems legitimate to me. They've never solved the murder of those two boys.

Trump was my pick from the start, because of that "Make America Great Again." And with the way Hillary Clinton screwed up everything as Secretary of State, I did not want that woman in power. Even as a woman, I didn't. I said, "If you are against Donald Trump and you want a woman for president, pick any woman but Hillary Clinton." She is not the right woman. Benghazi, that's the big screw up. If that was my family in the compound... whew. Let her answer for it.

Everything Trump promised, he's trying to do. But they're fighting him in every way! No matter what he says, they fight him. It's like my ex-husband used to say, we have a bunch of bleeding heart do-gooders in this country. It is all about what's politically correct instead of what's right.

We need to reform immigration, definitely, because we need to protect ourselves. Trump screening people that come in here? There's nothing wrong with that. Everybody should have a right to a better life, but if they can't pass a background check they shouldn't come in here.

And I think that we should stop handing out money to those countries that slap us in the face and spit on our flag. We have to cut them off. I have no problem with cutting them off.

Trump's not a political person really. I like that. He says what he thinks, and those are things that many of us are also thinking. I do wish he would stay off Twitter, though. That gets him in trouble a lot.

I didn't like Obama, but I would never have been blatantly disrespectful to him like people are with Donald Trump. Attacking his youngest child? Leave the kids out of it. Leave his wife out of it. She's a very pretty and elegant lady, I think.

NAFTA was wrong for our country. One of the vendors that our company bought stuff from closed their facility a year ago and have since taken it to Mexico. We still purchase from them, but I felt

---

[72] Yup, I've heard that a lot here in Arkansas.

so sorry talking to the workers. They had the opportunity to go to Mexico with the company, but of course they didn't want to because it's such a dangerous place. We sold ourselves out with NAFTA.

I paid more to have the 90/10 healthcare plan through my work. When Obamacare came in, we had to sort of align our plan with theirs. Now, it's an 80/20 plan. I can't get a better plan, I have to have a lesser plan for the same price. What's fair about that?

They say everybody can get healthcare. My friend's son couldn't get it. He couldn't get the healthcare. We don't know why. We don't know. Wasn't eligible for it. He could not get the Obama healthcare.[73]

Trump won't be able to achieve anything if the House and Senate don't back him. That frustrates me. They all need to work together and forget the party lines. I vote for the person, not the party. I'm sick of party lines determining everything for these politicians.

With immigration and refugees, I think if you come here for a better life then you should love America. If you don't love America, go live somewhere else. Go live in a Muslim country if you can't accept our ways. We should not change to suit them; they should change to suit us.

There's a lot of protests going on over Trump. I think that people that protest illegally should be put in jail. I think that people that have threatened Donald Trump should be put in jail. I think that people that destroy the American flag should be put in jail. If they would start making people be responsible for their actions, this might be a better world.

---

[73] This cannot be true, as *everyone* is eligible to purchase health insurance, including those with pre-existing conditions that may have deterred companies from insuring them in the past. This story is more likely about the son in question not being eligible for Obamacare *subsidies*.

CHAPTER THIRTY-ONE
The Clinton Mistress

June 23rd, 2017
Little Rock, Arkansas

The Clinton legacy stills envelopes Little Rock. This morning, Vickie touted the Trump party line with standard restatements of his natural gas policy, demonstrating a calm intelligence and full understanding of the industry while simultaneously explaining to me how she is sure the Clintons were running a drug importing ring out of small Arkansas airports. The alleged drug ring, however, did not stop her from voting for Bill Clinton, though it "was really a vote for Hillary because she has always been the brains behind the operation." The Clintons are Vickie's dirtied-up local celebrities, but she views Trump as a policy leader. Of course, she is drawn to his fame, too. I get the feeling they all are.

This afternoon, I'm to meet another local celebrity in the leather-adorned lobby bar of the posh Capital Hotel in downtown Little Rock. Sally is a former Miss Arkansas who claims to have been outed by a state police officer as having been Bill Clinton's long-time mistress. Speaking briefly on the phone, Sally tells me she has experienced first-hand the "dirty tactics of the Democratic Party." She goes so far as to refer to the Democratic Party as a hate group, refusing to trust them (us?) any further than you can throw a stick. Of course, these harsh words are delivered with the sugary charm of a Southern beauty queen who knows how to draw in her audience. I'm drawn in – fully, easily – and Bill Clinton surely was, too. It seems Sally was quite into the dashing, young Bill, but Hillary's wrath "forced" her to a decade-long exile in China. An exile? That can't be real, right?

Sally has agreed to meet me in the Capital Hotel today, but she's bringing along Steve – her friend and sometime bodyguard – because she can't be sure whether to trust me. She feels I might be duping her, that I may actually be part of a dirty Democratic tactic. Perhaps I should be?

###

SALLY: After being crowned Miss Arkansas, I had a lengthy affair with Bill Clinton. But that's not even my biggest secret. I'll tell you about Bill soon, but the real secret of my life is that my mother molested me from the time I was born, and she molested my three-year-old brother right in front of me. We never told anyone about that while she was alive.

I was raised in an era where you kept all the family secrets. You never exposed anyone. We didn't have therapists, and we didn't go to psychiatrists. We were afraid those people would lock us up in the insane asylum! I've always felt like two different people; there's a little girl inside me who's never grown up. I kept the family secret.

My mother was manipulative, and I was scared to death of her. Funny that it's my mother who signed me up for my first beauty pageant, and that changed the course of my life. I was a sophomore in college. She called me one night and said, "Guess what? You're going to be in the first Miss Pan World pageant. Some people I know are putting it on and they wanted your phone number. I told them you would probably say no because you're so freaked out about your flat chest and bird legs, but I think it'd be good for you so I filled out the application. You're going." She basically owned me.

After a few pageants, I was crowned Miss Arkansas. I was quite proud of that. I had to commit to them for a year, but my mother warned me, "At the end of this Miss Arkansas year, you better have a place to go. Either find a job or move in with someone else, because you're not staying in my house and I'm not supporting you. You're almost twenty years old and it's time for you to get out." I said, "But my daddy..." and she wouldn't even let me get the words out. She blasted back, "I control your daddy too, and it doesn't matter what he thinks."

My daddy was my salvation. He loved me; he never touched me, never spanked me, never scolded me. He was so supportive, and I probably honored him best by being a finalist in the Miss America pageant. From that day on, every time he introduced me to someone, it was, "This is my daughter, Miss Arkansas." I would say, "Oh daddy please, that's old news." And he'd look hurt! It was never old news to him.

As I got older, people would look embarrassed when my father spoke about the pageant. "Oh my gosh, she's forty-something years old. Why is he still calling her Miss Arkansas?" But it was an honor for him. It was a big moment in his life. He worked hard and supported me. He was a railroad engineer and ran a construction company; he did whatever it took to make money, and he probably liked working so much because he could spend more time away from my mother. She was a bitch.

I came home one day and saw a telegram that had already been opened. I grabbed it and ripped it from the envelope – angry because my mother was always opening all my mail – and it was from NBC in New York City. They were inviting me to fly to New York and audition as the first female host with Dave Garroway on *The Today Show*. I read the telegram out loud and my daddy said, "This is wonderful. This is so wonderful."

Of course, my mother said, "Absolutely not. She's not going anywhere. Only whores and sluts go to New York. This man Dave Garroway, whoever he is, just wants to sleep with her." My mother told me that I would not using any of her money to get there, but I told her, "Mother, NBC is going to pay my way and put me in a hotel. Everything will be free." She said, "No, that's a bunch of malarkey. They're not going to give you anything."

Years later, I looked at that telegram as I was going through boxes of my life and the little girl in me just started screaming, cursing my mother. I tore it up and put it in the waste basket. I saved so many of the documents that proved what I needed to prove, but I didn't save that one because I couldn't stand the thought of having to look at it again. When you get older, the thing that bothers you most is what you didn't have a chance to do. It's not the things you did and you failed at or the audition you bombed. It's all the things that you never had a chance to do, the missed opportunities. And you can't go back.

My mother let my father die. He had an aneurysm on the couch, but he lived two days and she never got him over to the hospital.

Ain't it interesting how timing is everything? The guy that you were in love with in high school was a farmer's son and didn't dress well? He grows up to be a billionaire and dresses superbly and all of a sudden you think, "Why didn't I go after him when I had the chance?" That's how I feel about my relationship with Bill Clinton.

I was in the halls of the Capitol trying to meet people and find work, and I ran into this guy with an Afro, a thin face, not particularly handsome, not particularly well dressed. That was Bill. He stopped me and said, "Hey, I think I know who you are. Weren't you Miss Arkansas a long time ago?" I said, "Well, it wasn't *that* long ago!" He was charming.

I started working for the 87th General Assembly. Through that work, Bill and I became friends. At the parties, we danced together, had a drink, and were all part of a group. Bill and I had an attraction as far as fun, and he was a good dancer. But nothing came of it. We had no real relationship then.

Bill probably didn't lose his virginity until he was almost twenty. I call that a late bloomer. And he would have been happy to be Arkansas royalty for the rest of his life. When he became governor, it was the pinnacle of success for him. But Hillary kept her hand on his back and kept pushing and pushing and pushing. She couldn't have made it as far as she did without pushing Bill ahead of her. He was her song-and-dance man. He knew how to warm up everyone in the room.

Ten years later, I'm going through my second divorce and he's governor of the State of Arkansas. I was drawing up plans for a public park project, and I proposed it to Bill. He liked the idea, and he liked it even more when we discussed it back at my condo while sniffing coke.

It's funny, Bill's a good old guy. He'd give you a pat on the back, "Honey, you're so cute, so pretty." He made me feel like my legs were the right length, my breasts were the right size. Everything I had was just perfect for him, and that's what I needed because I really was feeling like used toilet paper after my divorce.

My condo backed up to a city property called Reservoir Park, where the reservoir water system is located. It was so convenient to walk out on my patio, open the gate, and go about sixty feet to the road that wrapped around the park. Bill would have his chauffeur, usually a state trooper, pull in right there behind my condo. The light would be on and Bill could just come right through the back gate. The one time he came by way of the front, one of the neighbors saw him! She called me and said, "Was that Bill Clinton that I saw walk in your house last night?" I was dumbfounded. She said, "I was standing in my kitchen window and told myself that better not be the governor. I donated to his campaign and if he's fooling around on Hillary, I'm not going to give him any more money." She was livid.

So I had to lie, and I don't lie very well. "That was a guy I know who looks a lot like Bill. People tell me all the time about how he looks like Bill. But think about it: Bill Clinton travels with the state troopers. Did you see any state troopers?" I fooled her because that was the one time he didn't use a police car.

Bill Clinton was a good old boy, and he made me feel like a beauty queen again. He lived with a mother who was also dominating, so we had a lot in common in that respect. He was afraid of his mother, but he also had a little boy attraction to her. I wrote a book where I talk about this: Bill had some strange encounters with his mother. She would come home and have him rub her feet, take off her stockings. It turned him on. He even put her bra on one time and stuffed it. He liked to watch himself in the mirror with it on.

Hillary Clinton knew about my affair with Bill. I mean, I never wanted to be a mistress. I know how it feels to be married to a man who's running around. You feel like no matter how you dress up and fix your hair, you'll never be pretty enough because he's always looking at his secretary or he's looking at some great big boobs and you look down and you don't have the big boobs. It was only because of my mom that I married the man who cheated on me. So I wasn't the one that sought Bill out, and I know how Hillary must have felt. But that doesn't excuse how she would talk sometimes.

Bill told me how Hillary would speak to her own stomach when she was pregnant with Chelsea, saying vile things like, "If this baby inside me looks like a mongoloid or a freak..." One time, I was at the Easter Seals discussing children with disabilities and Bill said, "You ought to see Hillary when she talks about disabled children." Not kindly, I guess! I learned a lot about how Hillary speaks when the cameras aren't rolling.

In the meantime, this is the eighties now, I decided to run for mayor of the city where I grew up, Pine Bluff, Arkansas. I said to Bill, "Guess what? You're going to love this. I decided today that I'm going to run for mayor of Pine Bluff. But I'm going to run as a Republican."

Bill just stood there. Then he made fun of me and we had our first argument. An anger that I'd never seen before started coming out. He said, "You're not a politician. You're not a Republican. You don't know jack-shit about politics. What in the heck makes you think you're going to beat out our candidate? We've already groomed her, we've got money riding on her, we've got the votes. There's no way you're going to win." I said, "I'm sure as heck going to try." That made him angrier, like I was attacking *him* by running for office as a Republican. He slammed my patio door, got in his paid-for chauffeured life, and we were done.

I was so glad I got to see the real Bill, because I thought it was only Hillary who could get that angry! She was the one that was throwing chairs and dishes. She was the one about who the State Troopers said, "My gosh, this woman's got a violent temper." They never saw Bill's bad side, or if they did, they weren't willing to talk about it. I think he learned that temper from Hillary, frankly. He thought, "Wow, look at her. She can get all this attention from being brash."

The thing is, I wasn't really a devoted Republican yet. And the Republicans didn't support me. But what I saw very clearly was that I had to commit to that party in order to get in the race. I had to grab some sort of a position; running as an Independent was always wishy-washy to me. When you say that you're an Independent, it's like you're riding the fence. That wasn't me. The Democrats had already anointed their candidate and the Democrats own this state, so if I wanted to run for mayor it would have to be on the Republican ticket. And by the way, the Democratic candidate hadn't even graduated from high school, was over 300 pounds, and had never been outside the State of Arkansas.

Pine Bluff at that time was the second largest city in Arkansas, so this race was a big deal. The city's about fifty miles down the road from here in Little Rock. It was very, very expensive to run a race, and there were all these tactics used against me: my condo was flooded because the city wouldn't open the floodgates, my car was keyed, the vinyl top of my car was cut. It was a rough race! I got a call from one of my supporters, "Hurry, get out to this voting site. They're bussing people in to vote for the opposition. They're paying them. You can see them, they're handing them money!" Can you imagine?

Finally, I just realized it wasn't in the cards. The Republican Party had no chance in Arkansas. It was like we didn't exist. Liberals probably can't even imagine that the Democratic Party will do *everything* to win, regardless of whether it's an honest or dishonest.

I wrote about the tactics of the Democratic party in my book, but when I was trying to get it published editors were reacting only to the Clinton portion. They were saying, "You're really too hot to handle right now because the word on the street is that you're going to be talking about Bill's private parts." I was not, of course, going to talk about Bill's private parts... though I certainly could have! I did, however, want to include my impressions of Hillary.

My friend Steve here beside me – I like to say he's my bodyguard – he always says that Hillary was never a natural people person. He says you've got to kiss the damn babies to get elected! And Hillary just never came across as somebody who would want to pick up the babies or do the things you sometimes have to do at the retail level to win. Hillary was just not an actress. Had she been an actress, she could have made Bill feel like he was worthwhile and he wouldn't have sought attention elsewhere.

Let me tell you about how I went to China, came back, and then was forced to China again by Hillary Clinton herself. Ever since I was in the ninth grade, I'd dreamed of visiting the Great Wall. I was offered a chance due to my status as Miss Arkansas, and I took the opportunity to walk the full length of the wall. I kept a journal and wanted to publish an account of my experience. But when I returned to the airport in Houston, my mother was waiting.

"Get in the car. You're going home to Pine Bluff and you're going to take care of me. I've got to have hip surgery." I said, "But mother, I've got a publisher in New York who's interested in my book about the Great Wall. I have Shell Oil who still wants me to work for them. These are both wonderful opportunities." Mother replied, simply, "I am the one in control." It was childhood all over again.

She took the money from the sale of my condo, then kicked me out of her place when she no longer needed my help. I had no home. I lived in my Jeep with my cats for a week, then they arrested me! State troopers arrested me because I wasn't supposed to be in the park past six o'clock, but I had no place else to go. I had no money. I had nothing to get me to the next step.

My daughter in Atlanta wired me money, and I drove to Atlanta to stay with her. While I was there I got a call from my old college, Lindenwood outside of St. Louis. They'd tracked me to my mother's house, and even though whatever she told them would have been negative and ugly, they wanted to honor me. "We want to honor you at graduation with an achievement award because we understand you walked the Great Wall of China. And while you're here, we'd also like to talk to you about the possibility of finishing your degree. We'd give you a job, a stipend, a place to live." I cried. That's all I needed.

About two months into my stay at Lindenwood, the phone rang in my little apartment. It was an Arkansas reporter saying, "We're going to run a story about you tomorrow. Would you like to comment?" I thought it was about the Great Wall, but he said, "No. It's about the fact that a state trooper has come forth with all the details about your affair with Bill Clinton." I knew then that the gig was up. Ron Tucker from the Democratic Party called me and offered me a lifetime federal job if I stayed silent, but I knew that job would never materialize. That was just a tactic.

I started receiving death threats and was fired from my post at the college. I'm certain Hillary Clinton was responsible. I had no place to go, again. I actually moved in with a student, can you imagine? One-bedroom apartment and I slept on his couch.

To make ends meet, I started working for a home for adults with mental and physical disabilities. I changed adult diapers. No one can ever say, "Well, she thinks she's hot stuff." No, I've been to rock bottom. And through all this time, the Clintons are hitting me from all sides. The back of my Jeep was shot at, and I knew it was just a matter time before they were going to shoot *me*. But they found a different way to get rid of me instead.

I got a call, "Would you like to come back to China to teach at the Broadcasting Institute? Could you do that and live on $345 month if we give you free room and board?" I would have said yes to probably *three* dollars a month. I said, "How soon can you fly me over there?" They said, "Within twenty-four hours." I shot back, "I'll be ready."

Hillary Clinton was behind all this. She forced me out of the country. She would have killed me. She would have had me shot if I had not left the country. So when the call came, I was gone the next day.

I spent years in China, but when I finally came back to the States, Hillary and her gang were still on me. I found out my computer was hacked, my phone was hacked, and you're not going to believe what else. I was sitting on my bed one evening in Pine Bluff and I had this new TV connected with Comcast. My grandchildren were visiting, so I click on the TV and there we all are on the screen. My two little boys said, "Look, we're on TV!" That little Comcast box had the capability of watching *me* while I was watching television. I went crazy.

When Hillary's national election race started at the end of 2015, I had all these Comcast trucks hanging out in my neighborhood for about two weeks. I finally knocked on a few windows and asked, "Why are you here? None of my neighbors have called you and I haven't called you." "This is our new resolution," they said. "We're giving good service before it's needed." I called the Comcast office and they said, "This is a big customer service promotion." I replied, "But you're not in other people's neighborhoods, you're just in my neighborhood. Am I the only customer you have?" Somebody was keeping an eye on me. The Clinton machine never stops.

Now let's talk about Trump. I've studied Donald Trump for years, and I've met him. One of my good friends, a former neighbor in Arkansas when we were growing up, became an attorney with American Airlines. (I thought that a marvelous way to be successful.) When I was planning to go to China, he saw my picture in the paper. He called my mother and she told him, "Sally's got some crazy idea about the Great Wall that she's been hanging onto for years."

He said, "How can I get in touch with her?" He was in New York, and I was living in New Jersey at the time. He said, "I'm going to send my chauffeur to get you." I thought, "God, that sounds wonderful." The chauffeur comes and he even had the chauffeur *outfit*, the whole thing. Everything is beautiful. There was a telephone in the car.

My friend had now moved on to become the president of advertising to women. I can't recall the company, but he was doing very well; he and his wife had seven floors on Fifth Avenue. I think his wife was the one who developed, *"You're not getting older, you're getting better."* Everybody's heard that! Unfortunately, he had an affair with the woman in charge of his tax department and when he wouldn't marry her, she called the government and said, "I can tell you how he's been cheating on his taxes." On the weekend, he was dragged to prison. He's a complicated man, but a wonderful friend.

So one day this friend and I were having our lunch at the Four Seasons and he said, "Hold on just a minute, there's a buddy of mine. Don, come over here. You want to join us for lunch?" It was Donald Trump. A young Donald Trump.

Trump was dashing, charming, very serious, and still married to his first wife. We talked, we visited. At the end of the meal, Donald Trump shook my hand and wished me well. I did the same. My friend said, "Sally, I want you to watch that guy. He's going places."

When I was voting in the primary, I could just almost hear my friend's voice ringing in my ear, "You're making a great decision, and remember I told you to watch for him." Trump was and is all about success. He is about knowing how to take something that's iffy and make it a rock-solid success. In my life, I've had to take a lot of almost nothing or just a little something and try to make it into something big. And what I gleaned from Donald Trump was that he loved a challenge. When he says, "I want to make America great again," I know damn well that he can do it, and I also know that once he starts something, he has too much pride to let it sink. He's intense, and I like that. He's thinking constantly. Yes, he has affairs with women. Yes, he eats too much. Yes, he doesn't exercise. But you know what? Inside, he's Mr. Success. And he's got so damn much pride that he's not going to let himself be connected with failure.

Trump has already exposed the corruption and hypocrisy that exists in Washington. And it's not only with Democrats; it's even more with the Republican party! We all want a better country, but it's like the people we've elected have forgotten who we are. That's just as true here in Little Rock. The people we elect say, "We're going to go up here and do that." They've been promising the same stuff for thirty years, but they don't do any action. Donald Trump is a man of action. I've been so frustrated with politicians these days that I only vote when I'm passionate about the candidates. I was very passionate to vote for Trump.

Also, I'm impressed by the First Lady! I think her role is what she said a long time ago that it would be: she's there to be a mother for her son. I think the role of the First Lady might be a secondary situation with her. She's a mother first, and that's much more important. She represents us well internationally. Jackie Kennedy was like that, too. She didn't open her mouth very often, but she was a presence. We've had a few First Ladies that were not so great, some that looked like they'd had too much to drink. Melania Trump is not at all like that, she's just plain classy.

People are tired of traditional politicians. My daughter worked on the floor of the United States Senate as a reporter, so I got the inside connection on all of these politicians: what they do, where they get their hair cut, all the perks that they receive. I was appalled. They say, "The government pays for these perks." Well, who's the government? It's *us*, the taxpayers, and we don't have a choice. We can't make a decision whether we want them to have a barbershop and a beauty shop in the Congress building and not have to pay for it.

Trump was born liberal. And in many ways, he is still basically that: a New York liberal. He's adopted some positions that are conservative, but Trump's not winning on ideology. There are no ideologies with him. It's more practical politics from a CEO point of view rather than a political stance.

There's a lot of forces already against Trump, and that's just unfortunate. If he had free reign, he could do things his way and get them done. If the Democrats would just back off and give him a chance to start some of his projects, we'd all benefit. And then if he didn't get them finished, they could point the finger and say, "You loser." But they should be giving him a chance.

My opinion on Trump has never wavered, and it's not changing anytime soon. I've heard people say, "Well, I'm off and on about him," or, "I was off and on about Hillary." The worst are people that say, "I'm loyal to the Democratic Party. I'm always going to vote for a Democratic candidate." That's a mindset I'll never be able to understand, and I don't even bother to challenge it. It's locked in concrete, right?

I didn't vote for Trump because he was a good-looking man or because he had an empire in New York City. I saw in him what I saw in my hard-working father, a determination. He would not set himself up to be associated with failure. I don't think even Donald foresaw how the liberals would try to hold him back with bulldozers and firing squads. I don't think he was prepared for that, but I think he's handling it well.

He's got traitors in his own cabinet. He's got people there that are prying and spying, but he knows that. He's a smart man. He didn't just fall of the turnip truck.

Our biggest problem in America right now might be that we can't get rid of the politicians that have made it their life – the hanger-ons – because we don't have term limits. We can't force them out, and it's almost like we're being held hostage. They've got the gravy train, and we don't get to ride it.

Even liberals have to know that there is a lot of trash out there, and we need someone to carry the trash out. Trump can do that. He can carry the trash out.

CHAPTER THIRTY-TWO
The Planned Parenthood Nurse

June 30th, 2017
Fayetteville, Arkansas

If the stories Sally told me back in the Capital Hotel about Bill Clinton are true (and her autobiography certainly claims they are — there are even more salacious details in there), then it makes her support of Donald Trump all the more interesting. Revengeful? Not quite, but definitely interesting.

Sally is Little Rock celebrity, but Linda is Fayetteville gentility. After the most gracious, polite phone call I've had on my entire cross-country journey, Linda invites me to visit her exquisite home at the top of Stone Mountain in northwest Arkansas. She greets me with a slice of homemade strawberry shortcake that her husband made from scratch for the occasion. He's there too, mostly silent and deferring. The sweetness of the cake, the sweetness of her voice, the sweetness of her demeanor, the sweetness of... distraction. Linda intrigues me because of her insistence that she is an absolute social liberal, but how can this be? Is the sweet Southern charm a distraction from more serious disagreements we may have? I'm starting to really understand a lot of these pro-Trump arguments, but I don't like the distraction of personality and kindness. I admit that there are certain things likely to make me look positively on you; thankfully, desserts aren't usually one of them. I can avoid desserts. Distracting me from analyzing our conversation will be more difficult than shortcake... wait. They're opening wine. They have the most amazing, brass wine opener attached to their counter. It's gorgeous. It's funky. I'm distracted now. They belong to a high-end wine club, they say. I'm more distracted now. They love to chat and drink and talk gently about the issues of the day. I'm...

###

LINDA: I was born on a farm that's been in our family since President Polk gave us a land grant back in the early 1800s. My family, we're the McKennons; Captain Arch McKennon fought in the Civil War. He also was one of the people that founded Hendrix College down in Conway and one of the first territorial governors in Oklahoma.

We lost our farm in 1965. The McClellan-Kerr Arkansas River dam flooded it. My family bought land in Conway and Folk counties. My brother and I still farm there. We have crop farms: soybeans, corn, and occasionally wheat. I attended the University of Arkansas. I have a bachelor's degree in nursing. I also have a master's degree in nursing from the University of Central Arkansas. I have a certificate licensing me to be a women's healthcare nurse practitioner, and I got that from UCLA. Nursing and health care are my passions.

I have two sons. Brad teaches at Southern Methodist University in stage and production management, and we lost my son Kyle a few years ago. He had graduated from the Brooks Institute in Santa Barbara, and also from the Music Institute. My husband Bill here has a daughter that we share and her name is Jessica. She's given us the most darling little grandson, a year old.

I spent thirty-seven years of my life in California because I couldn't make a living teaching nursing in Arkansas. I was the chief nursing officer at a number of hospitals. Finally, at the age of forty-two, I didn't want to do management anymore, so I've been a nurse practitioner ever since.

Bill and I moved back here to Fayetteville four years ago after a very long and deliberate search for where we wanted to semi-retire. I just took a new position which I won't be paid for, but I will be working as an officer of the court representing abused or neglected children. I will be making sure their side of the story is heard. It's a personal mission of mine, and a volunteer position.

My parents were Southern Democrats. Daddy was in the state legislature at the time of Governor Faubus here in Arkansas. Most people don't know that Governor Faubus was a socialist. His father was one of the main people in in this state trying to form a union. The union was for foresters. They were cutting wood. We adored Faubus;

my entire family adored him. I wrote to him until he died. People totally misunderstood him.[74]

Every time somebody starts talking about integration in Little Rock, I say, "What about Boston? What's better in Boston? Who were killed in Boston?" It really… it offends me.[75]

In any case, Daddy was a Southern Democrat, but he was known to vote Republican for national offices. He had an extreme dislike for the Clintons, and with good reason. We don't want to offend anybody – we know absolutely wonderful people that are Clinton people – but many of us here in Arkansas are vehemently anti-Clinton. Bill Clinton had so many girlfriends! There are videotapes of him with Arkansas State Police driving him around while he's making out in the back seat! I also think what he did with Monica Lewinsky was unforgivable; she was so young. And then he lied; oh, how he lied. I think that he is smarmy, and I can't even think a word for Hillary. She just wants to be anointed.

I define myself now as a Republican, an Episcopalian, and the proud mother of a gay son. Do you know much about the Episcopalian Church? It's not just that we don't just believe in the Pope. It is the most liberal Church in America. We believe in a little bit of everything. A little bit of everything is good for you! The first time I ever voted for a Republican was in 1978 against Jerry Brown. I had moved to rural California, a farming community. (Our farm looks small compared to the 10,000-12,000 acres that these people farmed.) The very nice people there in rural California were vehemently against Jerry Brown. Why were they against him? Because he was so liberal! He just wanted a welfare state, which now he has.

Even as a Republican, Planned Parenthood hired me. I was to work part time, but then there was a problem. I developed breast cancer. I missed some time. Things were made very uncomfortable for me. There was a young woman just graduating at the same time I was diagnosed, and they really wanted her. In the end, I was forced to leave Planned Parenthood over a disagreement about my refusal to

---

[74] I must be one of those who misunderstand him. Governor Faubus famously acted against a court ruling and had the National Guard block nine Black students from entering Little Rock High School in 1957, ludicrously claiming it was to prevent "property damage, injury, or death." Is there really any more to understand?

[75] A federal judge ruled in 1974 that Boston's schools were deliberately segregated. On the first day of de-segregation in South Boston, hundreds of white protestors attacked busses of Black students with bricks, displaying signs that read, "Niggers Go Home," and flaunting pictures of monkeys. Suffice to say, I do not believe Boston de-segregation is a counterpoint to Little Rock; rather, I believe it is the same sort of racism on display seventeen years later. I still cannot understand Linda's defense of Governor Faubus.

give Truvada. Truvada (PReP) is a combination of two medications that you can give young, gay men who are HIV-negative. If they take this drug, they have an 85% chance of not acquiring HIV from a positive partner.[76] I refused to administer this drug. But understand: the important part is the side effects! One of my dearest, oldest friends is a hospice nurse in Hollywood. She stuck herself with a needle on a HIV-positive patient. She had to take Truvada for two months. She said it was the meanest, most powerful drug she's ever had to endure. Planned Parenthood didn't care that I don't believe the drug is safe or healthy; they terminated me.

Also, Planned Parenthood didn't like some of my teaching for domestic abuse. I tried to teach responsibility to the young women that came in, those that had passed out and been date-raped. While I was sympathetic and sent them to the Rape Crisis Center, I also talked to them about personal responsibility. Planned Parenthood didn't like that at all, but I have spent my life teaching responsibility. I lost my first cousin to AIDS before the world knew about the disease. I lost my secretary in San Francisco, he was an early person to die from AIDS. It's really touched me. I don't want to give any young man a drug that says, "You've got an 85% chance of being fine." I don't do that. I don't want to do that.

Planned Parenthood has lost some of its direction. The organization was founded to get birth control to women so they could plan their children. That's how we were founded by Margaret Sanger in 1921. Ben Carson thinks Margaret Sanger founded Planned Parenthood in order to control the Black population. I don't know. I've never read that. What I do know is *birth control*, and that's what I did for Planned Parenthood. I believe in that.

Do you know that only 2% of our patients are abortion patients? 98% come just for birth control and that, to me, is our mission. If you're quoting me, please don't leave out that there are some fabulous people in Planned Parenthood, but the fanatics there are distorting our mission.

Health care provided for everyone is not going to be easy, but I do have to tell you that my work with Obamacare was sad. People – poor people – would come into Planned Parenthood and proudly say, "I have health insurance now." We'd look it up: $6000 deductible. This was very difficult to explain, even with the free preventative care that the Affordable Care Act was promoting. Medicaid wasn't

---

⁷⁶ The CDC reports a 99% effectiveness when taken daily.

working at Planned Parenthood either because we weren't getting paid; our governor decided not to pay Planned Parenthood at all. He didn't understand that only 2% of patients come in for abortions! We were providing excellent services, but not receiving payment under Medicaid. When I started working there, the state had not paid us for a year. But we still provided services. We still said *yes* to the people walking in the door.

Trump was not my first choice in the primary, Jeb Bush was. He's brilliant. Of all of the Bush siblings, he is the most brilliant man. He is not really far to the right, which I like. But the same is true for Trump! I kept trying to tell everybody that Trump is sophisticated New Yorker. Trump's mission is going to be *jobs*. It's going to be decreasing the budget. It's going to be about getting people from welfare to work. He's not a crazy right-wing politician!

On Election Day in 2016, we decided to go to the most wonderful place in Arkansas, Gaston's Resort, to go trout fishing. I went to bed early, and the next morning my husband said Trump won. Well, the look on my face! I just was so surprised! Let me tell you: Fayetteville is a liberal little town with wonderful people, but a whole lot of the people we love here are Democrats. Some people we are very friendly with went to New Hampshire to support Hillary there. I think that's just great. They're wonderful people. I wouldn't do a thing in the world to insult them. I just happen to disagree about some things politically. And I was taught that, fundamentally, you can disagree without being disagreeable. So in this liberal town, I was quite surprised by the election results that morning.

President Trump is boisterous. If I were Melania, I'd take his Twitter away from him. Being in the South, we see a lot of men that do the locker room talk. I don't care. I think it would be better if Trump didn't do it, but I don't really care. Also, he's too thin-skinned. If he's going to throw it out there, he should be able to take some hits back, right?

What I admire most about President Trump is his family. My perception, and what I've read in the *New York Times* and *The Wall Street Journal*, is that he has been able to maintain this incredible relationship with his children through multiple divorces. These children are really educated, sophisticated people. They've gone to Wharton; they've gone to Georgetown. His young child has already been admitted to Cambridge, to Oxford, to Harvard, and he's eleven! He just won a national science project based on studying the heat dynamics of shale underground at Lake Porter, Arkansas. That's why they kept him in New York, because he was working on this. Trump's family is terrific. A lot of what I admire about him is what he's created in his personal life.

Let's talk immigration. I believe everybody should immigrate to America through a process. I have seen, for years and years and years of being a farmer, that we need a work program where these people can get a license to work every year. That much is obvious. We need the workers in California. Immigrants are wonderful people and they work hard. They work harder than anybody I know, back-breaking jobs. If you drive up Highway One in California next to the ocean, you'll see them bending over at their waist, picking your strawberries. A licensing system would let them be appreciated but controlled. They shouldn't vote, they shouldn't drive; they should be housed properly, fed properly, and taken care of. Healthcare, they need it. But I don't think we should have them just streaming across the border like these hundreds of thousands did. I don't agree with that.

I want to regulate immigration and have a way for the federal government to better track every individual. If you've been here too long, you go home or you reapply. You and I go to China, the Chinese know where we are. Go to Russia, the Russians know where we are. But workers coming in illegally and sneaking back over the border with cash in hand? We have to stop that. And they do sneak – there's no doubt about that – both ways. They send billions of dollars to Mexico. You'll see homes that are three-quarters built all over Mexico. Three-quarters built out of cement blocks, and that's where they're sending their money. They're building their retirement homes. A lot of American money goes back to Mexico.

I went to see my grandmother McKennon, who was almost one hundred years old, and I said, "Nanny, I have a problem. I love my housekeeper, Maria, but she wants me to sponsor her. That means that if she's sick, I take care of the bills.[77] She lives with some Iranians down the street, but she's worked for me for a long time." Nanny said to me, "Linda, do what's in your heart." So I sponsored Maria. And I'm very glad I did. I would do it again, because I loved her.

We never should have gone into Iraq or Afghanistan, you know? I think we should have left them alone. But now we have to

---

[77] The I-864 program does allow for sponsors to be sued for the reimbursement of medical expenses under certain circumstances, but it is not so clear-cut as Linda states here.

clean it up or get out. My husband says he doesn't think it's a matter of having better armed services, but a matter of realizing our past mistakes. Trump has created a cabinet that understands history and where we went wrong. Trump said early on that it was a mistake going into Iraq, and he won't let us get bogged down again. That's why he's trying to stay away from regime change, because regime change we've seen. It's evidenced by Libya. The devil you know is better than the devil you don't.

ISIS knew we were going to pull out of Iraq, so they were biding their time. Then, all of a sudden, they're taking over. A lot of companies made money off of that, but it hasn't been good for the families. The worst thing in the world you can do is bury a child. We buried the most beautiful twenty-eight-year-old, and I feel for people who have also lost their children.

Trump is brashy, a businessman, and pragmatic in terms of what works and what doesn't work. I was encouraged by the appointments he made to his cabinet. Some people are worried because he's marching in all the generals, but I think that these generals are well-educated and they're all pragmatists, too. They have a good sense for what works and what doesn't work, without being political about it all. They don't want to lose their sons and daughters. Do you know how many sons of Congress went to Iran or Iraq? One. I trust the generals more than the politicians.

Trump doesn't want to fight in wars, but he says, "If you step on my foot, I'm going to step on yours, big time." He is a rough-and-tumble, knockabout New Yorker; he is never going to be a Southern gentleman.

You know who *is* an absolute gentleman? Jared Kushner. He has been given one of the most important things in our lifetime to try to accomplish: peace between the Jewish state and the Palestinians. And he is an Orthodox Jew! Have you ever seen him touch his children? He has a soft side.

I have a gay son, and a lot of people see my political views as a contradiction because of that. But even with the guy everyone says is anti-gay, Mike Pence... Can you tell me one thing Mike Pence has done that has adversely affected my son? No. Sure, when Pence goes out to some small town in Indiana and there are born-agains, he says that he agrees with them. But is he really going to do anything about it? That's what I keep trying to tell people: look at what their focus is. It doesn't matter what Mike Pence might *say*, it's what he does. Politicians pay the piper and sound off their opinions, but they're not out there trying to ban gays, they're not out there trying to change the Supreme Court law allowing gays to marry. That's never going to happen.[78] I think some people thought the world was coming to an end when Trump was elected. I didn't think that at all.

All those social politics aside, I want to be clear that I think the most important thing Trump can do is fix our healthcare. People deserve healthcare. The question is, "How do you pay for it?" Only way to pay for it is cutting other things or increasing the taxes. That's the difficult part. The Republicans always want to cut taxes to stimulate the economy, but somewhere out there is a fine balance. Bill Clinton raised taxes forty-five times while he was in office; that's not balance. Here in Little Rock, we pay – I think next to New York and Chicago – we pay the highest sales tax. I think that's unfair taxation because it puts the burden on the poor. Now the liberal in me is really coming out! But I believe that.

----

[78] In 2015, Mike Pence said, "I'm disappointed that the Supreme Court failed to recognize the historic role of the states in setting marriage policy. Nevertheless, our administration will continue to uphold the rule of law and abide by the ruling of the Court in this case. Under our system of government, our citizens are free to disagree with decisions of the Supreme Court, but we are not free to disobey them. As we move forward as a state and a nation, Hoosiers may be assured that our Administration will respect the law and the dignity and worth of every Hoosier and every Hoosier family."

CHAPTER THIRTY-THREE
The Minnesota Contractor

July 13th, 2017
Minneapolis, Minnesota

Up on Stone Mountain in Little Rock, Linda's dessert – baked from scratch by her husband – was a gesture of kindness and civility. The invitation into their home was a gesture of openness and diplomacy. This is the kind of experience and discourse that I wish for us all to have. In fact, this is the very point of my journey across conservative America. I'm understanding the nuanced perspectives of some of these folks. Linda worked for Planned Parenthood because access to birth control is so important to her; she left Planned Parenthood because she didn't like administering a certain drug to gay men. I'm not on board with Linda's opinion on the drug, but I can at least see her reasoning. And her reasoning does not directly contradict her general social politics. Linda believes Mike Pence, one of the most openly anti-gay politicians I can think of, will not actually do anything that will harm her gay son. I still disagree with her, but I'm glad to see she has given the issue deep thought and isn't reflexively judgmental or simply bigoted. I didn't see bigotry. I saw a decision that I happen to disagree with. Linda chose Trump for reasons relating to health care, immigration policies, and his "rough and tumble" pragmatism.

Also important to point out: Linda is vehemently anti-Clinton. So many of these Arkansans are vehemently anti-Clinton.

Time to move to a drier climate. I panted and sweated on my walk down from Linda's home atop Stone Mountain, and am happy to fly to Minneapolis for a week. Hopefully it's cooler there. More restaurants. More cosmopolitan. More liberal? My people.

I'm to meet Jeremiah, a contractor and driver, in the 5th floor lobby bar of Marriot City Center. It's a busy enclave in a busy part of town. Jeremiah arrives with a calm, centered energy. A lot of the folks I speak with are energized, pumped, bubbling to talk. Not Jeremiah. He's reserved. He needs a bit of a push. He warns me in advance that he views himself as pretty liberal, so might not be the best subject for my book. He's very pro-immigration, he says, except for the fact that Minnesota has too many Somalis...

###

JEREMIAH: I had a construction business. We were running other crews, acting as sort of a middleman for other contractors. We did pretty well in that. I bought land in Hawaii and lived over there eight years before having a couple of kids. It was a little tougher there with kids. Schools aren't very good in Hawaii, and we lived pretty remote. Then my dad was lost at sea. Not in Hawaii, but off the coast of Florida. They never found him. I flew around trying to figure out what was going on – his wife wasn't very forthcoming – and the mystery brought me back to Minnesota for a while. Then we just decided to stay. The whole thing cost me thousands of dollars in last-minute airfare.

My kids are happier here in Minnesota. They're taking drama classes now; that's their big thing. My stepdad's side of the family, they're all big into theatre. My uncle is a lighting guy, my aunt's a choreographer, and their daughter is traveling right now in a major production. Me, I'm just a contractor. I hate my job.

I want to work for someone else. I'm sick of being self-employed.

The artistic side of my family hates my Trump posts. I think I've lost about a hundred Facebook friends since Trump got elected. My brother is a hardcore Trumpster, though. My other brother is a hardcore liberal. His wife hates me for voting for Trump. That's the only real stress in our family.

I'm pretty liberal. Yes, that's right! I wouldn't be a Republican, but we have to pick sides and I was into Trump right away. All the real Republicans, I think they liked Cruz and everybody else. But I'm sick of being conned by politicians. In Hawaii, it's super anti-business, so nobody can start anything. They make it almost impossible. They're 100% run by Democrats. They don't even have a Republican office.[79]

You can't become a contractor in Hawaii. You'd have to have three other contractors sign off on you. That's like wanting a fast food restaurant right next to McDonald's, Taco Bell, and Burger King, but having to get them all to approve you. It's impossible.

I do believe we need these oil pipelines like Keystone. I don't work in the oil business or anything, I just believe it's something the country needs. Forcing us out of oil so fast is not good for us. America is a good place to do business because of low energy costs. If we keep raising energy costs, we're going to keep losing jobs.

Early on, I remember Trump being so shocking with the boldness of what he would say. That appealed to me. I thought it was funny. I still think he's hilarious. He pisses people off, but I think that's on purpose. I honestly believe he would have run as a Democrat if they didn't have superdelegates. He couldn't have won as a Democrat because the party wouldn't have let him, but without the superdelegates he could have had been a challenger. I don't think Trump is as set in his conservative beliefs as people say.

I don't go for the hard-right guys, and I'm not religious. At all. I'm not into church. My best friend passed, so I went to his funeral. Other than that, you're not going to catch me in a church.

Bernie got screwed, but he's too much of a socialist anyway. I don't like socialists. I don't think it works. If everybody gets the same cut of the pie, nobody's going to work. There should be winners and losers. People who work harder should do better. I honestly wouldn't want to see only the Republican Party in leadership forever, though. I'd probably end up trying to get us to bounce back a little.

I really hated Obama. Racism has gotten way worse since he was elected. What bugs me most about liberals is that, like racist people in the world, you all judge everybody by what group you are. You separate everybody into groups. I really think liberals are the most racist because they're always the one talking about Black people, white people, Mexicans, poor people. The talk is always about suffering, but everybody's always separate. Why do we all have to be separate? There's no fighting for the same cause. They're just fighting for their own.

I really don't care if Trump builds the wall, but I also really don't think it's going to happen. It's funny campaign stuff, "build that

---

[79] The Republican office is located at 725 Kapiolani Blvd. in Honolulu.

wall, lock her up." Who's actually going to lock her up?! But that boldness works. He was pretty smart.

I have no problems with the Mexicans. What I would prefer is that people with families already here, people waiting on the list, could get in faster because we could allow more leeway to them. We need them financially. We should take more immigrants from Mexico since they're closer to us, and they logically have more family here. They assimilate a lot better. I can tell you what's happening since they brought every single Somali to Minnesota. It's not good. It's definitely not good. The Somalis have been here forever, and they won't assimilate. They stand in your way, they're not polite, never hold the door. Everything has to be their way. I've seen it firsthand. Go get in a cab and see how rude they are.

When we just take mass amounts of one group at a time, they don't tend to assimilate. They tend to all move together and just recreate where they came from. If I moved to France, I wouldn't do that. I wouldn't just hang out with a bunch of Americans. I would learn the language, assimilate, learn their culture. Somalis don't tend to do that at all.

I'm pretty socially liberal, but liberals made Trump. They pushed and they pushed and they pushed, just too hard. Trump is the blowback. Liberals push a huge social agenda and believe there is no compromise. I have daughters, six and eight, and now they're trying to pass these transgender bathroom laws? First of all, if you change yourself into a woman, that's fine, ok? But if you look like a man, if you are a man, you shouldn't be in there with my little girls. Now, of course most of them are not bad, but what about the couple percent that are? And now they're in there with my daughters, and I have to stand outside? It's like, I didn't have any problem with gay marriage, but as soon as liberals get what they want, they try to push even more extremes down your throat. That's why I push back.

I love it when liberals block traffic at the protests. It's great for my side. Terrific advertising, because they're pissing off a whole bunch of people. I sometimes drive for Uber and right after the election I got caught driving in the middle of this huge protest. It's just stupid college kids or whatever, but I'm stuck, can't move. I call the people I'm picking up and I'm like, "Where are you? I'm here. You might as well come and meet here." They tell me they're scared to come to me in this crowd. So I get out and walk down the block, leaving my car in the middle of the street. I find them – they're college kids – and I walk them through the crowd back to my car. Eventually,

I get out of the mess of people by following a fire truck. Four blocks later, I ask my passengers what they were doing in the middle of all that anyway. They say, "Oh, we were protesting. We came for the protest, but then it got scary." I was like, "Are you shitting me?! Get the hell out of my car." I kick them out of my car. Why in the world do you call an Uber in the middle of your own protest?

Trump's tweets are hilarious. Piss people off. He knows it; I think it's on purpose. He was a genius at the election. He didn't have to spend any money, and his name was all over TV. As soon as the name started to fade, he would go out and say something crazy, and then – boom – he's all over TV again. Guy's a genius. I don't think he honestly believes half the crap he says. I think he's just creating media attention with these tweets. If you can get a whole bunch of the other side acting like complete lunatics about you, well that just shows their bad side, so you get more free advertising. I think that's what he does. I can't believe liberals just keep falling for it! It works. Why's he going to stop? Why would he stop? They want him to stop, but he'd be an idiot to stop. He'd just be a normal, boring old man if he stopped saying crazy things.

I don't have any health insurance. Obamacare's horrible. It only *works* for people who *don't*. I know that's a slogan, "If you don't work and you're poor, Obamacare's great." For everybody else in the middle class, we get completely screwed.

I used to buy insurance at $120 a month for me. Wasn't the greatest coverage. It covered my doctor bills, and then I had a decent-size deductible. But if anything real bad happened, I would have been better off. Well now they don't even *offer* that. I can't just go buy myself some crappy policy. It's horrible. They've ruined the whole market. There's no more free market and everybody's getting screwed.

At least my kids are lucky: I have them on what they call Minnesota Care, which is amazing. You don't pay for anything. It's great healthcare. If we all had that, that'd be something. But I'm not allowed to be on it because the income limits are so different for parents. With Obamacare, the whole family has to move to Obamacare to be on it, which means my kids would lose their insurance for us to get ours. It's a fact. So for me to sign up for Obamacare, our family deductible would have gone up to $14,000, I would have been paying like $750 a month, and my kids basically wouldn't have insurance. I decided, screw it. I'll pay the fine just so my kids will have good health insurance.

Four months ago now, my daughter's appendix went out. It was during the Super Bowl, exactly during the Super Bowl. She had stomach pain, and halfway through the game I was checking on her when she pointed out the pain. I Google it and say, "Oh, crap. Appendix." I ran her over to the local hospital, they transferred her over to Children's Hospital. The experience is great. They did surgery, everything's fine. It didn't cost me a penny. If I would have signed up for Obamacare, I would have been screwed on that deductible. I literally dodged a bullet there.

CHAPTER THIRTY-FOUR
The Somali and the Irishman

July 13th, 2017
Minneapolis, Minnesota

It's midsummer in Minnesota and, contrary to my preconceptions, the wet heat feels more oppressive here than it did in Arkansas two weeks ago. Our president spent yesterday trying to work through his own heat, and again called the ongoing Russia investigation the "greatest witch hunt in political history." Donald Trump, Jr. released the email exchange he used to set up a meeting with a Russian lawyer, Natalia Veselnitskaya, and his father is moving boldly to Jr.'s defense. Was the meeting illegal? We can't be certain yet, though one thing is crystal clear: no conservative on the ground seems to care.

The intricacies of campaign law and foreign contacts do not matter at all to those who voted for President Trump. These are people who viewed the campaign as a battle, and Trump as a warrior. His son's meeting with the Russian lawyer? That was just a weapon in their arsenal. The thing is, I can buy that argument. Blatant breaking of the law would backfire, of course, but when you're in the fight... I must admit I can see myself defending the Clinton campaign trying to dig up dirt wherever it could.

Just this morning, my breakfast with contractor/driver Jeremiah reaffirmed that many do not follow or concern themselves with intricate campaign rules. When we were parting he said, "Trump's pushing back hard. He fights hard. He's gonna come out of this the champ." Jeremiah just doesn't care whether the Russian meeting has legal significance. He also reminded me, during his tirade against them, of the vast Somali refugee population in Minnesota. "They don't assimilate," was Jeremiah's principal complaint, though I'm now heading out to meet one of the most assimilated-seeming former refugees I can imagine.

Abdi is a prominent member of his Somali community here in Minneapolis, and I'm introduced to him by Rick, an equally prominent member of his local Republican community. I travel a few miles into the suburbs through thick air, arriving at a pristine home with a poolside back patio. There's shade, music, a cold beer, and two well-dressed men waiting for me.

RICK: First off, welcome and thanks for being here. We're both glad you were able to make it and when that beer is done, I'll get you another cold one.

My name is Rick Rice and I just turned sixty years old. This is where you go, "No way, Rick, you're not sixty!" Abdi here was invited to my birthday party, but he didn't come. The party was during Ramadan and I was serving pork and a *lot* of alcohol! Obviously, Abdi's not into that. But I'm an Irish Catholic; we like to drink.

I'm the youngest of five, but the only conservative. All the rest are liberal weenies. They whine a lot, thinking the sky is falling all the time.

I've been a life insurance salesman for thirty-five years. I got into the industry because I didn't want to have a boss; I don't play well with others and I don't like people telling me what to do. I like the opportunity to have unlimited income potential, and I believe strongly that people should be self-reliant. My father died when I was eleven years old and I saw what not having enough life insurance does to a family; that's what gave me the daily motivation to do what I do for a living. It's important to sit down with people and encourage them to be personally responsible. It's my mission to help people take care of their affairs so, in the event something happens – probably not going to because we're all going to live to be one hundred, I get it – but in the event something happens like it happened to my family, there are adequate economic resources to maintain a decent standard of living. Doesn't have to be anything fancy, but it would be nice if you don't have to sell your car and move out of your house after a tragedy.

I wasn't always a conservative, but Rush Limbaugh converted me. Prior to that, I actually worked on campaigns for Jimmy Carter, Walter Mondale, Michael Dukakis. I was working on "Get Out the Vote," door knocking, yard signs for numerous Democratic candidates. Then, being a political junkie, I started listening to talk radio. It was then that I realized, "Oh my gosh, the media has a spin to it." It had never dawned on me that I was being spun my entire life! In particular, I looked back and realized *60 Minutes* was spinning me on a regular basis just by the stories they chose to tell. That really pissed me off. I was thirty-one years old and coming to the realization that I had an invisible ring in my nose and was being led around. I didn't know that ring was there because I was too trusting.

In Minnesota, you grow up trusting. You trust somebody until they mess with you. I just assumed the best in people, so I assumed the news was telling me the truth. When I saw that it wasn't, my political shift started.

I worked for Ross Perot in 1992 – so I wasn't quite Republican yet! – and did the full conversion with Newt Gingrich's "Contract with America" in 1994. I've been a Republican ever since. That was my evolution. I had to pass through Ross Perot on the way.

I remember how I used to think Republicans were the nasty, greedy guys. But I've always considered myself open-minded and willing to listen. My wife was saying, "Why are we listening to Rush Limbaugh? That's not who we believe, that's not how we think." And I said, "Yes, but I'm interested to hear what he has to say." At first it was like *Godfather*; I was listening to Rush so I could keep my enemies close. But I was drawn in by him.

It's always important to know why the other side thinks what they think. You have to listen to the opposite viewpoint, and that is why I invited you over today. If we don't keep a dialogue going, you're never going to understand Republicans, and you're never going to understand Trump supporters. If I isolate myself, I end up in a bubble. It's a very comfortable bubble, but it's still a bubble. I try to stay true about being open-minded.

My brother and I have robust conversation about specific issues, but I can barely talk to my younger sister. She just went crazy off the charts with all the Trump controversy. She won't listen. For instance, I'm driving her to the airport one morning and the radio station has a Rush Limbaugh update. I probably turned it up because I want to hear it, but she reaches over, turns off the radio, and says, "How can you listen to that? He's a racist." I ask her if she's ever actually listened to him, and she says, "No, I would never listen to him." So it's rather obvious who's the narrow-minded bigot here. If you want to really learn, you have to go listen to what the other side has to say. I listen to NPR all the time, and you can't tell me that's a conservative outlet! I have more than enough exposure to Democrats.

I have two sons and they've both been to Afghanistan. My younger son is in the Army National Guard right now and a Black Hawk Medevac crew chief. I raised them right. I encouraged both of my kids to be involved in something bigger than themselves, whatever it is. You can accomplish much greater things when you belong to an organization than you can accomplish alone. I raised them to understand that with all of our boils, bruises, and warts, this is still the greatest country in the world, and it's the greatest country because of our Constitution.

Abdi and I were talking about this earlier. Our Constitution protects us from excessive use of government. Government is just human beings, and human beings have a tendency to want to grow whatever organization they belong to. That's human nature. But as government grows, people become smaller and more pliable. I was reading Abdi a quote and asking him if he could figure out who said it: "This year will go down in history. For the first time a civilized nation has full gun registration. Our streets will be safer, our police more efficient, and the world will follow our lead into the future." Do you know who said that? It was Adolph Hitler.[80]

You won't get my gun out of my hands. "You'll pry it from my cold, dead fingers" is the saying I like. And I'm not even a big gun guy! I have them, but they're probably dusty because I never look at them. The point is that I believe in the Second Amendment because I don't believe in in giving up all power to the government.

Our Constitution is what makes us a great country. We're lucky. Abdi is lucky to have emigrated here, and you and I were very lucky to have been born here. I, for one, am very grateful.

ABDI: My name is Abdi. I'm forty-three years old, Muslim, and I feel very lucky to be here in America. I was born in Somalia, and I'm living here in the United States not because I chose to, but because your government chose *me* from a refugee camp.

I don't have relatives in America. I don't have nobody to give me an affidavit. I was in a refugee camp in Kenya and when you

---

[80] No, it wasn't.

become refugees, random countries choose random people. Your file can be picked up by Australia, some of the European countries, the United States, or Canada. I'm very proud that America picked up my file. I didn't even know what America looked like at the time.

I was about twenty when I left the refugee camp. I landed in upstate New York. Rochester is where I call home because, in America, the city where you were born is your home. I always feel excited when I meet somebody from New York. That's home for me.

I moved here to Minnesota in the year 2000, got married... luckily married! I have four children. I don't know what the political parties in this country stand for that much, but I love seeing the people voting, exercising their rights. This is something that never happens where I was born, or in most of the third world countries. All we usually know about the government is that somebody's the leader and you have to like him. Otherwise, you pay the price. It doesn't matter whether leaders in Somalia do good or bad; if you don't like what they're doing, they see you as a rebellion.

In America, it's different. I was extremely very delighted to be utilizing the opportunities this country offers. Being a refugee and having friends in almost all of the countries where refugees are sent, I know there's no place comparable to the United States of America when it comes to the freedom and the tolerance people have, even when it comes to race. It's worse in Europe and Australia. And the Somalis who live in Saudi Arabia cannot have anything *close* to what they can have here in the United States. It's not a secret, it's very awful there.

I'm surprised by the founders of this nation. How did they come up with this plan? How were they smarter than us back in that time? Their ideas still echo today. I am very proud to be here, so I'm building some small businesses. I've had a successful business already with an interpreting service company, but now I have a new idea I'm working on. See, too many people always complain. Instead, everybody needs to be responsible for their own life and work hard; that's what I'm doing. And when you work hard, you deserve to get what you work hard for. This is our Constitutional right.

My new business is an autistic daycare center. See, the usual daycares don't accept autistic kids. If you have autistic child, finding daycare is a pain. I don't know why, but it's just not there at all. And the kids having autism is three times higher for Somali children born here in Minnesota than any other group next to them.[81] They don't know why it's happening. Some people are arguing it's because of the immunizations, but there's no good proof for that. It doesn't actually matter how we talk about it, there's a child getting sick every minute. That's the point. We're targeting the Somali community because everybody knows that we're leading the entire country with autistic children. This will be the first daycare like it in the state, it's going to make history. It's a good deed mixed with good business.

The best thing a person can do in life is solve somebody's problem and have somebody say, "Thank you." I don't care what you did for them. Whether you give them water, give a job, it doesn't matter. Somebody has to feel that you take a pain out from them. Whether you make money from it or not doesn't matter. My children, they don't have the autism, but I know the pain because I've been interpreting for people in the medical field.

If I can say, "Hey, I'm here. I have this center for you," then the parents can go to work! And we can give the kids all the other things they need while they're in the daycare. Whether it's therapy, or any other service the child needs. It's a win-win.

Do you agree this daycare center would provide an important service to my community? Of course, you do. So why does our Democratic government make it so difficult to get started? Why do they make so many regulations that I have trouble doing a good service for my people?

We've seen the Democratic leadership fail. Obama did not do well at all. As a businessperson, I assumed he was going to bring more business to Americans, but instead every single company is heading out of the country. Me? I'm trying to create jobs *here*.

I was very prosperous under our previous governor, a Republican named Tim Pawlenty. Under him, the ethnic community was thriving. We were doing very well. Our current Democratic governor is a great guy when he's talking, but not when it comes to business. They investigate our businesses and they shut us down for nothing. If I dream and work hard to build a business, and you shut me down because of small mistakes with your hundreds of regulations, then I'm going to end up sending my kids into the welfare system. No one should want that.

---

[81] Indeed, Somali and white children in Minnesota have rates of autism at three times the national average, and Somali children have consistently more severe versions. Hispanic and non-Somali Black children in Minnesota are more in line with the national average.

With welfare, they just give it to you, and I can't discipline my kids like that. I wouldn't be their father. In my culture, in my Muslim faith, I can only claim to be a father when I am the provider for my family. It doesn't matter if I'm a biological father. If they tell me their needs and I can't provide them, then I'm not their father. If I know somebody else is feeding them, that person will lead them, and I will be just a toy. My wife would never respect me. That scares me a lot. We all pay the price when parents aren't able to discipline their children, we all pay the price together. If they do a crime, if we send them to jail, it's a wasted human being. I need my business to thrive so I can provide for my family, but my business cannot thrive with over-regulation. That's why I prefer the Republicans.

When I was having my first child, I picked up a lady while driving a cab. The lady was a great-grandmother. I don't even know why, but I asked her, "Since you're a great-grandmother, can you tell me one thing? Why are people having children? Leave alone their passion, their love life... put those things aside. Can you tell me the one thing that's best about having children?"

She gave me an answer that I never anticipated. It was not even in my brain, and it still echoes in my mind. She told me, "The best thing about having a child is to see what kind of person you add to the community. Some children come into the world and benefit other people. But some children just don't. Some children grow up and hurt other people."

I almost stopped the car; it broke my heart. My child was a month old. Is he going to be a person people are scared of or is he going to be a doctor, a good leader, a policeman, somebody to help people? That's the question I have. I might add a violent human being into the community, or I might add a successful human being. It's a testament, and it shakes me.

I have to be sure I'm not adding an unblessed human to the world. Why would I want to raise him on my money and not make absolutely sure he is going to be good? I wrote down what that great-grandmother said, and I keep her words with me at all times. It is what inspires me to make absolutely sure my four children are thriving.

I received that message at the opportune time. And I see Trump sending us messages at an opportune time, too. He is talking about de-regulation, which is exactly what I need to grow my business and make sure my children are never on welfare. There's a lot of negativity in my community around my support of President Trump.

There's shock. But we can't all agree on everything a candidate says, we just have to agree on most of the things. That's where I stand with Trump. If I am looking to choose somebody that I agree with 100% of the time, I'm not going to find that anywhere.

I've seen the worst kind of leaders. There is no need for outrage about President Trump; he is not the worst. In Somalia in 1991, the entire government collapsed. Rebels wanted to get out the dictators, but then the rebels fought themselves over who was going to be the president. I'm among the families who fled first. We saw violence coming, and we were right. We left Mogadishu and went to Kenya. I become a refugee and lived in Kenya seven years. I think Somalia will come back, East Africa will come back. But that kind of upheaval has been prevented in America by the founders. They prevented the dictator, they prevented the kingdom, they prevented anybody dominating anybody. And that's why this country is amazing. Trump is no kind of dictator. Not even close.

Friends back in Somalia check in on me, "How are you doing? Are you stressed?" I say, "How can I be stressed? I am living the best life! I haven't seen any life before that is better than this!"

RICK: Abdi is so appreciative of what our country has to offer. Now let's talk candidates. I have to tell you that I was actually a Ted Cruz supporter right up to the day that he dropped out. He's a Constitutional Conservative and, as you heard me say earlier, the Constitution is what makes America great. Without our Bill of Rights and our protections, without our structure of government, this country wouldn't be what it is today. Constitutional protections free the human spirit up to be entrepreneurial, to write a book if they want to write a book! If they're willing to hustle their butt off and work double shifts or, in your case, to go out and talk to people like this, it's the Constitution that enables you to succeed. You don't have to be doing this. You could be back at the hotel *reading* a book if you want instead of writing a book. I think it is very cool that you have that kind of ambition. That's very American.

So I was a Ted Cruz supporter, but my wife and I loved what we were hearing from Trump the whole time. Actually, I guess some days we *were* Trump supporters, and other days we were Cruz supporters. Half the stuff Trump said, we were like, "Oh, God. Did he just say that?!" And the other half, we were like, "Yes. Somebody's finally saying that out loud."

He just said the most obvious things, like in Detroit to the Black community: "Just look around you. Your cities are crumbling. You've got heroin addicts running around the streets, your schools are a mess, your kids have a 30% graduation rate. Who's been in charge around here for the last fifty years? It's all Democrats. What have you got to lose by giving us a try? I don't think we can do any worse. That's for darn sure."

ABDI: Rick's right, they couldn't do any worse. But unlike Rick, I was a Trump supporter from day one. What inspired me is that he's a great family man. I like his family. I put *my* family first, and Trump obviously does, too. He's a great father. And like most people, I love that he just says what he thinks and he's not a politician.

RICK: Don't you love the way Abdi pronounces "politician?" His accent makes the word sound like "bull-itician." Which sounds to me like "bullshit!" Abdi makes politicians sound like bullshit!

ABDI: Don't make fun of me, Rick. I don't see you being able to speak any other language.

RICK: You're right, you're right. Ok, so my biggest issues are jobs and the economy. And Trump is good on both of those. Just look at what's happened to the Dow Jones – just yesterday another record high – as people are feeling so optimistic about our economy! A psychological lift for three hundred million people happened just like that.

I know there are a lot of Trump Derangement Syndrome people out there freaking out, but those of us who are sane and busy doing our jobs don't have time for that silliness. The reduction of regulations is going to go a long way toward helping entrepreneurs expand their businesses without having reams of paperwork to satisfy some bureaucrat. That endless paperwork – no one's ever going to look at it.

I'm burdened by over-regulation in my field. For example, though I don't sell health insurance very often, I did have a couple of group cases recently. After Obamacare went through, the medical loss ratio – we call it the MLR – squeezed out any compensation for the distribution system. The MLR lets only 20% go toward overhead, while 80% has to go towards benefits. Guess what? Our offices cost more than that. Congress basically said, "Okay field force, you are now going to work for free." Our compensation was dramatically affected.

There's also something called a fiduciary and suitability standard that came about under Obama: we now have to work under a fiduciary standard, rather than a suitability standard. What that does is increase the liability for the *advisor* and their ability to help people with retirement planning. In the event that plans set up twenty years ago don't turn out perfect, the advisor can be held liable for the investment performance. And that's absolutely absurd. First off, when you set up a retirement plan, you base it on what is suitable or appropriate for the client at the time. Then you review the plan on an annual basis and make adjustments. They made the liability go from non-existent to *lifetime* for advisors handling retirement funds. And that fiduciary standard was implemented by the Department of Labor via regulation, not legislation. They just changed the rules on us. They didn't give our elected officials time or opportunity to debate it. Thank God Trump stepped in to delay the change. Maybe he'll even get it eliminated.[82]

My trade association has been lobbying against the new standards, but we're lobbying against the Department of Labor – that's Tom Perez, the chair of the DNC. They look at everybody in the private sector as out to make money off the public, never mind that we're providing a service *to* the public. Most everybody we work with wasn't doing a very good job saving until we came along and said, "Look, you're not saving for your retirement and you need to do that." We helped Main Street America take care of their personal financial affairs by making them do the stuff they're supposed to do to be properly cared for in retirement or if something tragic happens. People just don't save like that unless you get on them, so our job is to get on people to do simple stuff like saving 10% of their gross income. You want to be independent of, not *requiring*, your Social Security.

Most of the people I've worked with didn't come to me wanting to set those plans up. I had to get referred to them and then I'd take them out, buy them a hamburger, get to know them, and

---

[82] According to Investopedia, "Fiduciary is a much higher level of accountability... Suitability meant that as long as an investment recommendation met a client's defined need and objective, it was deemed appropriate. Now, financial professionals are legally obligated to put their client's best interests first rather than simply finding 'suitable' investments. The new rule could therefore eliminate many commission structures that govern the industry." So, we must conclude that Rick's commission will be negatively impacted by a new duty to put his client's best interests first. To be more clear: Obama's administration believed people like Rick should put client's interests first, whereas Trump's administration believes Rick can include commissionable interests in his advice.

develop a relationship and trust. Only then could I help. But lately there's just too much regulation getting in the way of the private sector (me!) being able to make a living.

I'm an establishment Republican, I'm not far-right. Of course, I'm religious, but I'm not religion-based. I'm a Republican because of the economics, the freedom, and the protection of our citizenry. I'd even say the first job of a government is to protect us against foreign invaders, and Trump sees that. Our guns can get dusty because we won't need them with Trump in charge.

ABDI: Well, I'm definitely *not* an establishment Republican, but I wanted Trump in there because Hillary has just been around for too long.

Looking at my race, my religion, and my status as an immigrant, I know that I seem like the last person you'd think would support our President Trump. It's no secret that most people think Republicans are rich, white males. Well, I'm not rich and I'm not white. I am male, though, 100% or more! I just think Trump is going to do a better job. Please excuse my language if I'm not saying things right – I'm not that civilized – but I am more scared about the liberal movement than anything else.

One of the most scary things about you liberals is that transgender bathroom thing. Liberals concentrate on very small issues like that instead things like creating jobs. When Trump spoke to African-Americans in Detroit – "What do you have to lose?" – it was extremely powerful to me. Because it's the same here in Minnesota. What do we have to lose?

Somalis are almost all Democrats. The majority of ethnic communities are Democrats. I think it's because the Republicans aren't doing a good enough job telling people who they are and what they stand for. When people say they don't like that I'm a Republican, or don't like me because I'm Black, I don't care. I will never worry if somebody likes me or doesn't like me for those kinds of things. I must only take care of myself; you *will* like me if I become successful. The point is this: how can I raise my family, how can I take care of my problems, how I can make you need me as a person because of my *quality*? That's what I see in the Republican message, and it's a better message than the Democrats are putting out. The Republicans aren't saying it clearly enough; that's their problem.

RICK: Can we talk about Russia now? This thing really is a witch hunt, just like Trump says. The Russian attorney that Don Jr. met with, I understand, was given an emergency visa to get into America by the Obama administration. We don't know the whole story, but it doesn't bother me in the least. First off, there is no crime. It's not illegal. Don Jr. is not a government official, and he certainly wasn't back then. He's just the son of the president. He's running a business. And having been in politics, if anybody calls me up and says, "I've got really good dirt on your opponent," I would say, "Are we meeting in my office or yours? How soon can we do it?" Because that's just part of the game. The reality of life is that the dirt will get used on you. If they've got dirt on you, don't think they're going to be Mr. Nice Guy and keep it under their hat to save you embarrassment. That's the way the game is played.

ABDI: As a Muslim, I'd like to talk about this supposed "Muslim travel ban" and get my thoughts on the record. This is one of those things that I actually have a question about. I question Trump's decision on this, and I'd like to see what kind of advice he's getting and where he's getting it.

RICK: Well, we got the advice from Obama. The Muslim-majority is irrelevant. They're restricting travel from high propensity *terrorist* countries. That's it. That's the only thing this is about.

ABDI: Yes, I understand that, but I question it. If you were asking my advice, I'd say, "Don't allow travel from the Kingdom – from Saudi Arabia." Saudi Arabia is the only country I wouldn't allow people to travel to the United States from. America is struggling right now and every broad action, every major terrorist action, is coming from Arab areas where they have wealth and money.

So, choosing seven *other* countries to ban, I don't like that. But I also think it's not something we have to concentrate on, because there is a better way to solve it. We can solve it with a prosperous America! If we let people prosper here, we can help the Muslim leaders educate their own communities. Those leaders should be taking responsibility for what's happening. When you specifically talk about seven countries and you label them, it just divides communities. I don't like anything that makes us divided. When you're solving a problem, you have to solve that problem. If I solve one problem and create a bigger problem, that's not solving anything. That's unintended consequences. Trump is creating unintended consequences with this travel ban, because it's dividing us.

With visas, I guess don't know how they do the vetting. But when people come through a refugee camp, the United Nations has a file on that person for *years*. They know that person. When I was coming to the United States, the UN had my file forever. They knew always who I was, what was I doing. Then they give it over to a third-party American agency and they do their part. Then the INS comes. What more vetting of refugees could you want?! But with visas, I don't know. I didn't come from a rich family, so I couldn't come with a visa.

Trump wants a ban on travel from Somalia, but Somalia has a new government now. They elected an American as president; a guy from Buffalo, New York is the president of Somalia. And the Prime Minister of Somalia grew up in Europe. There's a new generation and I believe they can solve problems if Somali and Western governments collaborate. I would have handled that travel ban differently than President Trump because I place most blame for terrorism on Saudi Arabia, but we can't agree on everything.

RICK: A lot of times during the campaign I would put my hand to my head and go, "Oh God, did Trump really say that?" But that unpolished quality is endearing. I've met a lot of Trump supporters, and they all feel the same way. I did eleven highway overpass rallies for Donald Trump. I was a flag-waving enthusiast on those highway bridges. When you're standing on an overpass waving a Trump flag and half the people are honking their horns, the truckers are blaring and making the overpass vibrate, you know there's something going on. I could feel he was going to win. It's a movement! I'm more of a gut reaction type of person, and my gut told me that he was going to win easy.

I like what Abdi said about Trump being a strong leader. After eight years of fatuous leadership, I feel we have a real *man* in charge. Whether that real man is a man or woman, I don't care. But somebody that's got some testicles is finally in charge of our country. Is he going to make mistakes? Sure, he is. Name me the perfect president. I'd sure like to meet him. Name me the perfect human being, I'd like to meet him, too.

I can tell you that it took testicles to pull out of the Paris Climate Accord. That wouldn't have even been *considered* by anybody in the Bush family. Not that I'm an expert on climate accords, but I'm guessing that what Trump did is the right thing. Of course, nobody wants dirty air, nobody wants dirty water, nobody wants to see our environment polluted. I've been doing an adopt-the-highway pickup for twenty-three years now. Three times a year, I go out and pick up garbage on the side of the road with my headphones on. I'm as much of an environmentalist as anybody else. But Trump is bringing some reality to that subject. The sky is not falling. The world is not boiling. I thaw in air conditioning in summer and I need my heater in the winter. Everything's fine, so calm the fuck down.

I'm sorry to use that kind of language in front of Abdi. He's more religious than I am. But I just love being provocative.

ABDI: I am religious, yes. And I find it extremely troubling when somebody harms another human being and claims he's a Muslim. Whatever religion you believe, there's no way you can please God by harming another human being. It has no place. But cold-blooded killers give themselves all kinds of justifications. These killers harm more Muslims than any other community. Muslim countries are suffering the most.

I don't know where this germ is coming from. Killing does not please God. Believing that you're going to go to heaven after it, I don't know where this comes from. It's a sad time, and we need to educate the communities where this begins.

I would love if the Muslim leadership around the world put a little more heat on Muslim-American scholars. The Muslim-Americans need to lead more. They should not be so quiet about unfairness in Saudi Arabia and other major Arab countries. Those countries get away with whatever they want, and the poor people pay the price. It's insane, and I'm trusting Trump will do something about it. I know about all the problems in third world countries, and I know these problems are having the biggest impact on poor Muslims, but these problems don't come from sky. These problems come directly from rich Arab countries. It is countries like Saudi Arabia that we need to focus on, not the countries in this travel ban.

CHAPTER THIRTY-FIVE
The Prodigy Bluesman

July 15th, 2017
Minneapolis, Minnesota

With Abdi from the last chapter, I had a typical liberal preconception: how can a member of a minority group — he's a Somali-American Muslim — be passionate about President Trump? Abdi forcefully disagrees with Trump's attempted travel ban, however — and here's the part I'm learning to understand — there are parts of Trump's agenda that simply matter more to him. The social issues that I tend to focus on as a well-meaning liberal are not the defining characteristics of Trump's plan for many others. For Abdi, shaking up the Washington administration is far more important than any social issues he may be inadvertently voting into place.

The conservatives, even those who disagree with some of Trump's objectives, have dug in. They want action and change, and they still believe — six months in — that Trump can deliver if only other officials would stop blocking him.

I'm headed north of Minneapolis now to visit another conservative voter whose demographic surprises me. Leon is an old-school blues musician, and I've been invited to speak with him in his basement recording studio. His wife warns me that he's quite a talker. I tell her, "I'm trying to be quite the listener."

The steps to his studio are darkened, and the rooms themselves candlelit. There's plenty of audio equipment and instruments, a well-appointed bar, and an oversized poster of Frederick Douglas. Leon's waiting on a funky couch that was probably

###

LEON: I'm a Black man. A proud Black man! Born in '54 and, let me
tell you, I have learned quite a bit in this life. I've got some wisdom to
share, and that wisdom brought me to Donald Trump. Let me tell
what I'm all about.

First off, I'm a passionate musician. I've played for over fifty
years in some of the best and the worst nightclubs in the country. I
was what you might call a prodigy when I was coming up.

I started out on piano and really had something there, man. I
was seven or eight years old and getting into competitions that I
wasn't officially old enough for. My teacher was getting me in
anyway, man, and I was winning! Went on to graduate from
Oklahoma State University. I'm from Muskogee, Oklahoma, an
original Okie from Muskogee! Straight up business, man! Straight up
business. Back then, boys playing a piano meant you were a sissy, so I
stopped playing. That was the *worst* thing I ever did, stopping the
piano back then. I've never played as well as I was playing when I was
a kid.

I hit high school, and I'm feeling something about music
again, so I join this summer band. Didn't tell my parents. Just decided
to sneak out from home at eight o'clock in the morning every day for
practice. I'm an only child, but my parents didn't know where I was
from like 8:00 a.m. until 12:00 p.m. Four hours, I'm out-of-pocket.
My parents aren't used to nothing like this happening, and when they
figure out I'm not hanging up at Jim's or Sue's or Becky's, they're
worried to death. We lived in a nice 7th Street, north side
neighborhood, but now they know I ain't in it. My dad goes out
looking for me, doesn't find me, and later I come rolling home with
what? With a trumpet!

My mother was so upset, not because I'd gone missing, but
because she wanted me back on that piano, man. That's why I didn't
tell her about summer band in the first place. But I wanted to play
trumpet, so I got this school-borrowed one. I could only use it like
once a week, because other people also had claim to it. My daddy
bought me one before the month was over. He hooked me up.

So I'm playing on this trumpet when the band director finds
out I read both clefs. She says, "We don't have a tuba player in the

summer band, so I want you to switch." Now I've got to be afraid of what my mother's gonna say when I come walking home with that tuba!

But I get surprised, man. She says, "You're coming in here looking just like your grandfather." Turns out my grandfather was a tuba player at Tuskegee University. She said I reminded her so much of him. That was her daddy. I stuck with tuba for a long time.

Muskogee was not to be messed with when it came to music. We had a music department that was really untouched by anybody around there, it was more like being from a big city. When you got to looking at the history, one reason the music was so good was because it was coming out of the south, say from New Orleans, and coming up to go to Kansas City or whatever. It was what we called the Muskogee County pipeline! To get to Kansas City, you had to come through Muskogee. Muskogee was like a little, thriving metropolis. It was a crossroads for music.

The scene was hot, so I started a little combo. Little Leon was the leader of this hot combo, man. It was a nine-piece band, and everybody in it was a young prodigy like me. We were the Dynamic Souls! I didn't have a bass guitar, so I'm still playing tuba in this group. People were like, "Oh my God, these guys are good." And here's the thing: in band you had to read music, so we *could* read, but this particular group had some ears. One of my partners had a good set of music flappers, so we could just listen to a record and pick our parts off of that. Of course, I was having to pick up a bass guitar part and turn it to a tuba part.

When my parents saw I had something going in music, they absolutely supported me, even though it wasn't really part of who they were. My dad was a mechanic teacher at the high school. Taught for forty-two years and inspired my own interest in cars. (I rebuilt my first carburetor when I was eight years old.) We also had a hundred-sixty acres that we farmed, and about two hundred heads of cattle. Even though music wasn't their thing, my folks supported me.

Being a musician comes with its benefits and its curses. I worked a lot, all over the country, but there was always both celebration and troubles. I've got five kids by four different women. I know them all, though; I'm in their lives. I was married to my first wife, I've got a daughter I didn't meet until she was about twenty-five years old, and I got a girl pregnant down in Louisiana that gave me a son I work on music with today. He's my engineer. We started up a little music company and got stuff coming out soon.

These days, I'm not hitting the clubs. All my music is down here in this studio. But I did well, man. When I was playing out, every year we did a big party for the homeless here in Minneapolis. My band would play and we'd raise between $10,000 and $20,000. For ten years solid we did that. I like that feeling of helping people out.

I thought I could help out kids around here by substitute teaching, but I wasn't able to deal with the way society is going. See, I don't ask for respect, I demand it. And even though I had principals that were totally on my side, it didn't work for the parents. Remember, I came through school when, if you didn't respect the teacher, they had the paddles! No matter what anybody says, paddling works. That harsh discipline works. And I'm here to tell you – I could get in trouble saying this – *timeout* just don't work for Black people. I'm sorry, a Black child that gets timeout is just on his way to jail. They need more discipline than a timeout.

Now, I know some white people out there are going to say, "That's really disrespectful." But on the Black side, there'll be people saying, "Yes, he's right." The Bible says, "Spare the rod, spoil the child." Man says, "Just put the kid in timeout." Black people are going to agree with what God said, period. But in today's time, paddling is a no-no, so people won't agree with it in public. Behind closed doors, though, that's what they're doing. It's like with Trump. You ask some people what they think of him and they say, "He's the worst." But then they're going behind that curtain and they're voting for him!

I didn't vote for Obama. When he first came on the scene, of course I was tickled pink, "I'm getting ready to witness a Black president." But I like investigating stuff. The word "vetting" wasn't in my vocabulary, but that's what I was doing. I vetted Obama very well, and when I got to seeing what he was really about, I could not vote for him. Where did this Black man come from all of a sudden? You've been in the Senate a year and now you're running for president? Everybody knew that Hillary was going to be president in '08. So how the devil did you knock her out? I'm not a conspiracy theorist, but there's some stuff about Barack Obama we still don't know.

Somebody just released a fourteen-hundred page book on Barack Obama, and I'm pretty sure there's some good dirt in there on him. I guarantee you, the publishers would not have allowed that book to be published in 2008 or 2012. Think about this, if they vetted Barack Obama the way they're doing Donald Trump, Obama would've never got to be president. One thing I know – and a lot of Blacks don't understand this – the only way Barack got to be president was because he pulled in all the white votes. There ain't enough of us Black folk to elect a president.

It's Obama's associates that turned me off. Frank Marshall Davis, Bernardine Dohrn, Bill Ayers! Bill Ayers is a terrorist, period. And he teaches at a university now. This is what really pisses me off about you liberals. You all take terrorists, people that hate our country, and put them in academia. Go listen to Reverend Wright's speeches like Obama did; there's no way in hell you can sit in Reverend Wright's church for twenty years and *like* white people. "Well, I was just there. I really didn't hear nothing." Yeah, sure, Obama.

He did almost get me because of that diction, though. I used to say Obama's one of the best speakers I'd ever seen. I was putting him in the frame with Martin Luther King... until they pulled the teleprompter one time. Off the cuff, I found that this sucker can't speak no better than me! You couldn't trap Martin Luther King off the cuff. You couldn't trap Malcolm X off the cuff. But Obama was saying, "Uh-uh-uh-uh." He only sounds great when he's scripted.

Once upon a time I was a Democrat, but you see that picture on my wall of Frederick Douglas? That's one of my main idols. And Booker T. Washington. Those guys understood where we are. What Black people are doing right now is not what those conservative Black leaders had in mind for us. When I study how America was built, I see those early leaders were doing it right. Other countries have thousands of years of existence on us, but in less than two hundred and fifty years we just take over. We become the world's superpower in innovation, the world's superpower in *power*, in military. We had our problems, but when you have somebody like Justice Ginsburg going over to Egypt telling them, "If you want to mimic somebody's way of governing, you shouldn't mimic the United States." This is a Supreme Court Justice! She's got weight, and she's sitting up there judging Mr. Trump, my president. How in the hell is that happening?[83]

---

[83] The full quote from Justice Ginsburg: "You should certainly be aided by all the constitution-writing that has gone one since the end of World War II. I would not look to the U.S. Constitution, if I were drafting a constitution in the year 2012. I might look at the constitution of South Africa. That was a deliberate attempt to have a fundamental instrument of government that embraced basic human rights, had an independent judiciary. It really is, I think, a great piece of work that was done. Much more recent than the U.S. Constitution: Canada has a Charter of Rights and Freedoms. It dates from 1982. You would almost certainly look at the European Convention on Human Rights. Yes, why not take

Our press is one-sided. And they're on the liberal side. I used to think Walter Cronkite and all those guys were journalists. I didn't realize I was getting swayed news – one-sided news – their way. Then Fox News and Rush Limbaugh popped up. I'm in Oklahoma back in the eighties and I'm waking up listening to Rush early in the morning, thinking, "Who is this guy? Why haven't I ever heard this side before?"

With that respect for history in mind, you can see how the first guy in this last election that had me going – before Trump announced – was Ted Cruz. Ted Cruz is a Constitutionalist; he is a straight arrow. He stands up by himself for what he believes in, and that's just like me. I don't care about the majority. The majority of Black people loved Barack Obama without even knowing why! I'm not like that. And I'm not really good at doing what I'm told anyway. There's a couple white people I know saying, "Leon, you're one of those Black guys where if you were enslaved, you'd tell them, 'After you kill me, kiss my ass.' You don't care who you're fighting." I admire people who say what they think is right even when everyone disagrees with them. That was Cruz, and now it's Trump.

Trump spoke to all of us in the places you liberals call the "fly-over areas." He said everything we like to hear. I can go and start grabbing my neighbors out of the house right now and they're going to tell you the same. White boys around here, they're going to tell you the same. He spoke to me as an American. I'm the guy that wrote a song called *Love My USA*. Trump spoke to that. He spoke about living under our Constitution, rather than doing what Obama and his regime did trying to shred that Constitution. Yeah man, Obama did a really good job of shredding that Constitution.

Trump was talking about going back to American values. He is a man that's willing to go from continent to continent pushing American values, rather than being a president that went from continent to continent apologizing for what America did. Trump went to the United Nations and stood up for us. He took the Paris Accord and stood up for us. What if there is global warming? Well, we'll see. According to the Book that I read, it won't be no global warming that finishes us. Bible says it's all going to end a different way.

An ice cube breaking off in Alaska and floating down here is not going to do a damn thing but melt! That's all it's going to do. The Democratic Party has shunned God. They want to say the framers didn't believe, but that's another damn lie. The liberal media, the liberal people, have done too much changing of our history. Those framers were God-fearing men.

Let me talk about what Democrats did to my race. In the mid-to-late 1800s, during that time of Reconstruction all the way up to about 1960, my race was *the* race; we were thriving! We were number one in marriage; there wasn't no broken homes in my race. But then here comes the Democratic Party and it's, "We've got to help those Black people." Lord, help us. The Democrats never meant to help. They crucified my race.

I've got books here in this studio that I can show you about when my people couldn't read. They're working on construction sites and out in the fields as free men, but they can't read. So, they'd get in a circle and the one that could read would be teaching the ones that couldn't. They'd do this on their lunch break. Couple of white guys came in – Democrats, of course – and guess what they said? They said, "We got to do something. These people are getting too powerful." Those were the liberals, and actually it wasn't even just white guys. There were some Black sellouts. I'll call them "whitewashed niggers." Du Bois, for example, was a Black communist. He was an ace rival against Booker T. Washington. He respected white people and light people more than Black people. So Du Bois and this group of people – Nazis, communists, nigger-haters – got together and started what? The NAACP. Well, well, well. That's no good for me, man.

These liberals in Hollywood want to tell you about Trump being such a racist. Don't you find it strange that Trump *wasn't* a racist in 2015? Then, in 2016, he's worse than Hitler. What Trump is actually saying is, "I'm reaching out to you, Black people. I want you to do better than what you're doing." I tell you one damn thing, anybody that's Black and says they had a better life under Barack Obama is too damn stupid to vote.

The Russia scandal is a witch-hunt, pure and simple. I don't give a damn who Donald Jr. met with. Is there anyone that's dumb enough to think if Chelsea Clinton had the same damn meeting presented to her about Trump, she wouldn't take it? You think that, you're too damn dumb to vote! Just throw away your damn voting card and be done with it.

I follow the news pretty close. I've got the wisdom of experience *and* I've got the current information. As hard as it is to do, I actually listen to AM 950, which is a liberal station. I want to hear all sides, you know? But I have to be careful because I just got through with throat cancer and listening to those liberal stations can give me an ulcer. Here's the thing: I can hear something on CNN − the Clinton News Network − then go back and listen to Fox News and hear it rebutted. That means there's always another side to the story.

Of all the news outlets, Mark Levin is the greatest. He is a constitutional lawyer and has a great show. He doesn't know how to lie. I like him because he's like me. He's got this new book called *Rediscovering Americanism: And the Tyranny of Progressivism.* That book is teaching me a lot.

Our country was not built on a collective. We tried socialism at the beginning, and it didn't work. You and I are individuals, and just because you have and I don't does *not* mean that I'm entitled to what you got. I didn't work for it. Taxation is legalized theft. Me and my wife right now are at a 37% tax deal. When Obama got in office, we took a $25,000 hit. We still have a good lifestyle, but not like it was. Hell, before Barack Obama I was buying between $6,000 and $10,000 worth of music equipment every year. Not anymore, man. Not anymore.

We are a constitutional republic. We work under federal laws, not national laws. Big difference, okay? When you talk nationalism, you're talking about Russia. You're talking about China. You've got to be intelligent and educated to understand about being a Republican and caring about the individual. This country is built on the individual. We're built on having unalienable rights. We're built on God. In God we trust, not nobody else. If you come to this country − and we don't mind you coming − you have to *assimilate* to our ways. If your ways are so good to you, just stay home. Keep your butt right there in the middle of all that sand and leave us the hell alone.

You New Yorkers? God help you. Great place to visit, but you guys elected damn-near Stalin for Mayor. De Blasio just doesn't like Americans. A Black cop had just been shot, and he finds it more beneficial to leave his city and go support the G20 rioters in Germany. They were tearing the hell out of Hamburg, but De Blasio is over there supporting them.

Let me finish off by clarifying something important: there's been talk lately about the framers of our country being racist, and that's a damn lie. George Washington assumed his slaves from the death of his parents at age eleven; he didn't buy them. And you're going to tell me Thomas Jefferson was a racist while he was writing all that stuff about how all men are created equal? Thomas Jefferson loved God. He had a problem with God after his wife died, but the searching he did to understand God is what I like. Because I'm searching, too. I'm educating myself, and that education is telling me that the conservative movement is what's going to save this country. And our movement is tied right up with God.

God is real, man. I can't stand it when liberals say, "If I can't see God, then He doesn't exist." Well, I've never seen air, man, but I damn sure breathe it.

CHAPTER THIRTY-SIX
The Car Guy

July 21ˢᵗ, 2017
Lebanon, Pennsylvania

Let me tell you, the couple hours I spent in Leon's basement recording studio back in Minneapolis were some of the most enjoyable I've had on this project. He is flippant and captivating and provocative and just quite a cool cat. I'm reminded that my lesson is not to appreciate Donald Trump's point of view any more than is reasonable, but to more deeply understand the people behind his votes. I want to stop dismissing voters from the other side. My rousing conversation with Leon stepped me closer to that goal.

But we still disagree. Leon was distrustful of President Obama. Leon loves that Trump spoke against the Paris Climate Agreement because Leon doesn't believe in global warming. Leon believes Democrats have shunned God and created the NAACP to "crucify" his race.

Then again, Leon reads political commentary and American history fervently. He is fast and furious with dates and timelines, and out trivia-ed me countless times. My point: Leon knows his stuff, even if he interprets information in a vastly different way than I do.

The journey continues, today landing me deep in Pennsylvania. I have to do some extra convincing to get Robert to meet me; his wife warns him against "violent liberals" who have been physically attacking conservative guys like him. I assure him that I'm not violent and encourage him to Google me to see. He relents, agrees

###

ROBERT: I was brought up not to lie and not to steal. We never really needed *stuff*. What we didn't need, we didn't have. My parents had good family values, and instilled that in us.

I met my wife at a poultry plant. We were together only four months before getting married, and we just celebrated our thirtieth anniversary. It wasn't easy for her because I was wild; I had a hot temper. Everybody thought we would last no longer than a week. Well, it's thirty years.

My wife is ten years older than me. She asked me, "How come you want to marry such an older woman?" I said to her, "Well, I want to tell the guys I'm going home to the old lady and mean it." She slapped me on that one. I think our secret to success is making sure we don't say anything we'd want to take back, and not yelling at each other.

She is in pretty bad shape now, though. Dementia. Not doing good at all. It's an emotional roller coaster.

Anyway, my life's pretty much an open book. Truthfulness is an important part of who I am. I've been in automotive sales most of my life, and I can read people. I can tell when they're not telling me the truth. For that reason, I believe the man when he looks in the camera and says, "I have no ties to Russia."

I've been working on cars ever since I was sixteen. I learned from my father, and went up to building street rods, stuff like that. That is my hobby. Had at least fifteen old street rods, real race cars. I drove them down at the drag track. The last one I did was my dad's. He had an old '79 Chevy pickup. It was a rusted-out thing. When he had his stroke, he couldn't drive anymore. One day I got done doing a Chevelle, and I called my dad up and said, "Hey Pop, I want to go look at this truck all right?" and dad said, "Okay. I'll go with." I went and picked him up, but there was no truck to see. I just brought him into the garage, and I had *his* truck up on the lift. He goes, "What's wrong with that?" I said, "Nothing dad, I'm going to restore it." The bad thing is, he never got to see it. He passed away a couple of months later. But I got it done. I dropped a 454 in it with 650 horsepower in the back tires. That thing screamed. I did everything to that truck; runs better than brand new. I really wish dad had seen it done.

I had my own stroke about six years ago. Don't do much restoration anymore.

I used to sell cars down here at Ebersole's. I was there for about fifteen years. I have lots of awards from them, and my sales record still stands at twenty-nine cars in one month. But I worked twelve hours a day. I didn't miss any days of work. The only time I missed was when my dad passed. I used vacation days, and they fired me for it. You lose your first parent, it's really hard. I was a wreck. But it was a Saturday when we lost him, and Saturday I had off. Sunday, Monday, I claimed vacation days, and then Tuesday I came back to work. Got called into the office, and they let me go because they said that my conviction should be there and not with my family. They're supposed to be Bible thumpers, but they're not real Christians. They talk the talk, they talk the game, but they don't do the walk.

As soon as I heard Trump was running, I was in. People knock him for getting that million-dollar loan from his father, right? Well, we all have the same situation. If our fathers were millionaires, they would lend it to us, too. That loan doesn't make any difference to me, because that's family. As far as his bankruptcies, personally he had none. Business wise, he had three. Here in Pennsylvania, Milton Hershey also had three. Business is business.

Trump is a good man. A good, strong family man. I could care less if his wife came from Czechoslovakia, or somewhere in that area. It doesn't bother me. I didn't marry her. And he didn't marry her so she could become a U.S. Citizen. She talks six languages; I can't barely speak one! Everybody is looking out to find the worst in him. But you have to look at facts. Facts are facts, and he's good got facts behind him.

The healthcare that I have is good because it's Medicare plus a secondary insurance. I'm not covered by Obamacare or anything like that. It comes from what we worked for and we earned it. You want better insurance? Get a better job. You want to make yourself better? Do it like everybody else did prior to you: work for it.

Go out and do your job, save your money, do investments. Do it so you can say, "I did it my way. I made my own money. I don't have to rely on the government handing me a check so I can sit at home and do absolutely nothing and get my welfare and healthcare." I don't like these people who say, "Give me, give me, give me, give me. Pay for my education too while you're at it." This is not how we work here.

Trump loves his country. He sent a plane for that little girl who was dying of cancer. She didn't have the money. He heard about it, so he sent his plane and paid for her operation. This is long before he ran for president. You tell me if any of those clowns in there now would have done that? Trump helps. He's a very generous man.[84]

I'm ideologically opposed to Hillary Clinton. You believe she had nothing to do with Vince Foster's death? Come on. Vince Foster was right-handed. He shot himself twice in the back of the head with a nine-millimeter, they said. I have a gun permit and I am very active with my gun. I know that it's virtually impossible to take your left hand, point it behind your head and shoot yourself twice. But that was what they said happened. Come on.[85]

I hate her and I would never have voted for her. Even if it was between Mickey Mouse and Hillary Clinton, it would have been Mickey Mouse for me.

Our gas prices are going up again. Trump went over to Saudi Arabia. He didn't bow to the king, and he should never have to bow to the king. There's only one king you bow to and that's Christ, not that clown over there. That country has so much money, they don't need to be doing what they're doing with these oil prices. Why is it that we're paying on a stock market to buy oil? We have enough in this country to tell the Saudis where they can go. We can take care of our energy needs here, but we're afraid to get anything done because we got people who want to hug a tree, kiss a frog. I don't want anything to happen to the environment, okay? But if it means that we'll create jobs and be independent of oil from other countries? Then it's worth it.

Would you be able to live off the land? I don't think any of you liberals could. I could, though, because I went deer hunting, I

---

[84] Robert has all the details of this story wrong, but the true version is actually quite nice. When commercial airlines refused to allow three-year-old Andrew Ten to fly with substantial life-support equipment, Trump allowed use of his private plane for the family to travel from Los Angeles to New York to visit specialists. This was in 1988.

[85] The official autopsy revealed that Vince Foster shot himself just once in the mouth, and with his right hand. He used a .38 caliber, not a nine-millimeter. Robert seems to believe otherwise.

went fishing, trapping, and all that, with my brother. To this day, if anything would happen, I could live on my own. I'm not worried about that. If I have to shoot Bambi, I'm going to do it. Donald Trump couldn't survive either, I guess. He's probably one of the ones that will starve, like the liberals. I guess I just started talking about my life. Got off topic. Sorry about that.

Here's a picture of me and my wife when Trump came to the Harrisburg farm show. That complex is huge, and the line went from the front door, all the way down, over back, down, all the way around, and over again. They couldn't get all the people in. The neatest thing I seen there is Trump coming over the top of the farm show in his airplane. The Harrisburg airport is right down from there. The pilot came in slowly; it was awesome. He got there about an hour later than they said he'd be, but it wasn't his fault; it's because of security. When he finally came out, people went crazy, including at least one up front that seemed dangerous. If you watch Trump, he has a couple of bodyguards, but one bodyguard is a tall, skinny guy, bald hair, always to his left. That guy – I've never seen anything like it – that guy jumped off the podium, off the stage, up over four or five people, and managed to tackle this crazy guy within seconds. The state cops weren't even there yet. That bodyguard had the guy down and zip tied. He just jumped and did this Jimmy Superfly Snooker move. The rally was electrifying.

The immigration thing that gets me is that I will not bow down for any Muslim person trying to push what they believe in on me. Okay? There's only person in this world I'm going to kneel to, and that's Christ. All the other ones can kiss my American ass.

To be clear: there's good Islam, there's bad Islam, there's good people, there's bad people, there's good whites, there's bad whites, there's good Blacks, there's bad Blacks, whatever. But the Quran has nothing to do with the United States. I have read the Quran, though I guess not the whole thing. That part about the female mutilation and the beheading of people? That was pretty much where I stopped. I'd had enough up to that point. But before you criticize something, you've got to learn what it is; that's why I was reading.[86]

---

[86] The Quran does not mention FGM (female genital mutilation) at all. The Quran *does* mention beheading, but modern teachers view the passage in the context of war. Much like the Bible's call for murder in John and Chronicles, the violent passages are usually viewed in a larger context. I'm not convinced Robert actually read the Quran.

When you think about it, the way to get through to people and help people learn about stuff is through Facebook and Twitter. Trump knows how to work that. He did very well with that. That's where he got a lot of his votes, I'm sure of it.[87]

You know what I would like to do? I would love to be able to get into Congress and talk to them. All I need is ten minutes of their time. They want to know what the American people want? I'll tell them what the American people want: we want them all to sit down, shut up, and listen to what we're saying. Don't tell me that that starving child there in Africa needs food. Yes, I know. But why are his mom and dad making more babies? Learn to be self-sufficient. Don't tell me that it's okay for my grandson to have to go to school and learn Islam. No, it's not okay. That's a choice. You can't force him. If you don't want us to say the prayers, then don't force them to go learn some kind of Islam crap. We don't want to hear it. Go back to what founded this great nation, or we're going to lose it all.

---

[87] Those who created the Russian bots are sure of it, too.

CHAPTER THIRTY-SEVEN
The Top-Secret Clearance Tech

August 2nd, 2017
Durham, North Carolina

Up north in Pennsylvania, Robert's doing a lot for his wife these days. Dementia, he said. That makes me really sad, because it was very, very obvious to me how much he cares about her. He's an old-school "guy," not wanting to show his cards or his emotions, but he had to pause for tears as we spoke. Beautiful sentiment. Beautiful relationship.

Then as I was leaving, Robert made a joke about Barack Obama being violently sentenced for crimes against America. He may have used the word "hung." Hard to discern on the recording, and I'm pretty sure it wasn't an actual, illegal threat to a former president, but still...

Empathy. I want to offer it. It's just hard to come by sometimes.

I'm headed down south again. Durham, North Carolina, a college town with large tech and art components. The New York Times calls North Carolina "the swingiest of swing states." But on my Facebook page I read, "Durham? Good luck finding any Trump supporters there!"

Hillary Clinton won Durham in a landslide, receiving more than four times the votes Trump did. But this is still the South. I know Trump's devotees are here. It's warm enough to meet Jo outside at a picnic table. Gentility and poise is her front. Let's see what she's really like.

###

JO: I'm the neglected the middle daughter! One of four kids born to a military man and a housewife. Growing up, my parents were pretty apolitical. The only political thing I recall either of them doing was my mom lighting a candle in support of the Solidarity movement. I didn't even know what that was back then. Now, I'm a political junkie. It drives my husband absolutely crazy. He's not even conservative. He's kind of a middle-of-the-road guy.

I ran off and got married really young, didn't finish college. That was a big mistake on so many levels. Didn't work out. I did get an awesome son out of it though. I struggled as a single parent, but I can honestly say it never occurred to me to get any sort of public assistance. Now I look back on my struggle and think, "There were all these resources available. I just didn't avail myself of any of them." Through hard work and maybe some divine intervention, anybody can succeed in America. I like to say that I have a PhD from the school of hard knocks.

I worked some minor jobs, but interviewed in 1999 for Cisco Systems. They took a chance on me, and it changed the trajectory of my life and career. I didn't have a lot of experience, and the job I was applying for was really a big step up for me. It's an opportunity that to this day I appreciate. They were very good to me. When they offered me an early retirement package, I took it and was able to use the skills that I learned there to get another job in two weeks. I now work for a data storage company out of Silicon Valley.

I'm a technical adviser, a consultant to the customer. I tell them what bugs they are at risk for and what firmware they need to be running. I manage their upgrades, make sure they've got everything in place when they're ready to migrate systems. It's kind of a technical role. But I must also point out that it's a very male-dominated role. Only about 10% of the people that do that job are women.

When I worked in the public sector, I had top-secret clearance to support special operations in Iraq and Afghanistan. Everything there is on a need-to-know basis. It's not like you just open these books have access to all the great secrets about UFOs, but with all of this drama around Hillary's emails, I feel I have a clear perspective based on my experience working in the field. And my meter goes through the roof on some of the things that I hear!

One of the first things you learn is that a lot of information that's posted online is classified; you can't share it. It's online and fifty million people may access it, but it's still classified information. If you are not within the clearance, you are not allowed to freely disseminate any of that information. You can *have* classified information, and it may not be marked, but it's the collective that matters. You may have one piece that doesn't mean anything, but when you disseminate the piece you may give somebody a picture that they're not supposed to have. That's why a lot of things are confidential. It doesn't look like they matter, but when you add all the other things together, people can glean information that can be used in a nefarious way.

Was Hillary complicit? Well... she was either complicit or so incompetent that it probably doesn't matter. She still mishandled it all. We have SCIFs. That stands for sensitive compartment information facility. It's where you handle that kind of information. You don't have it freely flowing on your BlackBerry! When I worked in that environment, there were signs all over the place warning us about the minimum fine and the minimum prison sentence for mishandling classified information. She was either extremely incompetent or extremely dishonest.

I've got a great husband. He's my son's stepfather, but you would never know. He is the best husband in the world. I've got three grandchildren and I like to say that's who I'm fighting for, my grandkids. That's who I'm standing up for. I don't know what state this nation is going to be in, but I'd like to think – and I get all emotional – but I'd like to think, "I tried. Kids, I fought for you. I stood up for what was right. I made my opinion known. I filled out petitions. I voted. I did all these things to try to make a difference."

I will say that I think the people on the left probably feel that they are right, too. They think they are doing the right things for their kids, and it's a shame that our nation has gotten to the point where we can't disagree in a civil way. I have friends that are on the other side. I have friends that are gay. I have friends that are Muslim. But I still have very set opinions about things. I like to think that I can keep those opinions and still love the people. I may not agree with them, but I don't hate them, and that's what we have to get past.

I'm a hardcore conservative. I'm as conservative as you can possibly get, and I don't necessarily think Trump is a conservative. I think he's more of the middle-of-the-road guy. A lot of the things he's fighting for, he probably can't give a flip about! But he ran on a conservative platform, and I believe he's going to keep his promises to the American people. So far, he's doing an amazing job. I know you probably can't stand him, but he's standing up for everything that I voted for him for, so I'm happy. If he's not really pro-life, that's something he and God can work out. But he's fighting for it, and that's what matters to me.

I want border security; I want to know who's coming in. I want to make sure that they are not here to do us any harm, but I'm not a prejudiced person. I actually have a charity to benefit people in a third-world country. I have a 501(c)(3) called Heart Threads International. In a nutshell, we provide clothing to children of Bangladesh, to orphans. The clothing is cut out here, then that piece of cloth is sent to me and my sister. We box it up, send it to Bangladesh, and pay somebody a very good living wage to sew the items. The finished pieces are then given away to the orphans.

We use any excess money to solarize and expand huts. We just dug a latrine, putting the first bathroom in a village of eight thousand people. We are getting ready to finish an orphanage that will house fifty kids. It's going to have twenty-five boys on the top and twenty-five girls on the bottom. We're getting ready to put solar in there too, and we're hoping it will open in January. Nobody takes a salary. 100% of the money goes directly to the cause.

How did we get started doing that? I met two Christian pastors in Bangladesh on Facebook. I watched the struggles they were having trying to help people in their midst. Their orphanage was basically just a few poles sticking out of the ground. I said to my husband, "We need to help them." We started helping out of our pocket but, as you can imagine, the need is great and the workers are few. I was showing my sister some pictures, and the kids were naked. A lot of them, just stark naked. They are like eight, nine, ten years old, with no clothes. We said, "We have to cloth the kids." That's how Heart Threads began. As a Christian, I feel like we are supposed to help our brother, and that's everybody. We don't give people a litmus test before we help them. Some of them may be Muslims, some of them may not be. A lot of them are. I actually think Muslims comprise about 95% of the population. But I want to leave a legacy of generosity. When I die, I want people to say, "At least she wasn't selfish with what she had."

We need some equal-trade policies like Trump says. That's one thing I've learned with this charity. Trying to get a package through customs in Bangladesh is almost impossible, and the cost is astronomical. But when I look at how they can sell things to us, it seems easy-peasy. There should be a balance there.

And we need energy independence. I'm not a huge fan of fracking, to be honest. Nobody has proven to me that fracking is any good. However, I think we have probably thousands, tens of thousands, maybe hundreds of thousands of acres out the middle of nowhere where we *have* oil. Let's get to that oil. Let's get out from under Saudi Arabia the best we can.

And we need freedom *of* religion not freedom *from* religion. Somehow, the Constitution was hijacked and now it's freedom from religion. You can't bring your Bible into class. You can't have a billboard that says, "Thank you, Jesus." [88] I just think it's misconstruing what the Constitution says. It doesn't say that you can't worship, it just says government cannot mandate a religion.

One big thing I like about Trump: he sticks his foot in his mouth a lot, but the guy is politically incorrect and I like it. It's refreshing. Everybody just needs to lighten up. We need to be able to say that we are going to stomp the hell out of ISIS and not have somebody go, "They are Muslims. You hate Muslims because you hate the Islamic religion." No, we just know that there are people in that religion who have hijacked and want to do us harm, so let's stomp the hell out of them! Obama said we need to get rid of ISIS, so what is different about Trump? Well, Obama didn't get it done.

The Syrian rebels are ISIS. The Syrian rebels are the ones that Obama was arming. So, Obama was arming ISIS. Nobody has convinced me yet that Assad has used chemical weapons on his own people. Call me crazy, but I think Assad is on the right side. I think we have been fighting the wrong side.

Obama might be a closet Muslim for this reason: he claims to be a Christian but would speak one thing and do exactly the opposite. When I see Obama, I see him as a radical Muslim sympathizer. Why else would he do some of the things that he did? Why else would he take out Mubarak, a moderate, and put in a guy who was convicted of crimes against humanity and sentenced to death? What possesses a president to do that?

Also, I'm a gun owner. I think that everybody should have the right to protect themselves. When you start taking the guns out of the

---

[88] You *can* bring your Bible to school. And you *can* have a billboard that says, "Thank you, Jesus." A drive through Kentucky will make the latter statement quite obvious.

hands of people, it in emboldens the criminals.[89] If they know that there is a .45 on the other side of that door, they are probably going to think twice about trying to break in. When thinking about the Second Amendment, though, let me just say that I don't necessarily support the Republicans. I'm a conservative. Most of the Republicans are not true conservatives. These establishment, lifetime Republicans don't always represent us properly. Their motives are different.

Look at the most restrictive cities in Detroit, Washington D.C., Chicago. I haven't actually looked at what their gun laws are, but I'd be willing to bet they are pretty strict. Their crime is out of control. I think it's because the criminals know that it's harder for people to protect themselves. It's easier to get in there and take advantage. It's a problem, and those are democratically ruined cities.

Our Second Amendment, our Constitutional rights, are God-given rights.[90] It's not up to man to take those rights away. They are endowed by our creator. While I don't disagree with the fact that Australia is quite a peaceful country, I do think that the people there take a big chance by letting the government take their good weapons away. There is no guarantee now what happens when they get a desperate person in office and he turns on them. We've seen that happen throughout history.

And these VA hospitals? Some of them have cockroaches, patients waiting months to get in. They're dying; they're committing suicide while they're waiting for treatment. That is absolutely inexcusable. Heads need to roll, and that's the other reason I voted for Trump. He is a businessman, and I think it's time for somebody to run this country like a business. We need some accountability.

Getting able-bodied people off of welfare and back to work is a priority. My own *son* is disabled, and he was reevaluated as part of Trump's hold to get people off of disability and back to work. But they came back and they said, "You are still fully disabled." I think a lot of people are not. There is a lot of fraud, and we need to fix that.

What convinced me to vote for Trump: he said, "I'm here for you. I'll fight for you, and I'll win for you," and I thought, "How many years has it been since we've had a fighter?" And then he said, "You've got one big, beautiful chance. This is the last chance you're

---

[89] This is such a frustrating argument. There are *no* Democrats saying they want to take away guns from law-abiding citizens. None. (Well, except me.)

[90] "Put your sword back into its place. For all who take the sword will perish by the sword." (Matthew 26:52) This quote is attributed to Jesus and seems to imply that owning a weapon is not a God-given right, but a danger to oneself.

going to have to elect somebody that's not bought and paid for by a lobbyist." That was what clinched it for me. Say what you want about Trump, he didn't take any money from any lobbyist and he won't be bought and paid for. The establishment Republicans are very comfortable in their swamp. How are they making $170,000 a year in Congress, but walk out worth $250 million dollars? That doesn't add up for me. Trump has almost as much money as God. Why would he sell us out for more money? He's on our side; anything else just doesn't make any sense to me.

CHAPTER THIRTY-EIGHT
The Gay Puerto Rican

August 9th, 2017
Tampa, Florida

Durham was filled with my kind of people: progressive, cultured, and willing to talk. It's an extremely liberal town, so the conservatives there have stepped up their debating game. Jo presented gentility and poise on first approach, but hit her points with strength. She hit especially hard when speaking of computer security clearance, a subject on which she is an expert. I never considered Hillary Clinton's emails to be consequential until I spoke with Jo. I admit, I'm now a little bothered by the security breach. Jo's attack, that Hillary "was either complicit or so incompetent that it probably doesn't matter," makes sense to me. It still wouldn't change my vote, but it makes me think. And that's the point of this whole adventure.

Jo is another in a long line of people who see value in Trump's plain-speaking and lack of political-correctness. There are degrees to this, of course — even Jo thinks Trump sounds like a jerk too often — but I am starting to like the idea of relieving the stress that absolute adherence to the most recently appropriate language can bring. If we lessen the negative impact of poorly chosen words, would we increase the honest feelings flowing spontaneously from our leaders? And wouldn't that be a great thing?

Strict loyalty to far-left political correctness might just be detrimental to our national conversation. Liberal friends, please forgive me! I have to admit my truth, because I've pledged to do so: I do agree with most of Trump's fans that rigid guidelines on our words can actually disguise the ideas we may be trying to convey, that lightening our fear of offending can force direct conversation about unconscious bias. I agree that Trump speaks like a jerk, but I also see how fast he can get to his point without fearing the specific words he is choosing. Oh God, did I just make an argument for Trump's way of communicating? I don't actually like it — it is not polite and does not represent us well as a country — but I do recognize the efficiency of his language. Though couching his statements in doublespeak, there's little doubt as to the emotion behind them. Though shading the truth on a nearly pathological basis, there's rarely any doubt as to what Trump is feeling.

In Democratic Durham, Republican Jo has inched me closer to understanding. Now, I'm off to Florida.

"This place is called Steam Heat! And I see why!" James is walking toward me in moist, ninety-five degree air. It's a sauna on the patio of this coffee shop, but I'm into it because the weather makes me feel like I'm on vacation. On the other hand, I'm wearing linen pants, a loose shirt, and flip-flops, whereas James is coming from work in dressier clothes that he is sure to sweat right through. He says he is used to air conditioning, but I'm keeping him outside because I fear I'll need some kind of advantage in this conversation.

James knows health care from inside the industry. James describes himself as a "gay Puerto Rican." I'm going to have to catch up, because this guy is one I would never have pegged for Trump. Well, not before working on this book, anyway. There have been many, many demographic surprises on this journey of mine.

JAMES: I'm born and raised in Puerto Rico. Came to the United States to go to school back in 1979. I'm now fifty-six years old, so I've been here longer than I lived in Puerto Rico. I still go back to Puerto Rico every six weeks, though, to see my family.

I've worked mostly in the healthcare field, managing and growing medical practices. But I also established a real nice real estate brokerage firm in Atlanta and ended making most of my money there. Life brought me here to Tampa when my mom got sick; I came to take care of her and stayed. Went back to college, just because I was bored, and finished another degree. That's when I met the two young men that I call my kids. These two kids are just my life now. I've very much guided them.

Currently, I run one of Tampa General Hospital's biggest clinics, so I know a lot about the Obamacare issue. I do the business side of healthcare, making sure we are maximizing our schedules, providing access to patients, meeting the measures that tell me our patients are taken well care of. Insurance companies score us on how well we take care of our patients. The compensation is tied our quality of care. If you're a diabetic patient, are we seeing you every three months? If you're a hypertensive patient, are we seeing you every six months? Are we ordering the tests that you need? Are you getting colonoscopies? How do we follow up? All that is what I take care of, making sure we are excelling in those measures. It tells me that our patients are getting the best care available, and we get compensated by Medicare and private insurance according to those scores. I'm very proud that we score very high.

What I see right now, and I see it every day, are patients that can't afford insurance. Obamacare would have worked if more people had participated. There was no commitment to get young people to sign up for insurance. So, obviously, you can't maintain the system. There's a lady who comes into my office, she has Deep Vein Thrombosis and has not been able to go to a doctor. No insurance. We have charity, so we try to help. She is in her late sixties, working part-time, taking care of three grandchildren because her daughter is imprisoned. This is a white lady. When you see her, you know her legs are swollen. For her to sign up on Obamacare is $1,050 a month. She can't afford that. She can't afford her medication, either; we are just giving it to her. Apparently, she doesn't qualify for subsidies because she works, but she's also taking care of the three kids. She can't prove they are dependents because, when she filed her taxes the last time, they weren't listed on there. We are doing what we can for her, but she needs so much more. So much more. With her chronic condition, she is going to die within the year.

I have liberal friends who insist they are so for Obamacare but don't even have insurance! One friend in Atlanta has some health issues she needs to deal with. I say, "Sign up for insurance." She says, "It's a $6,000 deductible; that doesn't work for me." That is the absolute reality. Healthcare is a mess. I believe in competition, and I think that the government should stay out of healthcare completely. Since the expansion of Medicaid, and I'm talking from experience, you just try to find a doctor within a hundred miles of you. And if you do, good luck getting an appointment within a few months. That's the reality of Medicaid.

Let me shock you: this is the first time I've ever voted in a presidential election. I voted for the first time because of Donald

Trump. It was the first time I felt there was somebody worth getting out of bed for. But I supported Obama at first! I remember crying during his first appearance after the results came in. I got chills. I cried because I thought, "Wow, this is going to unite the world." As time went by, I became disappointed. I've been hearing the same promises all my life. How many elections does it take to get it done? That's what attracted me to Trump, his attitude of, "Let's get this done." I've been a businessman, and I know that you have to *deliver* or you're not solvent. That's business. I'm tired of both Democrats and Republicans not being able to deliver.

The main reason I voted for Trump was because he was different. Granted, I don't agree with everything that comes out of his mouth. Sometimes, I prefer he wouldn't say certain things, but at least he is saying what he means.

When the tape came out about him grabbing the pussy, I said, "This is it. Man, he's done." But he didn't give up. He kept going! I couldn't believe that.

I am really dissatisfied at the level of dysfunction in our Congress. They're so politicized that I don't think they have the best interests of our nation in mind. They certainly don't put us first. Who goes on recess when you have a business to run? They're gone right now, why? There's so much to do. With healthcare, just lock yourself in a room and get it done. That's what businesspeople do. We have our meetings, we brainstorm, and we get it done. We come out of there with some product. It may not be perfect, but we don't just say, "I'm not going to do it. I'm going on recess."

I see all this analyzing, like, "What did Trump mean by his threat yesterday about North Korea?" I don't care. I think the statements from Kim Jong Un were extreme. Trump didn't start it. I think his remarks are all part of the negotiation, part of getting Kim Jong to the table. Do you think that we cannot take care of North Korea? I have no doubt we could. Maybe it's time to do so. I'm not afraid of that. My dad was a prisoner of war in Korea for four years, tortured. He wrote a book about the experience, *Trapped in Hell*. When I read it as a young man, I realized why nothing bothered him. Nothing could compare to what he went through in North Korea. I have no sympathy for that regime, and I feel sorry for the people there. But Trump will get it over with, one way or the other.

Those are foreign issues, but we have our own battles right here. I'm old-fashioned; I believe in law and order. What I see these days is complete disrespect for authority. We were taught to say, "Yes sir, no sir." If I get pulled over, I shake with nerves. I'm not defiant. I respect order. Why are we are teaching our kids to be disrespectful to law enforcement? That doesn't fly with me.

I see a brighter economic future. Trump can't directly take credit for it, but the stock market is doing great. I looked at my 401(k) and I've made $15,000 this month without doing anything.[91]

I probably would not have voted for any other Republican candidate. It was Trump alone. It was his, "Fuck you, I'm going to do it my way." If it offends you, too bad. We're all too freaking sensitive.

I'm a gay man, Hispanic, Puerto Rican. I always say I belong to three minorities! Within that, I'm a gay man who voted for Trump. Believe it or not, there's a lot of us. I don't believe the issues that could affect me – like gay marriage – are going to backtrack. The Supreme Court has already ruled. I don't fear those things going back. Even if we get new justices in? What are they going to do, reverse gay marriage? On what grounds? How many times has the Supreme Court gone against what they've already ruled?[92] That would be insane.

I had this argument back in the eighties or nineties with my gay friends that insisted they needed gay marriage. I said, "I'm not going to wait until they grant me marriage rights to live my life the way I want." If I want something legal, I'll do a legal agreement with my partner. It would probably be more solid and more comprehensive than a marriage, anyway. A marriage license doesn't guarantee you much.

And that cake thing is dumb. Would you buy a cake from someone that doesn't want to sell it to you? Would you even *want* to give them your money? No.

There was something yesterday about a gym owner outside of Atlanta who posted, "No fucking cops allowed." I said, "Look, I would not be a member of that gym any more than I would buy a cake from someone that doesn't want to sell it to me. I'll take my money where it's appreciated." Why make a big deal of that?

I grew up in an era where sexual orientation was not a top-of-the-list item. We were playing, having fun. I didn't come out until I was twenty-three or so, but I knew I was different since I was a toddler. I didn't know what gay was or homosexuality was, but I knew

---

[91] For perspective, the S&P 500 returned 1.93% in July of 2017, so James must have roughly $800,000 in his 401(k).

[92] The Supreme Court has overruled itself more than one hundred times.

I was different. But that just wasn't an issue. Nothing has ever stopped me from being who I want to be.

We grew up in a family that went to my grandmother's every Sunday. We were there with our cousins, uncles, aunts, and everybody else. We grew up in that entire family. We did the church thing every Sunday, so helping each other was instilled in us. Celebrating each other's accomplishments was part of our development. When my sister got accepted at Texas Woman's University, we all went to Denton, Texas and hung out with her that whole summer. We had that kind of upbringing.

I come from a very, very traditional family. In that sense, I can relate to Trump's family; everybody is in the same boat, everybody supports each other.

My dad, I told you, was a veteran of the Korean War. He was happy as a goat; a happy-go-lucky kind of guy. As counterpoint, my mother was a capitalist, a businesswoman, who instilled in us an appreciation for competition and excellence. I remember the one time I was second in my class in high school; that was not good enough. I was second in my class and she was like, "Why weren't you first?"

What I like about Trump is that he'll get information and advice from many people; I do the same. I don't attack a problem from one direction only, there are always multiple solutions. I deal with this every day in my business. There are issues we have with scheduling, for example, when patients do not show up for their appointments. That can take up a big block of our schedule. There are many ways to attack that: a phone call, a text message, an automated text message. I get feedback, what's working and what's not working, and I come up with the best solution. I believe that getting advice from people that you trust is a good thing and so does Trump. Do I think that there's nepotism? Who cares?! One of my best alliances is with my brother.

Have you ever learned to fly a plane from someone that's not a pilot? No. Have you ever learned to be rich from a poor person? Trump's advisors are the people that know what's going on.

Let's talk about compassion. I am fiscally liberal in the sense that I don't mind my taxes going to the government. But I don't like when it's misused and abused, and I see that every day. I'll give you an example: there are people coming to my clinic who just want doctors to fill out a form that will deem them unfit to work so they can collect disability. I have friends in *wheelchairs* who go to work, but then I have somebody who's twenty-one come to my office wanting disability. I say, "What is your disability?" She wiggles her finger. "Your finger? Are you freaking kidding me?" The same person is asking me, "Would you give me $20 for Pampers because I'm on my third freaking baby?" Twenty-one years old and receiving all this assistance? That is abuse.

Even employees of mine have lived with their boyfriend for years and have a family of two or three kids, but they don't get married because they'll lose benefits as single mothers. That bothers me, and it happens all the time.

Look, I'm in a small town just outside Tampa, but in just one clinic I see the abuse over and over again. You know how many clinics there are in Tampa? In the United States? You know how many people are taking advantage of the system? It's compounding, and I see it daily.

I'd rather help people in my own way. I'm compassionate. I've taken these two kids into my house. They don't have to pay anything. One is in med school, and one is a musician. I said, "First, go get your degree," and I was able to guide them. They come to me for advice. I taught them how to build their credit. They have better credit than I do, by twenty points! I've been able to do that for them. So, I'm a giving person. I actually give myself the least. But the fiscal abuse in our government is beyond control, and it disgusts me.

The border issue is all about controlling drugs. Do I think that many of our issues in youth come from drug abuse, from drugs that come through the border? Absolutely. I see it in our clinics and I've seen it in our communities. I know who the drug dealers are. When I was in Atlanta, I wasn't a saint. I knew where to get stuff and I knew they were Mexicans. The border wall can be a deterrent.

Trump doesn't have all the solutions because he doesn't *know* all the solutions yet. I don't have all the solutions in my own work, but I'm resourceful enough to know who I can go to. We have more than a hundred doctors and I say, "Why is *his* ophthalmology compliance much better than everybody else? What is he doing differently?" So I go and meet with that person and he says, "Oh, we're doing this and the other." I say, "That's a great idea, but instead of doing manually, I'm going to automate that process." Now we don't have to keep our papers in an accordion, pull them out, and make sure that we've got this or that. Nope, we're going to do an order on EPIC, which is then able to generate a report that tells me, "We haven't gotten this." When you go out and get those ideas, it improves your business. Trump gets those ideas to improve our country; it's that simple.

Trump is a businessman and he assigns tasks. Get it *done*, right? Trump says, "Just figure it out!" He empowers people to come up with solutions.

CHAPTER THIRTY-NINE
The Imprisoned Chef

August 18th, 2017
Cleveland, Ohio

James, back in humid Tampa, provided the most engaging conversation I've had so far. Please re-read his words. While I still cannot agree with his vote, James is a smart man with a logical point-of-view that completely surprised me. Perhaps more than anyone else, he helped me understand the disparate ways that one's demographic may not easily predict a vote. I cannot add anything to this conversation. I believe James was correct in his assessment of health care inefficiencies, and his social politics opened my eyes to logical reasons why the Democratic party doesn't necessarily have to be the party of choice for the socially-conscious among us. Liberals, just re-read his words. Please. We can learn a lot from his perspective. We can learn a lot about how to fight conservatives in our next Facebook debate, our next Thanksgiving dinner, and even the next election. Because James is a smart conservative who defies traditional liberal logic. See his point of view. Learn to debate it. (I'll try to do the same, but I'm getting too personally involved here and it's driving me batty. I'm starting to question my own politics. Not my vote! But my politics. Everything seems so middle-ground. So... centrist.)

I'm flying to another swing state, Ohio. The rust belt. The geographic area that many say lost the election for Hillary. Joshua is an executive chef at Clevelander Bar and Grill, the largest sports bar in downtown Cleveland. He's led me here with a story of health insurance: his premium jumped from $40 to $250 under Obamacare, but it wasn't until he had his teeth knocked out breaking up a bar fight *that he realized his deductible had risen, too. $500 to $3000 was not something easy for him to swallow, especially with fewer teeth.*

Joshua is covered in tattoos. He's got POW-MIA artwork, a seemingly impersonal choice due to his young age. But I already know that he's incredibly passionate. And he's probably a bit violent. See, I've Googled him and learned that... Eh, never mind. Let's let him speak for himself.

###

JOSHUA: I was born in the poverty-stricken neighborhood of Slavic Village. It was trash. By the time grew up, I was a semi-professional boxer with a chip on my shoulder. At fifteen-years-old, I caught a case – a scuffle – and went to the penitentiary for five years. I don't want to tell you exactly what happened.

Grew up in a conservative house, all veterans. Grandparents from World War II, uncle in Vietnam, brother just got back from Kandahar, Afghanistan. I come from a long line of military guys and I just love my country. Man, I'm telling you: red, white, and blue all the way.

The neighborhood I was in as a kid was 85% Black; I grew up a minority. I was discriminated on for being the only white person in the school I went to. There wasn't a white teacher, nothing like that. It shouldn't matter, but I was told that Black people can't be prejudice. They are, though. I lived that experience first-hand.

Most of my friends from back then are Black, of the Black persuasion. We got over it, earned a mutual respect for each other. My guys that work for me now, majority of them are Black. But the divide in this country today is worse than any other time in history.

After jail, I turned my life around. I wanted better. I'm in a situation right now where I'm trying to have a family. I've got a girl and I'm going to be marrying her very soon. I'll have kids, but I don't want my kids to grow up how I did. My dad was a single father, nine kids, and he raised us all alone. My dad raised *nine* children alone. It was chaotic. We governed ourselves. He was an open road truck driver. Truck driver meant he wasn't always around; we had to be in charge of ourselves. He was providing for us, though. Always had food in our stomach and a roof over our head. The last thing he got me for my birthday – my twelfth birthday – was a job. He told me, "Now that I got you this job at the restaurant, you can get your own shit." I never looked back. Today, I am the executive chef at the biggest sports bar in downtown Cleveland.

I've had no schooling, none of that. Never had any degrees. I have all on-the-job experience and I've earned what I have from just that.

We had a conservative household, but I did like Bill Clinton a little bit. My dad's business boomed when Clinton was in office. That metal crisis in the early 2000s when Bush got in and we started the war? Metal picked back up and the economy started going again. That helped my dad.

Abortion is the key issue for me. I'm a Catholic. I go to church every Sunday. So the idea of preserving life is something that hits home. Hillary wanted to go up to thirty-three weeks with abortion. My nephew was born at twenty-nine weeks; he's sixteen years old now, healthy, and lives with me. I'm providing for him. I take care of him because his father is incarcerated, but the choice to bring him into this world is just something I personally agree with. I understand there are some extenuating circumstances sometimes, but people often just don't want to take care of their kids. That's the problem.

I don't really care who knows how I vote, it's my prerogative. The only thing our government asks of us is to vote. It's the only thing they ask; they don't ask for nothing else. And that's what I believe in, man. Look at places like Texas, where abortion laws are so extreme, so strict. They cut abortions by 70%! Why? Because people start to watch what they do. Everybody don't spread their legs so much.

People in Texas are not out back with a coat hanger like most of liberal America wants you to think. That's not the way it works. People just become more responsible for their actions. You tend to pay attention more instead of thinking, "Hey, our government's going to pay for the abortion." That's not a good use of my tax dollars. If we have stricter abortion laws, people would be more responsible.

I sent the White House a brick to start the wall. That's exactly what I did. One of my conservative buddies was on TV saying we should all just start mailing bricks to the White House and maybe Trump will get the idea; that's what the people had voted for him in for. Open borders is not the answer. We can't accept everybody.

Though I'm in the restaurant industry, I have no experience with illegal immigrants. We don't pay under the table here; we don't do any of that. I'm sure other companies do, but I actually take pride in paying taxes and doing things right. I pay taxes to take care of the less fortunate; I don't pay taxes to pay for another country's less fortunate. We have too many hungry kids in America to worry about any other place.

Trump could do without the tweets; he needs to just shut his stupid mouth and keep doing what he's doing. Let the economy do the talking. He don't have to point out how good it's doing; anyone that pays attention knows how good it's doing. My numbers here are up 20% from last year at this time. No shit. 20% in just this one restaurant.

Leftists fight Trump every step of the way. I think, at this point, if he found a cure for cancer, liberals would dispute how many jobs got broke up because he fixed the disease.

I'm from a less-fortunate neighborhood, and yet I know mothers of six driving an Audi around, eating steak. That's my tax dollars. I drive a 2000 Mercury Cougar and I eat chicken four times a week. Let's get these people into job training. Let's drug test them. Out of my thousand Facebook friends, I'd say six hundred of them are on welfare. At least fifty times a month, I get people trying to sell me food stamps on Facebook. Who wants to buy food stamps for fifty cents on the dollar? *Cash* is the incentive for that. Because with cash, you can buy yourself drugs, pay your car loans.

People make a career out of welfare; they ain't never look for a job. Never.

Have you seen how good Bitcoin's doing? Oh, my God. My buddy is making $1,000 a week right now. He had the money to invest and everything's up, the Dow, NASDAQ, everything. What is it? A $3.2 trillion increase in the economy? Yup. Look where we're at because people are hopeful.

Every white person that voted for Donald Trump is not a racist. I have Black family. That's just like every Muslim is not a terrorist. You might as well say everybody with a hijab on is going to blow me up, or every Black person steals. These are stupid assumptions. First of all, do you know who personally funds Black Lives Matter? A man by the name of George Soros. He's one of the richest people in the United States of America. His net worth was $27.2 billion in Forbes last year. He's a white male, but he's funding this Black Lives Matter project. No color of any skin should matter. I believe that the Obama administration pushed the race agenda.

The second Trump took office, the agenda completely changed. You don't see as much white on Black crimes; you definitely don't see the numbers we saw before. But Black people commit 65% of the crimes in this country, you know? Let's report on *white* people that were killed by white cops. Why does it only matter that a Black man was killed? Why is this such an issue? We all bleed red.

Everyone should have health care. This is something that both sides agree on. But it has to be paid for. Obama took office and gave everyone that didn't work a check. Me or none of my men got checks. Did you get a check? No. You know why? Because you have a job. There's a problem giving people a check when they choose not to work. Where does this money come from? The backs of blue-collar America.

My sixteen-year-old nephew tried to convince me to vote for Bernie Sanders. I really ain't with that. I'm not paying for kids that are going to end up flipping burgers anyway to go to school for four years; I'm just not doing that. The liberals have gotten so used to this cushion they've been given for the last eight years that they go ballistic when Trump cuts things.

I have a six-year-old nephew who's Black. He don't know anything but a Black president. So this race issue that people are pushing has no *effect* on kids today. My nephew sees a white president and says, "Hey, why is he white? Isn't the president supposed to be Black?" That's out of the mouth of a child. They only know what we teach them. And we've been teaching them too much hate.

I don't box anymore. But I was good at it back in the day. Very good. Really, really good. Just not anymore. I cook; that's my passion now. I quit going to school in the seventh grade but as you can see, I'm pretty well educated. It's a misconception that all Trump fans are ignorant. We're really, really not, and not all of us support him fully. But he is our president. I didn't complain about Obama once. I sat back and I shut up. I clearly remember "We Won: Get Over It" bumper stickers. And I clearly remember "We Won Twice: Get Over It Again." Now, *we* won. It's your turn to get over it.

I bet I'm probably one of the most interesting people you've met on this project.

CHAPTER FORTY
The Poly-Sci Veteran

August 22nd, 2017
Kansas City, Missouri

Joshua, the ex-con from Cleveland, is Catholic. He spoke at length about abortion, reminding me again how many people in this country latch on to that issue as a deciding factor. In this modern age, shouldn't we be getting more health-savvy, more science-minded, more concerned with a woman's right to control what happens to her own body, and less religious about it all? Religion has been the dominant feature in so many conversations I've had on this journey, and young people like Joshua who believe in a personal God still surprise me. To repeat we atheists' best argument: believing in a God that is both loving and all-powerful means that childhood cancer is either something God thinks is a loving thing for a kid to die from, or something that God chooses not to use his power to prevent. It means the shooting in Sandy Hook was something God chose not to stop, or something God believed was a kind event to offer His people. How can so many people believe in a God like that? How can so many let that God guide their vote? It just doesn't jive with me. I can understand the tradition attached to older folks and their religion, but I can't wrap my mind around younger people like Joshua who still believe. And as long as Republicans continue to brand themselves as religious pro-lifers, it will be hard to break people like Joshua away from conservative politicians.

Joshua's other key point was about welfare reform. Are there really that many people on welfare driving beautiful new cars like he said? No. I'm sorry, I believe that is bogus. I can get behind welfare reform or welfare fairness, but not behind alarmist assumptions. A family of three, at the time of this writing, must have a gross income of less than $1700 per month in order to receive SNAP benefits. We *can argue that the income number should be adjusted up or down, but arguing against people using the system as it stands seems disingenuous. Instead, let's vote in politicians willing to look at the system and adjust it when needed. Easy to agree on, right? For the record, both Donald Trump and Hillary Clinton have expressed a strong desire for welfare reform. The problem: most past reform has only increased extreme poverty and disproportionately impacted Black and Latino families. This is not my definition of fairness. Reform is needed, but intricate reform is difficult and I haven't seen any prospective, nuanced solutions from either party.*

Darting across the country has been eye opening, but the end is in sight. I'm travelling to Kansas City now, my last stop before heading back to New York and trying to reach some temporary conclusion to this adventure. William was quick to respond to my meeting request, and quick to agree on my proposed time. This is a guy who acts fast. We meet in my hotel lobby because the burger joint next door — my preferred spot — is closed due to a power outage. (Flash floods swamped Kansas City last night, destroying their electrical grid in the early hours.) William tells me of his time in two branches of military service, and his son who is currently a paratrooper with the 82nd Airborne. William doesn't understand why, after hours and hours of questioning, Hillary's opponents still couldn't charge her with anything in the Benghazi attack. I commend her for her defense; William condemns the committee for not hitting her hard enough.

###

WILLIAM: I'm from around here. Grew up mostly in Kansas City. Went to school here. Was in the military for about ten years, but came back and finished my degree at the University of Missouri. A law degree. That's about it.

Actually, I'm a weirdo. I was in both the Air Force and the Army for a little bit back-to-back. I started off in the Air Force, but when I left they had what they call a "three year obligation." They could call me up anytime they wanted. I went to an Army recruiter and said, "Look, I'd rather do this obligation time with you guys. Can I do that?" He said, "Sure," and took all my paperwork. Then, after I'd been in the Army for about a year, the Air Force said, "Wait a minute, you can't do that," and dragged me back for the last two years.

Now, I'm running a restaurant. Pizza. It's called Minsky's. If you're in Kansas City, you can't avoid Minsky's. We're pretty famous.

I don't think there should be such a thing as a professional politician. Just don't think it should exist. I don't think it was ever *intended* to exist, and Trump was the only one out there that wasn't one of those pros. That's why I was initially drawn to him. I identify more with the Republicans in the past thirty years, but I'm not automatically voting that way. My family was always Democrats. My grandfather was a small-town Democratic politician in the 1930s, but as the party moved further and further left it was moving away from *us*. I think I'm actually registered as a Democrat right now, but that's only because a guy I went to law school with was running for prosecutor here in town. When he was in the primaries, I had to register as a Democrat to vote. That's not really indicative of any commitment to the ideals of the party.

Most of the things Trump had to say, I generally agreed with. When I listened to the press talking about what he just said, most of the time they were lying about it. I got fed up with that, and being fed up actually pushed me further toward, "This is the guy." The press was lying about things he actually said, lying about quotes, lying about interpretation. The one that comes to mind mostly is immigration, trying to claim – and they're still doing it today – that he was some sort of racist. Now, based on everything I've seen and read about before he became a politician, that's just not true. I'm done with the press lying. For our society to function and survive, there has to be some kind of disinterested party that's just going to tell you the truth and the facts. That has gone away, mostly. I would say it exists more in the conservative media, but even they have big problems.

There's another branch of why I liked Trump so much: Hillary scared me to death. Hillary was, in my opinion, a complete liar and a criminal. And you didn't get the press saying, "She lied about this, and this, and this, and this." You only heard that about Trump. The press had picked a side and they were going to stay with it. That causes a problem, because if you and I can't look at some news and see what the facts are, then we can't have a discussion about it. If you've got one set of facts you think are true, and I got one set of facts that I think are true, and they're completely *different*, then we're screwed.

Clinton was criminal. If it hadn't been Trump, it would have been someone else besting her. Even if I didn't like them, I would have voted for another Republican just because I'm not voting for her. This is beating a dead horse, but it's a fact for me: Benghazi takes her out of running all by itself. She lied about what was going on, which I find criminal and contemptible, and she lied about what caused it. Then the entire administration lied about being able to do anything about it. Anybody who's ever had any connection with the military knows that's not true. We have huge numbers of troops stationed in Italy, including the 173rd Airborne Brigade. And my son is now part of the Global Reaction Force with the 82nd Airborne out of Fort Bragg, North Carolina; from Fort Bragg, they can have an entire brigade, boots on the ground, anywhere on this planet in eighteen hours or less. Hillary and Obama want people to believe that they couldn't get somebody from Italy across the Mediterranean in time. This isn't remotely true. And that lie destroyed it for me. If you're in a position of power in this country, you don't leave people to die. Even if you think there's nothing you can do, you try anyway. If it was unavoidable, it's unavoidable, but you better *find out* it's unavoidable when you have airplanes in the air almost there. And then you better go clean it up the next day. They didn't do that. They didn't go in to fix things afterwards. A bunch of Libyans had to go rescue our people. That should never ever happen for the United States of America. We should never ever leave our people to die. Ever.

My degree is in Political Science. One of the first things you learn is the definition of "nation." To be a real nation – as opposed to a failed state – you need the ability to control your borders, to know who's coming in and who's coming out. There's a million reasons for it: criminals, disease, etc. Everybody wants to turn it into something racist, but you don't know what kind of diseases can make it across the border. And drug cartels are a huge problem. It's not about race; it's about disease and crime.

People are on talk shows talking about Trump's mental state. I think *they* are crazy. The left, unfortunately, has gone completely off the rails. They will say absolutely everything bad about someone they don't like, whether it's true or not, just hoping that some people will believe it. That's what's happening there. Democrats have gotten way too much of their base convinced that Trump ought to be impeached, yet there's absolutely nothing to warrant that. Either they don't understand, or they're pretending they don't understand, how impeachment works. There are certain requirements, and nobody has mentioned anything to impeach him for other than, "We think he's icky."

They're obviously trying for a 25th Amendment deal to impeach him with the insanity thing, and *that's* just insane. Trump's perfectly fine, he just disagrees with them. It has reached the point where the left – forgive me, not everyone – but the powers that be on the left think disagreeing with them means you are either evil or crazy. Trump disagrees with them, therefore he must be crazy.

At Charlottesville, after that riot, Trump spoke about human fault being on both sides, and I think he was right. I'm not sure he said it as clearly as he might have, but he was right. The way I understand it, both groups protesting had permits and both of them were supposed to be in different places. One of them supposedly is really evil. I think they *both* were, but for some reason the press has picked this white supremacist group as being the evil ones. The Antifa, whoever the hell they are, went to get them. If they had both stayed where they were supposed to be, there wouldn't have been any problems. And that's another place where the left goes off the rails. No matter how crazy they are, no matter how stupid they are, those white supremacists have got a right to express their views. The left has reached the point where if you don't agree with them, you're not allowed to speak. They're going to attack you with boards, weapons, chains, and hit women in the face with bike locks to keep them from speaking. That's where the left is going too far.

The whole idea of free speech is to protect speech you don't like. If it's not to protect the speech you don't like, then there's no reason to have it, because nobody's going to try to stop the speech you *do* like. Were these white supremacists scumbags? Absolutely. Were the other side scumbags? Yes, I think they were. They had beliefs that were horrible. They were violent. You put the two together, and it's just not good.

Was Trump qualified for the job when he got it? Yes. We're all qualified for the job. If you're thirty-five years old and can convince people to vote for you, you're the president, period. There are no other qualifications in the Constitution. Natural born citizen, thirty-five, there you go. The movement that supported Trump is a belief that America is good, and it's a force for good in the world. We believe America is trying to do something right. We don't always succeed – we haven't succeeded in the past, and we won't in the future – but we try. America is good and is probably the best hope the world has. We should be trying to bring the rest of the world up, rather than tearing America down.

We conservatives are lucky with Trump. I think we feel like somebody is finally on our side. But importantly, most of my liberal friends are very nice, good, well-meaning people. I think they've been hijacked. They've been hijacked and convinced of things that aren't true, because most of my friends who say they're very liberal are actually much more in the middle. The far-left establishment keeps trying to convince liberals to hate conservatism, and that's lousy. Centrists are much better. The good people I know are centrists.[93]

---

[93] I'll officially join this group now, in a footnote. I'm a centrist, probably a "radical centrist." Whew, it feels good to get that off my chest.

INTERMISSION: 2017

I was a liberal elite. I'm quite privileged, and I was pretty left-wing. I live in a fancy New York City apartment, have gay family members, and tend to believe some entitlements are requirements. In the days following Donald Trump's 2016 election, I joined protests, chanted "not my president" through Times Square, and − yeah, I'll admit it − shed some tears. Now? Realism is taking hold, and I've come to identify with radical centrism. In the words of John F. Kennedy, I proffer "idealism without illusions."

That's me: looking for the ideal while learning the bounds of reality. What if embracing empathy contains within it a notion that no side can hold a monopoly on virtue? What if embracing empathy means humility in the face of moral conviction? What if embracing empathy means listening and understanding must come before certitude?

Radical centrism is a less prideful position to be in. There's not much shouting from rooftops you can do when you're a centrist. It's not very catchy to chant, "I hear both sides, and I want to ask some questions! I hear both sides, and I want to ask some questions!"

Allow me to clarify: I'm not identifying as a radical centrist because I support Donald Trump any more than I did before this project began. Rather, I understand some motivations of the *people* behind his movement better than I did in November of 2016. That was the point, after all, and listening to them forced me to slowly re-evaluate my automatic adhesion to far-left ideas. I'm now spending hours thinking about market-based solutions to affordable housing, bold action on the environment without dismantling the oil industry, and equalizing public school district spending. Radical centrism: where the solution is not automatically in the center, but is discovered by active debate with right and left. Radical centrism: where we act as judge, supporting the best idea no matter the partisan group from which the idea was derived. Radical centrism: where doubt and skepticism are welcome until enough evidence arrives. Radical centrism: where no one holds a monopoly on truth, and convictions may be overturned in light of new facts.

Our president appears unusually unleashed as 2017 bumps its way into autumn. During the week I write these words, Trump has referred to Elizabeth Warren as "Pocahontas" while at a ceremony honoring Native American codebreakers and re-tweeted three inflammatory, anti-Muslim videos designed to be divisive and prejudicial. This is not refreshing. This is not somebody from outside Washington coming along and showing us how our country can be led with bolder ideas and fewer lobbying interests. (I can get behind those refreshing changes that Trump supporters are looking for.) No, this is our president casting a public f-you to any sense of unity or compromise or... centrism.

And there it is. This year, and this exploration of devoted Trump supporters, has drawn me to the radical center, but Trump himself is making it clear that he doesn't want anyone to be there. His support from the far-right is strong. His base still lives on that end of the spectrum, even though some reasonable people in these pages exist closer to the middle.

We need to continue our conversation with those on the other side of the spectrum. We need to understand their desires, and I hope this book can help achieve that goal. But do we need to continue attempting to understand Donald Trump himself? Do we believe there is a master plan behind the chaotic approach he takes to governing? Decidedly, I do not. Conservatives: I have new appreciation and respect for you, but not for your president.

In searching for a proper concluding analysis for this section of the book, I did a quick word usage breakdown. There were some telling results. For example, my conversation partners used Trump's name seven times more often than they used words like "country" and "America," demonstrating the continued strength of his brand. Hillary Clinton is called almost always by her first name, whereas Donald Trump is known worldwide by his surname. Should we attribute this to the patriarchy or branding?

Interestingly, my interview subjects referred to Barack Obama just as often as Hillary Clinton, the word count showing these mentions just single digits apart. It is no exaggeration to say, and in the word count lies some evidence, that many Trump voters use eight years of Obama as a primary reason to support Trump. It is not a straight Democrat-Republican divide, but a strong Obama-Trump divide.

Finally, my quick word analysis shows extremely heavy usage of the word, "money," and moderately heavy uses of "God," "Black,"

"Mexico," "illegal," "wall," and "Muslim." The hot-button issues are painfully clear.

Back in New York, I need to reconnect with my people. Where are they? Ah, yes. It is September 12th, 2017 and Hillary Clinton is releasing her new book with a signing in Barnes & Noble at Union Square. Wristbands are given out at 7:00 a.m., but many people have camped out overnight for the privilege of momentary face time. I speak to the second guy in line; he arrived at 4:00 p.m. yesterday afternoon. It's 11:00 a.m. now, so I've got no chance of meeting Clinton myself. I spend my time chatting. It's seventy-four degrees out, a beautiful day, and liberals are ready to talk. There is a line around the block, each chunk of it segmented by fenced pens. And there are many machine guns. Like, a *lot* of machine guns strapped to Kevlar-crusted men. Hillary Clinton will arrive any minute.

And what an eclectic crowd! A melting pot. I take a survey of those willing to share. In the first pen, there are two Korean-Americans, one Chinese-American, one African-American, one Latinx, and seven white people. In the second pen, one Chinese-American, three African-Americans, and eight white people. Each pen is split nearly evenly between male and female. What's driving them to be here this early? "She inspires me," I hear. "We don't want her to think we've forgotten her," they tell me. "I want to support her," he says.

Note the personal approach. These folks speak of Hillary Clinton on an intimate level, like they know her. Trump supporters have been doing the same for months. Each group feels a particular claim, an individual connection.

There's one Trump supporter in the mix. He's a pseudo-protester, wearing a Hillary mask and responding to her book's title with a sign that answers, "Trump Happened!" Every press rep on the block is trying to interview this man, as he's the only obvious Trump fan here. A street performer has set up a DJ station and is freestyle rapping about why people love Hillary; he asks for tips as the line moves away from him. Another guy pushes around his "Roving Anti-Trump Bandwagon," a cart that sells Trump-hating buttons; the salesman says his job "is the only one Trump created." I'm enjoying the scene, but Hillary arrives through a back door and I don't have a wristband. As the crowd shuffles in to meet her, it's time for me to walk to my own district and vote in the Democratic primary.

During my walk, I check the Facebook event page for the

book signing I've just left. So many good feelings were being tossed about in the line; where is the opposition? Ah, there they are, on Facebook. Barnes and Noble's page is inundated with Clinton attacks: "We want to read your emails, not your book." "Do you write about landing under fake sniper fire in Bosnia?" "What happened to the millions for Haiti?"

There's one online comment, however, that I can really get behind: "I'm super happy this badass woman will be available to tell her story in NYC!" So am I.

But if I'm still happy with Hillary Clinton's viewpoints, and if I haven't become a Trump supporter myself, what is the point of this book? Well, with the way Trump is lashing out, I'd like to think this book can offer Democrats another level of understanding. Liberals, if you see Trump and can't fathom how somebody could vote for him, this book *tells* you, albeit slowly. The answer is not clear or simple. And if the answer is not clear or simple, is there even any value in my listening or your reading? Can I draw a conclusion or tangible purpose from this epic project I'm just now starting to examine on the macro level?

Before putting this project aside for a few years, and still searching for a proper denouement for 2017, I peek again at the opposing side by paying $35 to join the New York Young Republicans. Instantly, I receive their introductory message: "The New York Young Republican Club is the oldest and largest Young Republican club in the country. Established in 1911, the NYYRC is a club rich with a history of advocacy, and we today continue the work that began over a century ago by educating our members and the community about important policy issues, by promoting the principles and values of the Republican Party, among which are limited government, individual responsibility, and fiscal responsibility, and by electing Republicans to office." I am a registered Democrat and plan to remain so indefinitely, but I'm about to go spy on some young republicans by pretending to be one of them.

The Young Republicans are having their monthly social gathering at Hofbrauhaus House on Third Avenue in New York, arguably the most stereotypical place for young republicans to have a social gathering. (It's beer. It's bros. It's happy hour. It's not my scene.) It's raining tonight, an absolute downpour. I duck into the gathering and am blasted back by a deafening roar coming from the second floor. Dripping up the stairs, I see them: smart-looking professionals, well-dressed, seven-deep at the bar, yelling to be heard over the other two hundred people who are, well, also yelling to be heard.

The entire floor is not exclusively for us, the Young Republicans. I'm glad to see that. Spending some time mingling, it seems there are maybe fifty members packed into the center of this pseudo-German beer hall. What brings them together?

"In liberal New York, we've got to remind ourselves that we are not alone. The conservative movement is alive and well here; we just don't have all the votes yet."

"This is just a great place to meet like-minded people."

"I learn a lot coming to these gatherings. The tide is changing, fiscal conservatives are finally earning a place at the table."

Then there's my favorite quote of the night: "I know it's loud here, but I come to listen to what people have to say. I'm sick of getting all my news online, hearing political opinions only from Facebook videos and pundits on TV. It's way better to listen to what real people have to say. It's way better to hear a person's voice, to see their face while they say what they want to say, and really pick out what matters to them as people. This is real life, you know? The internet and TV can be so cut and dry, but in real life our opinions can be messier." After almost a year of travelling across America, I've found my concluding statement articulated by a Young Republican on a rainy night in a New York City beer garden.

It's loud here in America, but we've got to keep leaning in. Our opinions can be messy, but we've got to keep straining to hear each other over the noise. If we still want to *insure domestic Tranquility*, and if genuine empathy can get us there, then perhaps having a real conversation with a real person from the other side is a collective first step.

(Now, please allow three years to pass.)

ACT TWO: 2020

Empathy is the theme I adhere to, but the years now passed have scorched the insular cortex where empathy activates and left me nearly incapable of understanding. What began for me as a noble project to listen to the other side has now racked me with guilt for even giving voice to supporters of a leader I can barely stomach. Empathy? Where it once grew is now blackened and charred.

Our president speaks in ways that directly dismiss BIPOC citizens when they are hurting most. Regardless of whether a strong economy has helped these folks, empathy for their pain has never once been on display from our elected leader.

Our president speaks in ways that directly dismiss unauthorized immigrants and their families when they are hurting most. Regardless of whether these tax-paying workers broke laws in travelling here, empathy for their pain has never once been on display from Trump or his own family.

Our president speaks in ways that directly dismiss those affected by COVID-19 when they are hurting most. Regardless of whether Warp Speed has expedited the process of saving future lives, empathy for their pain has never once been on display from a Trump podium.

Our president speaks in ways that directly dismiss those unemployed during the pandemic when they are hurting most. Regardless of whether it is fully partisan debate keeping additional stimulus away from these workers, empathy for their pain has never once been on display during Trump's negotiations.

I'm reminded daily of my privilege. My 401(k) is thriving even through the pandemic and my taxes have been much lower since Trump took office; is this why so many still support him? It's time to check in once again with many of the characters who make up the previous section of this book. While I planned to visit them all again in person, travelling to thirty cities across America during a pandemic is not wise. Here they are again, via a virtual visitation. As is my preference, I shall limit my own voice and let these disparate folks speak for themselves.

CHAPTER FORTY-ONE
The Prodigy Bluesman (Again)

October, 2020
Minneapolis, Minnesota

Following George Floyd's slow, almost nine-minute murder under the knee of a Minneapolis police officer, President Trump gave an appropriate – if measured – speech, during which he expressed, "I understand the hurt. I understand the pain." If that sounded like an invocation of empathy, his comments shortly thereafter ran contrary, calling the protestors "thugs" and repeating the violence-inciting, "when the looting starts, the shooting starts." In Minneapolis, of all places, I would expect the cloud of George Floyd's death to influence every deep thinker, especially a deep thinker who also happens to be a Black man.

I had a remarkable time hanging out with Leon in his music studio back in 2017. Minneapolis is home to many professional musicians, and Leon is one of the most entertaining of the lot. (Check out his catchy "Love My USA" on YouTube.) He surprised me with his view that conservatism is the most redeeming political philosophy for Black folks, but I have to imagine that the ensuing Trump years have had an impact.

###

LEON: Hey Dan, it's Leon, man, down in Minneapolis. Leon, the Black conservative! Yeah, proud of that, very. Okay, first question: how have my hopes been fulfilled? Well, I can answer that. My hopes has been fulfilled just past anything I could have imagined. It's so good having a non-politician come in and disrupt everything, changing the status quo. We learned a whole lot about our so-called Republican Party conservatives. They were Republicans in name only: RINOs – R-I-N-O – that's all they were. This man came in with his whole motto of putting America first. Think about that! Just bringing back that patriotism and being proud of where I'm from.

Rather than wanting to be just a little, measly part of the rest of the world, he put us back on top. Let's start energy-wise: I'm sixty-six years old, and for the first time – and I'm from Oklahoma, which is oil and gas country – for the first time in seventy-five years he made us an energy independent company… I mean, "country." I don't want to disrespect nobody that great.

We don't have to depend on nobody for energy! When Saudi Arabia saw what had happened, everybody just crumbled. And just think about the price of gas going down. I'm in Minnesota, which is a very high-price state to live in. (High-price just like New York! Though we see that during the pandemic that New York is empty, and people are leaving there in droves.)
And now we're literally able to sell our energy to the world.

Another thing – how my hopes have been fulfilled – was pulling us out of the Paris Accord. Pulling us out of something that we knew nobody else was really going to abide by. Nobody but the Western countries. India said they weren't going to. China weren't going to, and they pollute ten times more than us. And think about this: on that whole global warming aspect, emissions has went *down* since this president's been in office. We're doing the job, doing our job, and we're not even a part of the thing. We've got clean air. Where did that idea came up, that conservatives don't want clean air? Yes, we do. We just want it done responsibly.

Okay, next question. No, not next question. Let's stay on hopes being fulfilled and talk about the Middle East. My guy, think about this: we have this major problem with Iran, so we put those sanctions on them. And the best thing we did was we honored Israel with recognizing the capitol as Jerusalem, just like our God said it was. Not like the Palestinians wanted. Not like the Arab countries wanted. But this man, this president, did it. George Bush promised it. Barack Obama promised it. I think Reagan promised it, but nobody could do nothing. That man Trump went over in the Middle East and partied with those people and let them know there's a new sheriff in town, and it ain't Nancy Pelosi.

I've said this pretty much all of my adult life: why is it the

United States is the ultimate superpower, but we go in and we talk and act and fight wars like we're some third-rate country?!

Oh, this man! Dan, you know I can rant and rave pretty good, but this man! Think about what happened in North Korea. Barack Obama told this man, "Your biggest threat is going to be little Kim over there with his rocket launches." Well, when you have a president that understands that he's the president of a superpower, then you understand the power that you possess. This man says, "If you launch one missile on South Korea, the devastation that would be brought to your little land… you can't even imagine what's going to be done to you." This is how the leader of a superpower talks. What did Reagan say? What did all the real presidents say that understood peace through strength? You don't go start depleting your military to help somebody on welfare. Because guess what? You take that money away from the military, then Russia, China, and whoever else wants to is coming for you. That's something that a liberal needs to understand perfectly.

You notice, right now today in 2020, in the middle of a pandemic, you don't hear those Ayatollah over in Iran talking one thing about "death to America." Because you can do that with certain types of presidents, but it wouldn't be cool to do that with this one. And if you say it, you better say it very softly to where this president thinks that you're not a problem. Because once Donald Trump thinks you're a problem, you've got a problem. And it's called the American military. Lord help you.

Look at what's happening now. As of October the 25th, 2020, we have five nations signed on to this… I'll call it the Israeli Peace Accord. Sudan is the fifth nation to sign on. You've got all of these Arab nations from Saudi Arabia to Jordan. They're signed on to this Peace Accord and guess what? Little bitty Iran is sitting over there by themselves wondering what the hell is going on. Yeah, have my hopes been fulfilled? You damn right they have.

Now, it's funny that America is supposedly the most systemically racist country on Earth. I'm a Black man. And even back in the day, I didn't see that. There's racist people in our country; that ain't going to never change anyway. As long as you have people, there's going to be a difference of opinion. My deal is: I'm sick of my people running around wishing, "Oh, I want the white man to… whatever." Love yourself first. It's like back when Frederick Douglas and Booker T. Washington were saying, "We don't need desegregation, all we need is a level playing field." What did James

Brown say? "I don't want nobody to give me nothing. Open up the damn door and I'll get it myself." Systemically racist? No, that's not us. We fought a war to get rid of racism. And I'm so damn tired of the liberal media running around talking about systemically racist.

America first; think about that. My parents used to tell me, "Leon Jr., before you go telling somebody to clean up their house, make sure yours is clean first." Okay? You can't love and respect your own country first if you think that you're living in the most systemically racist country on Earth. I think the United Nations called us systematically racist, like they're some authority. Mind you, look at what China is doing to Muslims, Christians, and everybody else that don't agree with their way. Look at what China did to the world. And you know what? With all that they've done, the stupid Democrats – sorry – but the stupid Democrats are more upset with Donald Trump than what China did releasing this damn pandemic on the whole world.

Understand that I'm clinging to my family, my God, my country, and my gun. Because, yes, we do have a right to bear arms. And guess what? The framers put that in for us to be able to sustain ourself and protect ourselves just in case we get a tyrannical government. And looks like that's where we could be heading in the next eight or nine days, if that other guy gets in.

Okay, another promise he kept: Trump ran on this thing called "draining the swamp." Oh my God. We had no clue that the swamp was really a cesspool. And you just can't use Drano on a cesspool. We need dynamite. He's opened that cesspool up in four years to where we seen the power grab. Democrats and Republicans are standing together against him. Like I said, you can't call them Republicans. You call them RINOs, "Republicans In Name Only." They're standing with the Democrats, standing against our Constitution, standing against freedom of speech. Most liberal Democrats don't even realize they're trying to cancel out speech. Guess what? You guys talk too, and one day you're also going to be shamed for going against the status quo. I can't even listen to a decent, new comedian no more because of the speech police thing. It's ridiculous.

We now see how corrupt Washington really is. Everybody's employed by the government, and that's this man's problem. He couldn't be bought. Joe Biden's getting ready to come in already bought and paid for. We won't go there, because that's not what this conversation is about, but I think you're going to have to do another book, Dan! I'm losing my voice a little bit.

Anyway, my 401(k) is protected. In the middle of a pandemic, not only did I keep my job, but I got a raise. I don't think that would have happened under the Obama/Biden regime. I'm proud to be American. But most of all, guys, I'm really proud to be a Black American. When I walk in the room, nobody's going to try to play me like an idiot. "Oh, I don't even see what color is." Bull! And I don't have to go no farther than that. People need to wake up, stop the crap, and understand the road that's trying to be forced on us to get rid of this president. It's a road we don't want to go down. Not at all.

I love being a part of a man like Trump that understands the business realm and made his money somewhere else. He didn't have to go to Washington. It's amazing how we get all these broke people that we send to Washington and after they're there a few years, all of a sudden they're multi-millionaires. Oh my God, how'd that happen? But when you get a billionaire to come in office, then all of a sudden you upset about that. Come on people, wake up!

Why does he have my vote again? Because he's got a job to continue. I want him to finish it. I want the cesspool blown to smithereens.

Black people, look what he's done for our race! Joe Biden had forty-seven years to do what this man did in forty-seven months. Now, all of a sudden, if I give Biden four more years, he'll remember to keep my Black ass in mind? That's what all Black people need to understand. How in the hell is it Biden's going to do so much for me now, when he didn't do anything before. He wants to lead me down this Socialist path that most of you Democrats think is the proper way to go. Once upon a time, Venezuela was the fastest-growing, richest country on planet Earth. Now you go down there and you can't even get loaves of bread in the grocery store. Come on, Democratic Socialism!

All of you Democrats that think that you're so smart, so high and mighty? Where'd that come from? The universities; they've been exposed, once and for all. They've been exposed, Dan. You can now see the amount of money that they've taken from communist countries. I think the total figure now is that twelve universities − our major universities − have taken over six billion dollars from China, Russia, and places like that. What in the hell is an American college doing taking that kind of money from a country that swore to destroy it? Think about it.

Anyway, man, it's been nice talking to you. You know, I could do this forever because this is my topic. I hope you got enough to show what Leon's truly about. I love me some Donald Trump. And if you know what? If I could get him eight more years, I'd keep him. Our country needs a patriot. We need somebody that loves this country first and every other country later on. I was taught self-preservation is the first law of nature. In other words, before I can take care of you, Dan, I got to make sure I have taken care of me first.

Charity starts at home and spreads abroad, not vice versa. We won't be sending no more billion-and-a-half dollars to countries that's threatening to blow our heads off. "Death to America," and you hand them a billion dollars in cash on a palette. Think about it. Dan, that's like your next-door neighbor telling you, "Danny, no matter what, you just wait for it, buddy. I'm going to get you and I'm going to kill you. I'm going to blow your damn head off, Danny." And you come back the next day and give them a couple thousand dollars. "Here you go. I'm going to give you this money because I know you didn't mean that." Is that democratic sense or democratic stupidity-ness?

We don't educate nobody in this country anymore. It's all indoctrination. And you know that better than I do. It's something about you liberals, where you won't go against a trend. Even if you know the truth, you don't want to do nothing about it because you can't go against the mob.

There's two words I never hear come out of a Democrat's mouth: freedom and liberty. Wonder what's up with that. If you find out why Daniel, let me know sometime. All right, brother, love you to death. Hope your book sells like hotcakes. Be cool.

CHAPTER FORTY-TWO
The State Lobbyist (Again)

October, 2020
Indianapolis, Indiana

Leon accused liberals of not wanting to go against the mob, and I can certainly admit to jumping on the liberal bandwagon many times in my life. I'm learning – continually learning – to remain skeptical and take issues one at a time instead of reflexively subscribing to the party line. But Leon, devout fan of conservative radio, must accept the same accusation. When his talking points revolve around "patriotism," I hear the voice of Rush Limbaugh and Mark Levin.

A regular conservative commentator himself, Tony is introduced on the Sunday morning talk shows in Indianapolis as Vice Chairman of the 2016 Trump-Pence Indiana campaign. An immigrant himself, and with parents of Pakistani and Indian heritage, Tony is both an interesting demographic and the most "insider" person I've spoken to for this project. While one might say it is part of his job to speak positively about Trump, I have no doubt that Tony's views are deeply reasoned.

\#\#\#

TONY: There has to be police reform. What happened to George Floyd and others, it's horrific. But the racism, the talk of systemic racism? To me, I look at this country and see that I'm actually an example of it being the most accepting, the fairest, the least racist country in the history of the world. That's why we're a melting pot.

That's why people try to get to this country. People wouldn't want to be near my family if this was a racist country.

There *is* racism. I've seen it, I've experienced it. Maybe not as much as others, but more than some. That racism, though, is isolated. I'm a minority. I don't think of myself as a minority – in other parts of the world, I wouldn't be – but the way everyone looks at it, I am. And look at what I've done in the Republican party because I've worked hard, and I've built a good reputation.

Our president has also worked hard, and he's accomplished everything in the face of obstruction. I saw a bumper sticker that said, "I'm part of the resistance," and this resistance has been happening since before he even took office. We're finding out now that the Russian investigation was a set up and that his campaign was spot on. There were people in the FBI, not the majority, but people in leadership, that were investigating when they shouldn't have. The investigations were fake. And I don't mean to sound like the rhetoric! But I don't think it's rhetoric, I guess it's just truth. President Trump said, "fake Russia hoax," and that has been proven out. And the investigation cost more than $40 million taxpayer dollars.

Same thing with the impeachment; there was no reason for it except to bloody this president up before the election. Those two major attacks on the president from the left didn't result in anything because there was nothing there, but it distracted from his accomplishments. The president might be having a press conference on reducing the cost of prescription drugs, but in the news there's something about the impeachment, or whatever is going on, coinciding with his positive news. That's been going on for four years.

There was a news story in Chicago about parents having a Trump piñata and having their kids beat up this Trump piñata. I just looked to see where you could buy this piñata, and they're all sold out; the hate is spreading. And some people will say, "Well, it's both sides." I really don't think it's both sides. This kind of hate wasn't spread by the mainstream Republicans when Obama and Biden were in office.

I know the other side blames Trump for the hate, but I'm one that sees him as hitting back after he is attacked – just hitting back harder. Remember how low President Bush's approval ratings had fallen by the time he left office? That was because he was so viciously and continuously attacked – they called him "stupid" – and he never fought back. I'm not sure which strategy is better, because Trump's approval probably isn't much higher, but I'd rather have a President that fights back and is a bold leader. That's why I voted for him.

The big part of his message now is the accomplishments, and I think that's why Trump supporters that were there with him back in 2016 are still with him. He set out with a lot to do. In my role as Communications Director back then, I was on the phone with the national communications team every morning for calls, and then in the afternoon for another call, and they would set out policy initiatives. Those were the promises that he was making out on the campaign trail when we'd go see him. He set out to do a lot of things to help the American worker, and he fulfilled those promises...and then some. He even did things that he didn't talk about back on the campaign trail, like the creation of Space Force. I think Space Force is important, and it's fun for me as a *Star Trek* watcher all my life, but the Obama administration had cut NASA's funding to the point where we had to pay Russia and hitchhike on their rockets to get to the International Space Station. Now Space Force has been created and NASA has funding and plans to put the first woman on the moon; they'll go to Mars, put the first man and woman on Mars. That's just one of the additional things that he's promised and is on his way already to fulfilling.

On the economy, he gave us the biggest middle-class tax cut ever, putting thousands of dollars back into the hands of the average American working family. But he also cut regulations at the same time, encouraging businesses to grow, expand, and to hire more workers to come back from companies that had left to go to Mexico and Canada. He re-did trade agreements, which I think universally across the board is looked at as a major accomplishment. These trade deals with Japan, Canada and Mexico, these are major accomplishments! And the American people realize that.

The Obama administration depleted the military, but Trump has invested $2.5 trillion back in. At the same time, and this is important, he's kept us out of new wars. He's taken on the terrorists and the bad guys by taking out al-Baghdadi. That was a big deal to me because I remember – and I've still got a *USA Today* where the front page, the top of the fold, was a picture – the story about Kayla Mueller who had been captured and held by al-Baghdadi himself. Kayla's parents spoke at the Republican National Convention about how, if the Obama administration had acted quicker, their daughter could have been saved. They were convinced of that. From everything they knew back when Obama and Biden were in charge, they believed she could've been saved. And then the Trump administration went in and captured and killed al-Baghdadi! That's a big deal because I think of people like Kayla Mueller as anyone of us: my wife, my daughter, any neighbors, friends, friends' daughters.

Taking out General Soleimani who's from Iran, who's responsible for thousands of Americans being killed or injured in Iraq from IEDs, those kinds of things are important. But at the same time keeping us out of wars! Trump has said that a lot of these wars were just pointless, shouldn't have been started. And look at the loss of American lives, and all the wounded warriors that come home. Moving away from the previous few decades of wars led to him getting nominations for the Nobel Peace Prize. Also for bringing peace between the Israelis and the United Arab Emirates, the Israelis and the Iranians, his work in Kosovo, and then between the Turks and the Kurds. A lot of people don't know this kind of stuff. I follow it because it's important to me.

Building the wall was controversial, and obviously you don't hear as much about it now. The reason for the wall is to keep out gangs and drugs, and a lot of it's being built because a lot of folks do care about illegal immigration. Legal immigration, I'm all for it. As you know, I myself am an immigrant, being born in Manchester, England and coming here when I was three. We let in a million immigrants a year, but illegal immigration needed to be addressed. He's doing that, and doing it in the face of obstruction.

The Democratic party is moving more and more to the left. Maybe half my friends from my work at the Indiana State House are Democrats, but the Democrats that work here are not the ones moving their party to the left. A lot of them are having to go along with it, though. And by moving to the left, I do mean socialism. (I think it's even Marxism, but that's a whole different discussion.) It's dangerous for the Democratic party. Biden says there's a battle for the soul of the country; I really think it's a battle for the soul of the party.

And it's not your average Democrat going too far left, but it's some forces that are at the head making the calls and making the decisions. What's interesting is that many Trump supporters are also from the left of center, and I saw that in 2016. It's your blue-collar workers, your independent voter; it's your trucker, bikers, farmers, Vietnam vets. These are the folks we'd go out and meet with around the state, and they would tell us that they hadn't participated in the political process for decades; they were waiting for a guy like Donald Trump. Those same voters are still out there in 2020, and they may even be a little more hidden. They're not showing up in polling now, and maybe they're not going to have yard signs because there's a lot of intimidation going on, but they're still going to vote for Donald Trump. 56% in the Gallup poll a week or two ago said they're better off than four years ago. How can you say that when there's lockdowns, and COVID, and more cases and deaths? It's because the American public doesn't blame Donald Trump.

People were watching those coronavirus task force press conferences, those daily updates, so they remember that Trump was doing everything he could to supply the PPE, to get ventilators mass produced by using the Defense Production Act, to send the Naval hospital ships to New York and Los Angeles. The Army Corp of Engineers built hospitals, turned the Javits Center into a huge hospital for New Yorkers. Governor Cuomo and Governor Newsom back then were praising the administration's efforts. Voters remember that. And they know that Trump was the one that built that economy up to the best it's ever been. Even through COVID, it's already on the way back to where it was.

I was hoping that, once we got through the 2016 election, the American public would give him a chance. The folks on the far left didn't. I think a lot of Democrats did, but the party itself is trying to lead voters into hating President Trump, calling him a racist and all of that. I think he's going to win the 2020 election and it's going to be because voters are smarter than the Democratic party thinks they are.

And just real quick on the racism thing: I do this Sunday morning political show and the Charlottesville "very fine people on both sides" comment comes up often. I looked it up and saw that he was talking about folks arguing whether a Robert E. Lee statue should be taken down. Some were taking it down, some were against it, and those are the people he was talking about. Later, in that same talk, he said, "I'm not talking about the neo-Nazis and white nationalists because they should be condemned totally." The reason I'm bringing this up is that even Biden uses that incident and Trump's words, saying that's the reason he got into the presidential election. This is a false narrative for Biden. There are videos of Trump denouncing neo-Nazis and white supremacists and the KKK throughout and before his election, but that use of racism and the spreading of hate is what the leftist leadership in the Democratic party wants you to believe. My own Democratic friends are smarter than that.

I get frustrated when I see the hate, and I'm sure there's a bigger movement. It's not just Democrats; there's a bigger move. It's part of, I think, a socialist, Marxist movement. You can see what's happened in Yugoslavia, and also what's happened in other countries over the last several decades: Nicaragua, Southeast Asia. When this spreads – and it does – it takes the form of dividing people. That's what I think is happening in our country right now.

This country is at a crossroads. America leading the world in democracy and freedoms? I think that's in danger. We need to stay the course: this country has been the strongest country, the mostly economically strong country, and the country that others can look to and try to emulate. Other countries strive for our freedoms and our democracies and our liberties, but that's in jeopardy because of this Marxist socialist movement. If I sound like a conspiracy theorist – and I hope I don't – it's because I'd love for everybody to do some research on what's happening and connect the dots. China, a Marxist, communist country, does want to be the dominant player in the world.

You're party is different than the normal Democratic party that I grew up with. As a lobbyist, I work with Republicans *and* Democrats. These guys have been my friends for as long as I can remember, so it's not those folks. But there is a movement that is very dangerous.

One last thing, and it's actually the most important: Lily's thirteen now – almost fourteen – and Nolan's eleven. Lily's in eighth grade, Nolan in sixth. I've always done whatever I do politically for my family, especially my kids. When I think about where this country will be as they get older, I think about what's best for them. Ultimately, thinking about keeping them safe is why I want a President that keeps this nation strong. I thought that four years ago, and Trump has delivered by rebuilding the military while keeping us out of war, and by trying to achieve peace where it's not been for a long time. His support of our law enforcement is also critical, especially in the wake of all of the chaos and death and destruction in our cities. I talked about all of this before, but I want to emphasize the reason it matters most to me is because of my kids.

I think Trump's going to win Indiana by twenty-two points, more than the twenty I predicted that he won by last time. And I think he'll win the presidency again.

CHAPTER FORTY-THREE
The Natural Gas Rep (Again)

October, 2020
Little Rock, Arkansas

Tony's voice is one of reason. His facts and personal experiences speak for themselves, and yet his empathy runs opposite of mine. While I find myself regularly empathizing with those to whom Trump speaks unkindly, Tony's empathy moves to the president himself, discontent over the opposition Trump faces.

When we met years ago, Vickie was also discontent about the state of affairs in the country, though she placed a lot of blame specifically on Hillary Clinton. She's extremely savvy about the energy industry, having worked in natural gas her entire life. But I also remember her expressing, quite strongly, that jail time should be given to illegal protesters and those who destroy our flag. Empathy toward those who think differently didn't strike me as her default. She voted for Bill Clinton, but found true enthusiasm in her support of Trump. Has it lasted?

VICKIE: I'm sorry we kept missing each other, but I've been out working at the voting polls every day. Most of us here in Arkansas will be voting for Trump again.

I am retired and drawing five hundred dollars a month from my 401(k) money. Because of Donald Trump, the stock market has been good, the economy's been great, and my investments have been very stable.

He's fulfilled every promise – just about – that he made in his campaign. And anything that he couldn't do, it's because of all the things Democrats have done to stop him. He could have had a new healthcare plan, but they were so afraid of him undoing Obamacare that they fought him every step of the way.

Let me tell you about the polling. Yesterday, we had 530 people vote at the polling center I was at. Normally, they don't have 530 people vote the whole week! I think people are turning out in droves to vote for the president.

I had an eighty-something-year-old lady come in and vote for the first time – for Donald Trump – because they are Gold Star family. That's what she said to me. I've seen several young people come in that have just registered to vote. I've seen people come in wheelchairs. I've seen people come on crutches. I've seen crippled people come in, just to vote. I just feel like they're for Trump. I feel like Donald Trump got a majority here.

I met a lady from Sri Lanka. She said she'd loves Donald Trump, so her husband brought her in to vote. That was interesting. She's from another country. She knows what it's like there, so she loves America and she loves Donald Trump.

Also, this is the South and a lot of people hunt. They're afraid that Biden's going take their gun.

CHAPTER FORTY-FOUR
The Clinton Mistress (Again)

October, 2020
Little Rock, Arkansas

Vickie's last comment sticks with me: "They're afraid Biden's going to take their gun." Democrats continue to lose the propaganda war when it comes to this issue. At no time did Joe Biden or Hillary Clinton propose taking away guns, and yet so many in conservative America are fearful it will happen. Incremental, reasonable, bi-partisan changes to gun laws are all that Biden has ever proposed, but what does that matter if conservatives are convinced he is out to do much more? This should be a lesson in the dissemination of information, or at least a warning to more actively combat disinformation.

On the topic of disinformation, I'm back in touch with Sally, former Miss Arkansas. I've revisited her autobiography a few times over the years, pretending to be interested in her trek along the entire length of the Great Wall of China, but actually desiring to re-read the intimate details of her supposed affair with Bill Clinton. (Re-reading those details is a guilty pleasure.) Disinformation is key to Sally's current perspective, and the first bit of it disturbs me.

###

SALLY: I don't believe that George Floyd died. I believe he's somewhere with a new identity enjoying millions because he was "killed" by an actor, a guy who looked like a cop. Liberals created the hoaxes we've had in 2020; I think they shut down Trump's amazing economy because they couldn't stand that he was improving the country. America was looking damn good – people were happy and the economy was thriving – but Democrats had to throw a wrench in it. What they do best is create hate and divisiveness, so what better way to do it than through racism? I don't think America will survive if Trump doesn't get reelected.

You know from my book, *Sally Miller, The Beauty Queen,* that the biggest mistake I made was returning here to Arkansas. This is where my mother sexually abused me and my brother, this is where I had an affair with Bill Clinton. I came here to teach – I was a damn good teacher – but it ended up being a dead end because everyone in Arkansas knew my age, and how could I be a good teacher at the age of seventy-five?

I didn't want to retire, but here I am. I thought my teaching was so valuable; you know I qualified for Mensa when I was younger? But that conflicted with everyone's image of me; I couldn't be a beauty queen and be smart. Those two just don't go together, do they? I guess I was somewhat of a conflict most of my life and perhaps I still am. I live alone. There aren't too many "aloners" here like me, but probably I'm safer as an aloner. My daughters left me when my mother died and gave each one of them a million dollars. I guess maybe some of us are not meant to have a happy ending to our story, but I am determined to leave this world on a high note. I'll die with a smile on my face.

Now, back to Trump. I told you about my lunch with him many years ago. I was so impressed, and I still am. What makes him even greater is the fact that he has had to claw and fight every step of the way, not just to get *elected* president without being a politician, but he had to fight in order to *stay* president. Liberals have done everything possible to drag him down, to slaughter him, to kill his goals and play havoc with his life. I intend to vote for him because I think America is dead, it's gone, it's finished if he doesn't get reelected. Hate and jealousy is rampant among politicians; they feel entitled to strike back, hit, claw, destroy anyone who gets in their way. And Trump is getting in their way.

And these politicians become billionaires! You and I could write books all our lives and never end up with the kind of money these people get for doing nothing. My life has changed because I'm living on social security now, so I'm not doing what I really want to do with my life: to sell books and be a speaker. When I was a senior in high school, I had my own television show. Now? Well, sometimes we don't get exactly what we want out of life. I, like Donald Trump, have had to struggle every step of the way.

I've done things and been places the beauty queens never show up. And my goals have been realized in a way that beauty queens most often don't realize goals, like spending seven months on the Great Wall of China and averaging thirty miles a day to inch along. The parts that were climbable, I climbed. The parts that were runnable, I ran. And the parts that weren't there, I had to find them because I wanted this to be an absolute documentation of the Great Wall from west to east. Being alone on that trek was always frightful, and perhaps when I was alone in China day after day I was preparing myself for being alone when I was older... like right now. If I died tomorrow, I can say I had success throughout most of my life but, like Donald Trump, I had to work my butt off to get it. You can either be a survivor or a victim, and I never want to be seen as a victim.

I applied for an unusual job. Donald Trump removed the diplomat to China, and I know China well from having lived there, so I thought – just for fun – I'm going to write a little note to the White House saying, "Donald Trump, I feel as qualified as anyone to be the ambassador to China, and here's why." Now, I didn't hear from him, but perhaps that's because I also didn't send a resume. I just sent it as a little email to the White House and said, "Please get this to Donald Trump's attention." I could pursue it, and I still may, but right now he's in the fight for his life. He is in the shark tank game, and he's with the alligators and snakes. After he wins in November, he'll be back swimming in a clean tank without any swamp trash. At that time, I may decide to send my resume and officially apply. I think anything's possible.

Trump doesn't wear his age like a number around his neck. I don't believe he's ever had a facelift, but I do know that Joe Biden has had several. But the worst thing about Joe Biden, the thing that scares me most of all, is the videos – and I know they weren't doctored – of him playing with little girls' breasts. He likes to tweak the nipples of young girls. I'm talking girls that are seven, eight, nine, ten. He likes to tweak their breasts, their nipples, and that is seriously sick.[94] I want to distance every child in America from such sickness. And those aren't things you can ignore; those aren't things you can change. My mother was seriously sick in the same way, but in the days that I grew

---

[94] I agree that these videos are disturbing, though I disagree with Sally's assessment of deliberate "playing with" and "tweaking."

up people hid those kinds of sicknesses. Anyone who's running for President of the United States should be scrutinized.

CHAPTER FORTY-FIVE
The Poly Sci Veteran (Again)

October, 2020
Kansas City, Missouri

Much of what Sally said, I must take with a grain of salt. She's lost so much credibility because of her belief that George Floyd's death was faked. I'm having a hard time paying attention to any other viewpoint because of her bold stance on this one, but I recall my own directive from the introduction to this book: "Yes, many characters in this journey will repeat conservative media talking points that are categorically untrue. But they will do so because the talking points support their pre-existing feelings, and those feelings must be understood if our opposing parties are ever to achieve domestic Tranquility. If a liberal reader is open enough to hear the other side, I challenge that reader not to dismiss a conservative's entire story if a supposed fact is deemed false. The conservative media has power to indoctrinate, and we liberals have been unduly influenced by our own media, too. The underlying feelings are what interest me here, and empathy is a tool for understanding." Can I adhere to my own instruction? Sally has a vote, and her feelings are real. If for only that reason, I must consider them.

Three years ago, during a flash flood in Kansas City, William and I met to discuss our differing feelings. He fell in that specific, yet large, category of those who supported Trump due primarily to a strong dislike for Hillary Clinton. He felt her responses during the Benghazi hearings were unconscionable, whereas I felt them to be vindicating. He's a veteran with a son in the 82nd Airborne; I'll be curious how he feels about Trump's military actions.

###

WILLIAM: Trump was in the process of fulfilling most of what I had hoped for. Unfortunately, everything now is overlaid by COVID, a situation that – despite what the press has to say – I don't think anybody here in the U.S. can take the blame for. Including him.

He was doing a spectacular job fulfilling his campaign promises. Unemployment was crashed. There were more jobs than there were people looking for them. That's about all you can ask for.

My life has changed a little bit since he came to office. Making a little more money, but not tremendously more. Part of that is because of – forgive me – the unwillingness of the left to accept his election. He spent a lot of time and energy on stuff that amounted to nothing. I'm very disappointed that the left will not accept the election, move on, and let the administration function.

I think Trump has tried to expose a lot of things about the left that a lot of us didn't know, and that a lot of people who consider themselves Democrats didn't know. I know a lot of them don't want to admit it, but there are a lot of people that I have considered friends for years and years and years that are Democrats who are going to vote Democrat because they're being used. I think they're being used to trigger an agenda that they wouldn't really approve of.

Being rationally objective, we can see that President Trump has already accomplished some amazing things. But people have to look without already deciding, "Orange man: bad. I hate him."

Thinking he's "icky" doesn't really seem a good reason to hate the guy or to not vote for him. It doesn't make a lot of sense to me.

I quit talking to my friends on the left about this after a while, but I used to quote statistics. This is prior to COVID, because COVID put the pause button on everything. But prior to COVID, I would show them how we'd knocked down unemployment. We had record numbers from minority job participation, huge record numbers that the press didn't ever want to talk about. Gosh, I wonder why?! But the really sad thing to me is that the hatred on the left has gotten so strong that even people I consider intelligent, smart folks won't accept these statistics. The reaction is just so hostile. I've actually had people say to me that none of the job statistics are true. I would respond rationally and ask them to do the same. "Don't take my word for it. Never take anybody's word for it! Go look it up yourself." But from my liberal friends, what I get is, "I don't have to look it up. I know better." They're shorting themselves, horribly. And they're going to create a huge problem in this country.

The violence from the left right now is unspeakable and has to stop. And I don't really believe that my friends who are Democrats truly support that kind of violence, but on the other hand, I never hear them saying that it needs to stop. But it does have to stop. Or we're all in a lot of trouble.

Anyway, that's my two cents. I was surprised to hear you are using my comments! I'm very curious how they come across.

CHAPTER FORTY-SIX
The Red Cross Fundraiser (Again)

October, 2020
Detroit, Michigan

William studied Political Science, served in two branches of the military, and is interested in conversations with liberals around statistics. It can't be denied that Trump had some great economic and job numbers pre-COVID, but it can certainly be argued that they were trending upward for years, irregardless of Trump's actions. William's assertion that liberals don't want to listen to or investigate facts and figures? Let's hope that's not true. Skepticism, rationalism, and radical centrism all demand neutral questioning of every assumption, and neutral questioning is what I'm promising myself to continue to do.

The idea of promise-keeping is a common theme with those who continue to support President Trump. Though PolitiFact rates President Obama more successful, Trump has a decent record of campaign promises kept. These promises seem to matter more than anything else to Trey in Detroit. He's the one who works in fundraising and development for the Red Cross, a noble endeavor that pairs with his asking me not to make him "look bad" in print. I recall his enthusiasm from our first meeting; he's an exuberant young man who had a blast at a Pence event, describing the scene as a "pep rally" where he laughed and chanted, "Lock her up! Lock her up!"

###

TREY: My hopes have been restored in America! President Trump has kept every promise that he made before he went into office: building the wall, making sure there was a ton of economic prosperity before the pandemic hit, and not being a traditional politician. That's why I like him so much. He doesn't blow smoke. He does what he says. He doesn't speak how the media wants him to speak and he takes them head on.

My life is actually better now because his tax cut gave us more money. I saw a $100 increase per check under the President's tax cut.[95] My life is better now because I feel a stronger sense of pride in America. I feel the patriotism that was lacking under President Obama. And life is better because law and order is being restored, despite all the crazy riots and people trying to bring our president down.

The media, the deep swamp, and everybody else are so clearly against him! It's disheartening to watch the news so continually try to put out false narratives. And they're not really after President Trump as a person; what they're after is to change our way of life, to change our country into a socialist country. That's my view. That's what I believe.

Trump has kept his promises. Our country will always need a strong leader – not an apologist – and that's why I'm voting for him again.

---

[95] Me, too.

CHAPTER FORTY-SEVEN
The Planned Parenthood Nurse (Again)

October, 2020
Fayetteville, Arkansas

Trey's logic is simple enough to understand: he agreed with Trump's campaign promises, and he thinks that they are being fulfilled. The liberal counter to that might only be to combat the campaign promises themselves as they're being made. Did Hillary Clinton do that deliberately enough? Is Biden?

Up on Stone Mountain in Fayetteville, Linda and her husband offered me some homemade strawberry shortcake and a fine wine during our first visit in 2017. I recall a lovely afternoon of talk and debate, fueled by the headiness of afternoon Chardonnay. Today, Linda's mood is more deliberate; she's come with a written outline of what she'd like to share.

###

LINDA: I've lived in California, and the 9th Circuit was just so liberal! But now, more conservative judges have been appointed there and a high percentage of their decisions were overturned. More judges have also been appointed to district courts. If I have my numbers correct, and I need to fact-check this, but I believe more than one hundred district judge openings were not filled by Obama and came over for President Trump to do it. And he got it done.[96]

---

96 Fact checking on behalf of Linda, I see that she is technically correct. On the other hand, the reason Obama had empty judicial appointments for Trump to fill is that they were largely blocked by a

The Trumps have shown families across America how to work together and how to bond. They're a beautiful family. Budgets for the White House staff are interesting. Especially look at the number of staff and staff costs of Melania versus Michelle. I think Michelle had about twenty-eight people on her staff and – fact-check – I think that Melania has only four or five.[97] Also, the Trumps go to vacation in New Jersey or Florida, and the Obamas had to go to Hawaii. Think about the cost of operating Air Force One.[98]

Since Trump took office, my life has not changed that much. However, lives for other people have improved, particularly the opportunities for low-wage workers and for Black Americans. I'm glad to see that. If it weren't for COVID-19, we would be seeing record breaking improvement for jobs.

Trump carried through with the border wall; we have four hundred miles of new border-crossing protection. He pointed out that Obama built the cages for Hispanic children. Trump did not build them; Obama built them.[99] He has worked closely with science and the CDC to manage COVID-19 without causing hysteria. When you have a national and international pandemic, you want Trump standing up there saying, "We're going to take care of this. We're going to take care of it. It may happen sooner rather than later or later versus sooner, but we're on it." He closed travel from China, which all the Democrats were very critical of, because it was the right thing to do. It was a very insightful thing to do.

Trump showed that the Democrats had no sense of humor. For example, when he said, "Maybe we should drink Clorox, or maybe put Clorox in our veins and it kills it." That was humor! But it was just ridiculous how the Democrats jumped on it and talked about how we kill people. Give me a break.

Republican-controlled Senate. On the *other* other hand, both Reagan and Bush managed to get through more judicial appointments than Obama when they faced an opposing-party Senate.

[97] These numbers are found on a popular Facebook meme, but they are not accurate. Michelle Obama did have more than double the number of staffers as Melania Trump, but PolitiFact reminds us that Michelle Obama also had a much larger public agenda to support.

[98] At the time of this writing, Trump's vacations have cost about $36 million more than Obama's.

[99] Correct. Linda has got me fact-checking everything she says, and it is true that the 72-hour holding "cages" were approved and built during the Obama administration. However, Obama's policies did not force the separation of children and their parents in these cages, whereas Trump's "zero-tolerance" policy split up families regularly.

CHAPTER FORTY-EIGHT
The Southern Northerner (Again)

October, 2020
Norfolk, Virginia

My promise is to remain skeptical with both parties, and Linda's encouragement to fact-check her led to either 50% or 75% (in her favor) on the truth-meter. Inviting my theme of empathy to come back into play, however, it bothers me to see Linda dismiss Trump's comments about disinfectants being used in the human body as a joke. Trump was not joking; he was riffing on results of a real study that he — apparently — did not fully comprehend. I would not fault a scientist for exploring outside-of-the-box ideas, but I expect more empathy from a leader in time of crisis. Riffing on unrealistic possibilities… is that empathy for those suffering? Or is it dangerous, false hope?

What I remember most about Dave is his empathy for the plight of his wife as a dedicated public school teacher, and what I perceived then as befuddlement over his own support for Donald Trump. I really enjoyed Dave as a person and felt that his Christian-centered outlook was constantly forcing him to re-balance his political views. I suspect his support for our president may have waned, due to years of what I perceive as immorality in Trump's judgement. Will Dave be the first one here to change his vote?

###

DAVE: I do remember our nice chat in downtown Norfolk, and I'm sorry to learn you're still a liberal New Yorker! But I hope you've survived the pandemic and not been affected by the ravaging of it in New York. And I hope you've been safe even as crime has increased in New York thanks to a defunding of the police. I just hope the economy survives in New York since a lot of people seem to be leaving due to high taxes and general safety concerns. Anyway, I do appreciate the chance to follow up. I never thought I'd hear from you again.

The main reason I feel my hopes for President Trump have been fulfilled is that our country is strong and respected on the world stage again. Trump took the handcuffs off the military and increased their funding. He removed us from a multitude of what he and many feel were bad deals for America, and just took overall positive steps for America in so many areas.

For example, once he let the military loose, we recovered all the ground that had been lost to ISIS under the Obama administration. We don't hear too much about ISIS anymore. We're slowly bringing our troops home from the Middle East. (That's something I wish would happen more; it's not happening fast enough.) I'm very pleased that we moved our embassy to Jerusalem and that we're now supporting Israel rather than its neighbors. I'm glad to see the recent announcements of a Mideast peace deals with Israel and some of the neighboring countries. And we're told the more that is on the way.

Trump's obviously been very strong against China, Russia, and North Korea, trying to engage where possible, but being firm where necessary. China has been killing us by stealing our intellectual property and forcing companies that go into that country to be under the monitoring of the Communist party, but things are turning around there and I think that's really good. Gosh, we're out of that Iran nuclear deal where we gave them all that cash, the Paris Climate Accord, the Trans-Pacific Partnership. None of those deals were good for our country; they could have been better deals. I think we have a much better "new deal," so to speak, with Canada and Mexico.

On the home front, the liberal opposition has been just unbelievably fierce, corrupt, hate-filled. The Democratic party and others dominate so much of our society now, unfortunately. Until the virus came in from China, so much had been accomplished. Our economy was very, very strong. Unemployment was very, very low. Why? I would say because we lowered our corporate and individual tax rates and we cut a lot of unnecessary regulations that had grown and grown and grown over the years, making it so hard to do business.

I'm very pleased to see all the federal judgeships that have been filled. We need judges who will interpret the existing law, which is what a judge is supposed to do, rather than trying to take on the job of Congress or the legislative branch and put their own spin on the law.

I'm very pleased that illegal immigration and border security are really being addressed. We've got the border wall construction, we've got great enforcement now on the border, we've ended catch-and-release. Mexico is really supporting us and putting troops on the border, too.

What I think about most is our schools, since my wife is retired schoolteacher and I know her challenges and troubles. We have so many examples of poor inner-city schools, and the Trump administration is trying to address that by making school choice more available. It's a tough battle when most of the cities have liberal governors. And then the teachers' union takes dues from all the teachers, no matter what their beliefs are, and gives donations to the Democratic party! So, school choice is a tough row to hoe.

Trump's policies have given a lot of help to the minority community with job training programs; that doesn't get a lot of talk. We have heard about better funding for historically Black colleges and universities. He's also addressing criminal justice through the First Step Act. All those things are very helpful for the minority communities.

Another big positive for Trump is making our country energy independent while still being environmentally sensitive. I think carbon emissions have dropped.[100]

He's trying hard to replace Obamacare but hasn't gotten that done. That's a disappointment, but at least Trump has gotten rid of that individual mandate tax. We must, must do everything possible to avoid the true intention of Obamacare, which was to drive us to a single-payer, government-controlled health system. Not good. That would be a disaster.[101]

---

[100] Carbon emissions have decreased slightly during Trump's administration, but at a slower rate than they decreased during the Obama administration.

[101] 86.2% of Canadians don't think this would be a disaster, according to a current Nanos Research poll. And I wonder if Americans think it would be a disaster mostly because of Wendell Potter's decades-long disinformation campaign on behalf of CIGNA?

A hope I had that has not been realized is that our nation would become more unified these past few years. We had the perfect opportunity: a non-politician, a man with a great family, a man who seemed to be loved by all on the left and the right. But it just hasn't happened, obviously.

Little did I know in 2016 that, to distract everybody from her destruction of thirty thousand emails and numerous electronic devices, Hillary Clinton would be the one secretly devising the "Trump colluded with Russia" strategy. And little did I know back then that the Obama administration would actually spy on the Trump campaign. They basically weaponized the federal law enforcement and criminal justice system to attack the Trump administration. And we all know what that led to: the Mueller investigation, impeachment. All crazy, crazy stuff that came up empty! But they harmed Trump, harmed his administration, and harmed our country immeasurably.

And our media, good God, has forsaken all semblance of objectivity and are now actively promoting the Democratic party and the leftist agenda. They pretty much ignore everything positive that the Trump administration does. If they do a story or an article about something positive, the wording just always has a negative slant. Their headlines never really tell the story. They're just all slanted in a negative way.

The two so-called "town halls" that Biden and Trump participated in were a metaphor for lack of unification and corruption of the media. You had one on ABC with George Stephanopoulos serving up softballs and cotton candy to "hidin' Biden," and then on NBC you had pit bull Savannah Guthrie foaming at the mouth. She posed over forty questions and basically turned a town hall into her private debate with Trump. She only allowed ten of the citizens attending that town hall to ask questions. The way those two town halls were orchestrated is a perfect illustration of what's wrong with our country.[102]

And now we have all the stories coming out about the Joe Biden family and Hunter Biden and their connections while Biden was Vice President. The family got rich through Ukraine deals, through Russian deals, through Chinese deals. But it's not news! Can you imagine if Trump and his son were doing what Biden and his son

---

[102] During these Town Hall debates, Trump was asked nine questions from the audience, compared to Biden's eleven. Why? Biden's event was a full thirty minutes longer. That seems equitable to me.

did? It would be front page news in the boldest letters you've ever seen. Now it's being hidden from the news; it's not on TV, it's not in my newspaper in Norfolk. And you know the social media folks like Twitter, Facebook, and Google are hiding it; they're doing everything they can to hide it. It's literally shameful and despicable. That's what it is.

So let's wrap it up. How is my life better? Well, our country is stronger and we're now promoting traditional values and helping stem the tide of a shift to radical socialism. You know, maybe that radical socialism is gonna be our future. History says democracies don't last forever, and I can certainly understand why based on the country I'm living in.

We've got crazy ideas like the Green New Deal, the hatred of AOC and the Squad, Antifa, and the good sentiment behind the Black Lives Matter movement that's – unfortunately – backed up by an organization that is anti-American.

We've got rioters burning and looting with no consequences in our cities, and now we have Joe Biden who is allowed to tell Black people when they're Black and when they're not! It's just amazing.[103]

The leftist agenda has got Nancy Pelosi holding up the second coronavirus relief bill that would get checks in the hands of people because she wants more money to bail out Democratic states. We keep reading about George Soros funding liberal district attorneys and county prosecutors around the country. They no longer want to support law enforcement. They no longer want to enforce the law. And they no longer want to put criminals in jail. I don't think that's what most of America wants.

We've morphed into a world of cancel culture. We no longer have tolerance for people with different views. In fact, not only do we no longer tolerate different views, but we actively oppose them. We actively disallow them. It's just funny how the diversity crowd can't handle diversity of thought and will do anything to shut it down.[104]

Everything seems to be about race now. Every issue has a racial component. "Everything white people do is racial. Everything white people have done is racial, and they're bad people just because

---

[103] Joe Biden on The Breakfast Club, a radio program: "If you have a problem figuring out whether you're for me or Trump, then you ain't Black."

[104] I consider myself part of the "diversity crowd," but I keep Dave's words intact because I too believe in diversity of thought. He makes a point against "cancel culture" that interests me, and I hope he'll view this book as me putting my money where my mouth is, allowing for diversity of thought on my own platform.

they're white." That seems to be the message. I reject that. Obama was elected by a racist country? Elected not once, but twice?

What an opportunity Obama had, only to squander it. He said he wanted to fundamentally transform America. That kind of sounded cool at the time. But combine that with Hillary calling all the Republicans "deplorables" and it clearly shows that the intent was not honorable. The intent was not pro-America. The intent was to tear down the traditional America that has taken us to where we are today.

Obviously, Trump has my vote again. He's the better candidate. He's got a better family. He's healthy. And I know it drives the left and the Democrats absolutely bonkers that he got the coronavirus whipped in a week and was back on normal duty. The man works from sunrise to midnight every day with an incredible energy for somebody his age; you have to contrast that with Joe Biden who speaks once or twice a day in front of small crowds. And Biden has a history of a funny behavior around women, a funny history of racial commentary.

The big thing that makes it easy for me to support Donald Trump again is that Joe Biden selected Kamala Harris for a running mate. I believe most people will categorize her the most liberal United States Senator. She is she is actively raising bail money for those protesting and rioting and looting in our cities.[105] She has a reputation as a prosecutor that didn't do a very good job. I read an article recently of her total failure prosecuting the pedophilia aspect of the clergy in Los Angeles and San Francisco. Normally, I wouldn't consider the choice of running mate a big deal, but given Biden's health, age, and weak mental capacity, the prospect of Kamala Harris being our president sooner rather than later is a scary thing for me.

Anyway, I thank you so much for being willing to listen further and I hope I've been helpful. I'm not a very theatrical person like you. I guess it comes from being an accountant and CPA.

---

[105] From their website: "The Minnesota Freedom Fund believes that every individual who has been arrested by the police is innocent until proven guilty, and if a judge deems them eligible for bail, they should not have to wait in jail simply because they don't have the same income or resources as others with more privilege."

CHAPTER FORTY-NINE
The Car Guy (Again)

October, 2020
Lebanon, Pennsylvania

Well, Dave is certainly not changing his vote as I suspected he might. In the intervening years, I'd forgotten Dave's very real fear of Islamic terrorism, and I see now that the absence of ISIS in our daily news is something that he feels quite tangibly. My job is to learn from this, to empathize with his fear and the fact that it has been largely absolved. But what of his comments on racism? He fundamentally does not believe racism exists systematically in this country, else Obama would not have been elected twice. While I understand his strict point, I find it difficult to empathize with his complaint.

Robert in Pennsylvania was spending much of his time caring for his wife when we met years ago. Dementia was taking her slowly, and the toll on him was obvious. Sure, he brought a gun – and a friend with a gun – to our public meeting, and sure he made a violent joke about Obama as we were saying goodbye, but… Empathy is difficult sometimes, but I do wonder how Robert's wife is doing.

###

ROBERT: My wife of thirty-four years passed away January 6th, 2020; she was a Trump supporter, too. I know that the stock market's going up and the economy is already picking back up during the pandemic. My life has improved financially, as far as it goes. Business wise, yes, my life has improved. But losing my wife was the worst thing that I could handle. I'm trying – trying – to move on.

Trump has been of the best presidents we have ever had, and he's delivered on everything he promised. The problem is that Democrats are fighting him all the way, especially Nancy Pelosi, Chuck Schumer, and all the other crooked bastards that are down there. And that you can put in as a quote.

I will vote for Trump again, and I will vote for his daughter when she runs. (Either she's going to run or Donald Jr's going to run.) No matter what, I will never ever, ever, ever, ever vote Democrat for any position in this great United States of America; never will I do it again. They are corrupt, they are communist, they are not good for the American people and not good for our country. So, that can be a quote also.

Right now, I'm watching a "Make America Great" gathering down at Willet, Pennsylvania. I'm actually watching from my basement because I wasn't able to attend.

You know, I see a lot of people here going back to work. If Governor Tom Wolf would open the state, our economy would be going through the roof. But all Democrat governors are keeping our states shut down, lying about the numbers, lying about this so-called virus. People are dying, yes, but it's not because of the virus. They're dying of everything else, like the flu or suicide. I had a friend got killed in a car accident – head splattered – they said he died of COVID.[106]

Trump is the man; he has my support. Does he lie? Yeah. Is he bold? Yes. Does he care about what anybody thinks of him? No. And that's why I'm voting for him again: the man loves our country. I don't care what he does in his personal life; that's his business.

If Trump loses this election, it's due to the corrupt Democrats with this virus and this mail-in voting; it's going to be one of the biggest setups you've ever seen. My wife's got four – count them – *four* votes now. "Ballots," as they call it. My wife has been deceased since January 6th of this year, and I've got four ballots for her. How many other people like her are the Democrats sending out ballots to?[107]

I will vote for Trump again, my son, and I have umpteen businessmen that will, too. I can tell you about fifty names that are

---

[106] This is difficult to verify as true or false without asking Robert to reveal his friend's name, which I don't feel is appropriate. But it is quite easy to find reports of car accident victims in Pennsylvania who were brought to a hospital only to test positive and die of COVID during their stay. I find it hard to believe that a victim who died on the scene of an accident would be counted as a COVID fatality.

[107] Of course, signature matches are confirmed by teams of bipartisan election officials to prevent mail-in ballots from being abused.

voting for Trump that are in the same business that I do. My tenants and neighbors all have flags up; I have flags up.

Even my sister's going to vote for Trump, and she's diehard Democrat. She's voting Trump because you have *nobody*. The Democrats have nobody that's even fit to be in office, especially Joe Biden. And that hoe that they want to bring, Kamala or whatever the hell her name is, I can't stand the woman.

I will not be a socialist; I will fight to the end. They *will* not take my guns, they *will* not take my freedom, and you can quote me on everything I said. You want to put in my address? Go right ahead, I don't care. I mean, I really don't care what these little libtards are running around crying about.

CHAPTER FIFTY
The Immigrant Fan (Again)

October, 2020
Syracuse, New York

Robert makes empathy challenging. His wife passes, so I feel sad and can understand his desire to connect with a community; conservatives sure can lift each other with pep-rally energy. On the other hand, he refers to Senator Kamala Harris as a "hoe," negating much of my softer feeling for what he's been through. One vote per person, though, and he's one of them. (In a battleground state, no less.) For that reason, I feel it's worth understanding his stance and offering him space to articulate it.

When I met Anthony the first time, the visit helped me articulate what I see as a trend in immigrant supporters of Donald Trump. The common mantra: "If I was able to get to America legally, why can't you?" He was adamant at the time, so I'm not expecting any change in his vote in 2020.

\#\#\#

ANTHONY: We have an outsider now, and it was refreshing to see someone get elected and actually do what they said they were going to do. He kept all of his promises and more, which was really, really gratifying. I'm proud of the fact that he's stabilizing the world; he didn't create World War III like a lot of people said he was going to do. In fact, he's become a peacemaker. His "peace through strength" philosophy seems to be working. He's working with a lot of different countries, teaching them how to get along and how to develop trade deals.

Take a look at ISIS: he got rid of the caliphate; you don't hear about ISIS anymore. He's got South Korea and North Korea somewhat stabilized, he's holding China accountable, he's got a lot of sanctions on Russia, he's got a peace agreement with Israel. Look at the United Arab Emirates, and Kosovo, and Serbia. And he's been nominated for the Nobel Peace prize three times. I really, really like his foreign policy.

Before the pandemic hit, we had a hundred-sixty million American people working, the most in our history. Unemployment was at a record low for all different races. Black unemployment was the lowest it's ever been, and Asian, and for women. He really had it going on prior to the pandemic. This pandemic came out of China, and I can't imagine what was going through President Trump's mind. I mean, here comes something that we don't know anything about, and his instincts were to put a travel ban on China in January because he's got hundreds of millions people to worry about. He wanted to send our people over to China to find out what's going on, even while Dr. Fauci said this wasn't going to impact the United States.[108]

As we start learning about this pandemic, we find out that it's a disease that spreads really fast. So Trump uses the private sector, and uses FEMA, and uses the military, and he got all kinds of PPE, gowns, and face masks, and had all kinds of companies making ventilators, and he shuts the country down to flatten the curve. He built hospitals in New York and Louisiana, sent ships to New York. And really, when it gets down to it, it's the responsibility of the governors of the fifty states to keep their people safe and healthy. Trump did a tremendous job of providing everything that he could, but he's also got to worry about other things, you know what I mean? The economy, the livelihood of everybody, his stimulus program… His CARES Act gave money to all kinds of businesses to try to keep them afloat because it was nobody's fault; it wasn't their fault.

And what's going on in these Democratic states is just mind-boggling. Antifa is a terrorist organization. I mean, they don't care about Black lives. If they did, they wouldn't be burning down Black businesses and killing Black police officers. And everything that Trump has done now, despite the fact that from day one – from day

---

[108] In fact, on February 19th, 2020, Dr. Fauci said the coronavirus risk, "right now, today, currently, is really relatively low for the American public, but that could change." During the same interview, he also said, "This could evolve into a global pandemic, which would have significant implications for us."

one, they've tried to remove a duly elected president – they're spying on his campaign. They did the Russian collusion investigation for three years and there's no proof, there's nothing. They spent all kinds of taxpayer dollars to prove that Trump and his campaign colluded with Russia, and there's nothing. Then he makes a simple phone call to Ukraine, and they try to impeach him. Go all the way back to January, this man's got all this on his plate with the China virus, and what are the Democrats doing? They're trying to impeach him. That's what they're focused on.

I'm really concerned right now. I just don't understand the media, and Big Tech, and how biased they are towards conservatives. They are taking away our rights of free speech. They don't want to investigate fairly. We got all these things that are coming out about Joe Biden, and Hunter Biden, and all the stuff that happened allegedly with Hillary Clinton, and none of that stuff wants to be investigated by the FBI. I've learned through this process that our government is one of the most corrupt governments in the world. There's so many things that have been exposed because Donald Trump is not the establishment, and they don't like him because he's exposed them. It's totally unfair.

He doesn't get any positive press coverage, despite all of the things that he's accomplished. He brought prescription drug prices down, he's bringing our troops back home, he's given us the biggest tax cuts in American history, he brought the corporate tax rate from 38% down to 21%, the stock market is through the roof. There's so many great things, but it is overshadowed by what has been going on in Washington for almost four years. And it's not just the Democrats; Trump has hardly any support from the Republicans either. They're just as bad, just as corrupt. It's a swamp.

And the progressives have gone way, way, way to the left, so all of our principals are in jeopardy. Here in New York State, Andrew Cuomo has become a dictator. I mean, it's a fact. It's a fact that he signed an executive order ordering sick people to go into nursing homes. That's why we've had so many coronavirus deaths in this state.[109] I mean, we overcame fascism, we overcame communism, we overcame two world wars, plagues all over the place. America, we have inalienable rights! We are free people and our so-called

---

[109] Governor Cuomo's executive order around nursing home admittance is widely regarded as misguided, but certainly did not "order sick people to go into nursing homes." PolitiFact concludes, however, that many nursing homes "believed they had no other choice" under the order than to accept COVID-positive patients.

politicians, who don't understand that they work for the American people, are slowly trying to take away our rights.

Of course I'm going to vote again for Trump. We don't have a choice. You want a free, fair democracy? You're not going to get that with the Biden administration. Because even if Biden wins, he's not going to be there long. It's going to be Kamala Harris. And the Democratic Party is going to be running this country with that Green New Deal. They're going to raise taxes. China is going to start controlling us again. All the trade deals will be reversed. It's really, really scary.

Trump is probably the most liberal Republican that will ever be in office. He believes in *all* the American people, and the man is willing to give. He's willing to give back to the American people. He's willing. All over the place, wages have risen. Median income has come up $3000 to $5,000 per household. There's just so many positive things!

Three Supreme Court justices he's appointed are going to be on the bench, which is going to affect the next fifty years of our lives. All we want is for someone on the Supreme Court to follow the law, follow the Constitution, and not make decisions based on politics or feelings. Just based on the law, the law. The Democrats go on about illegal aliens, the border wall, and amnesty, while Trump follows the law. And the Democrats don't even try to change the law, they just want talking points. That's all they ever want: talking points. They don't do anything. For instance, they talk about Black people. What has the Democratic Party done for Black people in the last fifty years? Nothing. They just use them, *use them*, because they have no agenda. They never have an agenda. They never have policies. They just want to demagogue and obstruct, and that's what they did with Donald Trump for four years.

We have so much opportunity. It's just incredible that this could all be taken away, and we will be Venezuela on steroids. Nancy Pelosi trying to put in that 25th Amendment?[110] That's not about Donald Trump. That's about removing Joe Biden. That's what it's all about, because the radicals and extremists are going to run this country. They want to erase our history.

There will be a red wave on November 3rd. A red wave, and Donald Trump will be reelected in a landslide because people want

---

[110] I mean, the 25th Amendment was passed in 1965. (But that's just me being snarky; I understand Anthony's point.)

law and order. People want safe communities. This movement with so-called Black Lives Matter – which is basically Antifa – is what this country will look like if Joe Biden and Kamala Harris get into office. But it's not going to happen. The American people will rise.

Dan, you're a great man. I appreciate you giving me the opportunity to speak. As you know, I'm very, very passionate about this. I wasn't really into politics before, but it's consumed a lot of my time over the last four years because I'm liking what's going on and people don't even know about it. Trump has to use Twitter to get his message out because the media doesn't want to report it. They talk about, "Oh, Trump, if you lose, is there going to be a peaceful transition?" Oh, there'll be a peaceful transition, but how about the fact that you never, ever accepted the fact that that man was elected to be the 45th President of the United States and he's been mistreated from day one?

I'm a patriot. I really care about this country. I care about all people, all people, all people. We are this shining star on a hill, this beacon of hope for the world, and that's the reason people want to come here. But if Donald Trump isn't reelected, it'll start going the other way. People will just leave the country.

CHAPTER FIFTY-ONE
The Health Care Italian (Again)

October, 2017
Cranston, Rhode Island

Anthony believes himself a patriot. Time and again, Trump supporters have expressed how much they believe in the idea of country and American pride. Have their reports here illuminated any reason why they feel so strongly? Is there something about each individual that makes them see a businessman and television personality like Trump as representing national pride? Or, as I suspect, is it just Trump's excellent branding?

Victor spoke with pride about his Italian father when last we communicated. It is his father's work ethic that drives Victor to drive: he spends countless highway hours driving an expansive four-state healthcare sales territory because industry changes led to layoffs at his company, and he's got to get the job done. (Well, if I recall, he's got a lot of jobs to get done. In addition to healthcare sales, he owns vending machines, invests in real estate, manages rental properties...) I can only assume Victor was doing well in the strong pre-COVID economy, but I wonder what it is like as the pandemic draws on?

###

VICTOR: I'm not going to say that Trump's been absolutely perfect, but it's definitely been a fun ride these past four years, and I am excited about a number of things. I purchase stocks individually with any extra money that I accumulate; I always get in the market. I enjoy reading about companies and making a decision on whether or not there's going to be growth, and whether or not it's a good investment, and putting my money where my mouth is. The market's traditionally driven by investor confidence, and investors have had a ton of confidence in the Trump presidency. The markets have been unbelievable. The amount of return I've had just in his four years is greater than I've ever expected. There's some stocks, Amazon, Google, Facebook, where I'm up almost 100% on, which is unheard of. I mean, this is stuff that you hope to get over the course of thirty years, let alone four.

The economy is definitely the number one most exciting. Second, I'm happy to see what's going on with the wall. I don't know exactly how many miles have been built, but I do know that the wall is being built to some degree. I don't think it's as large as it needs to be, but the very fact that it's finally being addressed and is getting done, I believe is a good thing. I believe it's a good thing for our border security officers to have more protection between themselves and people that are trying to get across the border.

Whether those people be mothers traveling with their children or drug smugglers, they need to be able to feel as though the government is trying to protect them and keep our borders safe. There are mixed reviews as to how *much* of the wall's been built, but I'm just happy it's going on at all.

I'm happy about getting out of the Paris Agreement. I'm not saying it's something I would want to stay out of forever; I would certainly be open to us getting back involved if it made more sense for us as a country. But getting out is better than China being able to renege on it in five or ten years, and us having been stuck paying in the whole time.

I would also say that I'm very happy with President Trump's negotiations with Kim Jong-Un, and seeing an American president finally meet with the leader of North Korea. It never hurts to have a relationship with these countries that lead in a much different way than America does. I'm not saying that we should idolize them or try to model our country after them. But there's an old saying that I've always truly enjoyed: "keep your friends close and keep your enemies even closer." I'm sure you've heard that before. Despite what a lot of the media says about Trump, as far as him buddying it up with our enemies and ostracizing our allies, I feel like he always has an agenda. He's oftentimes a step ahead of everyone, including the media.

I will admit that the media's caught up with him with COVID. I do believe there's been a few times where the media's got a hold of him. But overall, I believe he's usually a step ahead, and I have no problem with the relationship that he's developed with Kim Jong-Un.

I also very much like how hard he's been on China, and the fact that unemployment pre-COVID was continuing to go down, month after month. There were historic Black unemployment numbers, the lowest African-American unemployment under any president.

Also, we had the highest Black home ownership under any president. Now, I'm a real estate guy. I part-time invest in real estate. I have a number of rental units. I have two-family and single-family properties. I've flipped real estate. I have my finger on the pulse of real estate outside of my position in healthcare, and I can tell you just from my own experience that I've noticed that there are a lot more minorities in the game in general buying homes and becoming homeowners. People that I used to rent to, that had no desire to buy homes, are buying homes now. It's great to see. I love seeing it. I always tell everyone that it's the best decision they could make. It's the single greatest step. Financial independence and building wealth is owning your own home. Under Donald Trump, African-Americans have the highest home ownership above any other president.

Another thing that I think goes without saying is that Donald Trump has finally decided to make permanent the funding of historically Black colleges. I never even knew that historically Black colleges had to go and beg for money – maybe "beg" is not the right word – from the federal government. I had no idea; that was something new to me. I believe he's granted them the ability to have this money for however many years it is moving forward, so at least they don't have to keep going back and forth asking for it. Black unemployment, homeownership, and colleges: just those three topics alone are reasons why I don't understand why people always say that this man is racist. But that's, I guess, a whole other topic.

I would also say that I am extremely happy in general with the Supreme Court justices. I feel as though what was done to Kavanaugh was an atrocity. I don't care what side of the aisle you're on. Blasey Ford, who is she? Comes out of nowhere with these accusations, things that never came up before. Thank God that Judge Kavanaugh was one of those people that kept daily planners and held onto them. I mean, this man was destroyed, his family was ripped apart. That was truly telling about how venomous the left can be when they don't like what's going on. It was awful.

What they did to Kavanaugh, and then what they've just recently done to Amy, is intolerable. What they don't like is the fact that she is a conservative female. The left always preaches tolerance, always preaches women, "Me Too," and everything. Unless you disagree with them. If you're a female and you disagree with them, the left's hypocrisy is blinding.

The reason Trump's voter base is strong right now is because of how the left has developed. They hated him before he got in. The media disliked him before he got in. And it has reached a point now where the media despises his very existence. I don't think that there is a person they hate more than Donald Trump. I think it's his exposing them, not playing into what they've wanted him to do, not answering all their questions the way they want them answered. The media is fed up, and that's why I also think that this Biden and Bobulinski situation is getting absolutely zero coverage. The emails have already been validated, and we're hearing nothing. You go to CNN's website and you search in the search bar, "Bobulinski," and it comes back with nothing. There is nothing found in the entire CNN website.[111] I ask one question of all my liberal friends: if this Hunter Biden situation were reversed, do you really think the censorship and lack of left-wing media attention would happen? For three years, the left talked about this Russian hoax like there was unequivocal evidence that the Trump campaign colluded with Russia, and it was a lie. For three years, we were lied to about it. But with the Hunter Biden thing we hear nothing.

It's because the left has such a hatred for Donald Trump after three-and-three-quarter years, that they are literally willing to do whatever it takes to get him out of office. They do not want him there, and they've actually become the biggest proponent of the Biden/Kamala Harris campaign. It's mind blowing. It's actually scary if you think about the media reaching a point of censorship at this level.

But I know I'm getting off the subject, because this was to talk about how am I pleased or not pleased with Trump's term. So just to get back to your question, because I think it's important that I follow your script, you know I have been fulfilled in the ways I've explained

---

111 This is true. I just tried.

to you already. There are reasons, too, that probably just aren't coming to mind right now.

But there are also ways I haven't been pleased. I would've liked to have seen something done with DACA. Why can't they put together a plan for DACA? I don't want these people shipped back; I just want Congress to do what it was supposed to do. That's what Obama did: he put it in the hands of Congress. Congress didn't do it, so he had to take executive action. I want something to be done. Just put something together.

Another reason to be displeased is — and I blame the Republicans for this — them not doing anything with Obamacare. They talked about getting rid of Obamacare, they had the opportunity to do it, and they haven't done it. Why is that? Why can't they seem to get it done? I don't want people going without healthcare, but I also don't want a one-payer system that's controlled by the government.

Those are two areas that I feel as though I'm not happy with. But I just think that it's not even comparable to the number of areas where I'm absolutely thrilled with the things that Trump has done.

Everyone in the world was shocked when Trump got elected. That's obvious. I even think his own party shocked. I think they were nervous at the beginning about how much support to give him. If you look over the course of the three plus years, his support in the Republican party has grown year over year. Now he's at a 93% approval rating in his party. He's got everyone behind him. I think that is fueled by the fact that the left has gone *all* the way to the left. It's become the "radical left" now. (I don't want to sound like a parrot for the things that Trump says, or the things that the right-wing media says, but a lot of times there's a reason why little slogans stick. It's because they're true.)

As the left has continued to push left, this divide has become immense. No doubt about it. I absolutely believe that the President could make that divide better than he has. But I also don't think anybody has even come close to reaching across the aisle to work with him. Nancy Pelosi is the cancer in our government; I personally believe that. Just seeing she stood up at the State of the Union address and ripped up his speech on national television, behind the President of the United States of America?! No respect for the position at all. Some people say, "You know what? President Trump doesn't give respect, so that's why he's treated the way he's treated." You know what? Fine. I get that. I do believe there are times he says things that are off-color, that he should not say. I just don't think a few core things ever leave this man: I believe he loves this country more than anything and he believes this country to be the best country in the world.

He has this burning desire to get the respect of the position that he has not gotten from day one. And that dovetails nicely into my position on COVID. Unfortunately, this is where I believe Trump messed up. I believe that at the very beginning, when nobody knew anything about this – and there's no doubt in my mind that the whole thing started because China was trying to cover it up – Trump did what Trump normally does, take everything that comes from the Democrats as a shot at his armor. He just went into it thinking that Democrats are going to blow this thing out of proportion, and COVID is no different than any other virus. I mean, I've never lived through a pandemic. I thought pandemics were things that happened because medicine wasn't as advanced as it is now a hundred years ago.

We have the CDC, we have the World Health Organization, we have science, we have brilliant minds all over the globe that are constantly working and trying to get ahead of anything that could come out. I'm in healthcare and I see it all the time. I see how physicians treat, I see how infectious disease doctors' brains think. I've had conversations with them, I've met with them. These people are geniuses. I never thought a pandemic could actually happen again. I'm sure Trump was in the same boat. He knew that the left was going to jump all over this, so he came out of the gates on the deep end. He came out of the gates saying, "I'm going to put this thing down. It's not as big as they say it is."

And guess what? It was the absolute perfect storm. Not because we lost hundreds of thousands of lives, of course not. But it was the perfect storm for the Democrats to allow Trump to either mess up on himself or have something to run on. Because they had absolutely nothing to run on going into this election.

The Democratic party was a mess. They had what? Eleven, twelve people trying to get the nomination. They thought it was going to be a battle between Biden and Bernie. If you think about it, neither one of them represent what the left supposedly really enjoys, or likes, or wants. Think about the left constantly preaching that they're sick of these rich, old, white men, and then what do they do? They bring in two rich, old, white men!

The funny thing is, I don't dislike Joe Biden. I think Joe Biden's a likable guy. I think if he's your next-door neighbor, he's not a bad guy. But I certainly don't think he's going to do a better job than Donald Trump. I just think he's pandering to the votes, he's pandering to the radical, far left, and there's no bigger example of that than when he picks Kamala Harris to run with him. He hits a home run when he chooses a Black female. Now he's perfect. Well, she stood up onstage and said that she believed Joe Biden's sexual accusers. Now she's in bed with him?!

These people that are rioting, doing these "peaceful protests," who do you think these people are voting for? Just answer that question. Do you think that if President Trump loses the 2020 election that there's going to be riots in the streets? Do you think that conservatives are going to take to burning buildings down? Or causing public destruction? Now if I ask the question the other way, if Donald Trump wins, what do you think's going to happen next? This is how radical that party has come.

Obviously, there's going to be these crazy, racist divisions of the conservative party; it's there, no doubt about it. Just like there's the Antifa division of the Democratic party, okay? You've got that on both sides, no doubt. But for the most part, your conservative friends are not going to start wielding a Molotov cocktail at the Providence police downtown. I'm not going to storm into the mall, I'm not going to set a car on fire, I'm not going to throw a frozen bottle of water at a police officer because my candidate didn't win. But that is what will happen if Trump wins, because that is where the left will go. Obviously, not all of them. But enough of them to where it happens in cities all over the country.

My life is different now in that I'm more embedded in politics than I've ever been. Moving forward, politics will always have a different appeal. I think it will force people to be more involved, whether because they hated Trump and they've got to make sure they don't mess up again and let someone like him get in office, or the other way around.

The past four years have been the most lucrative years of my life. I'm in the lab business. COVID has been unbelievable for me. I sell COVID testing. My company did a complete turnaround, thirty days in. We're a toxicology company that primarily does urine and oral fluids toxicology for the NFL Players Association, Major League Baseball, hockey, NASCAR, WWE. But we also work on a residential level: we're dealing with pain care doctors, surgeons, neurosurgeons, providers that are prescribing controlled substances that need to make sure that their patients aren't abusing, misusing, or diverting these meds. So as the virus rolled out, we went into a lockdown. Thirty days later, the company said, "We're going to roll out a COVID test." We are only one of two companies that got an HHS grant from the federal government. We went from doing zero COVID samples in March to doing sixty thousand a day, and our turnaround time is inside of fourteen hours from when we receive the sample.

I know that's bragging about my company, but you asked how has my life changed? My life has been embedded in COVID. Financially, they've been the best four years of my life. And not just that, Dan. My tax returns as a single male have been better than they've ever been. My accountant has told me that I was able to take advantage of the Trump tax cuts. I also want to

stress to you that in no way, shape, or form am I trying to brag. That's not my intention. There's nothing I hate more than when people brag about money. I'm only saying this because I'm talking to you and trying to answer the questions that you ask with truth. It's just the truth, that's all.

Some of the byproduct of me having good years is that I've been able to up donations to the foundations that I like. I've always been a big supporter of St. Jude; that's my go-to fundraising, is St. Jude's. I've also found myself donating to police officer foundations, firefighter foundations. That was kind of a change of pace for me.

First responders, they get money raised for them so that if they die in the line of duty, their families are taken care of. (If I get in an accident driving down the Cape to do my job, my family's kind of SOL.) I feel like this Trump presidency has opened my eyes a little bit to the first responders, and I'm trying to do what I can. That greater financial gain has also allowed me to spend more money: I've done more things around my home, bought a jet ski, bought a cottage with my brother down in Matunuck, over across the street from the Ocean Mist. We've been able to enjoy some good times down there.

When we're there, I'm spending money in restaurants, going out. It's not like Scrooge, where I'm making more money and just putting it all in this giant safe in diamonds and gold coins. It's actually getting out there; I'm making it, and I'm also spending it. And investing it. All of these things are great for the economy. That would be the best way I could say my life has changed.

How is my life different in a negative way? Well, unfortunately, I think some people maybe have got a different opinion of me because of being as outspoken as I am about politics. That's the only negative way my life has changed since Trump came in. I think that politics in general has consumed more of my time – trying to be informed, fact checking, trying to get things right. That's consumed more of my time than it ever has in the past. I guess you could say that's negative or positive. Because it's better to be informed, I guess.

I have a number of African-American friends; they've walked by Confederate statues their whole life and didn't even know what the statue was. They didn't feel like they were offended of the statue. Now, all of a sudden, the police are wrong all the time. I do not believe that there's systemic racism in this country. That might be a shock to you. Do I believe there's racism? Absolutely. 100%. Do I believe it's systemic? I think that it's situational. I think that it might be in certain areas. (Which I guess, maybe some people would say maybe that's systemic.)

I just don't think it's as bad as you hear about, when Joe Biden gets behind the podium, or Kamala Harris, or Barack Obama, and they sit up there and they just preach about doom and gloom. They preach about people dying, about division in the country, about people losing their healthcare. I mean, we were in an economic boom! Maybe not everyone was making great money or doing amazing. But the unemployment numbers don't lie, homeownership numbers don't lie, real estate values aren't lying, the stock market wasn't lying.

I think the problem here really boils all the way down to education. People need to know at a young age how to build wealth in their life, instead of going to a party all the time, or thinking school's not important, or not being able to get the funding for school. I think that's kind of more where we need to change things. I'm not going to get into individual races with you, but there's so much to be said for the African-American population that doesn't have dad at home in such a large percentage of families. There's so many different levels where we could address these issues.

I would just like to say that I just hope that no matter what happens on Election Day 2020, that there's peace in this country. Unfortunately, I feel as though the only way there will be is if Joe Biden wins. Because I think that if Joe Biden wins, conservatives won't do what liberals will do if Trump wins. Obviously not all of them; I don't think that *you're* going to go marching in the streets with a rifle and shooting people. I don't think that probably many people *you* know are going to be taking Molotov cocktails and hauling them at buildings. But I do think enough liberals will. I don't think any conservatives will. I think conservatives protest, but I just don't think their protests will ever become violent.

In a perfect world for me, I would see Donald Trump winning convincingly. I don't even want it to be close, because I don't want there to be a contested election. Then I would like to have Trump come out and say something like he did at his inauguration speech, when he talked about unity in the country, and he talked about making this country better and greater than it's ever been. I would like to see him start to spin that.

But it would be nice to have him have four years where it didn't matter what the left said or did. He would be able to focus more on now building a legacy. Every president is concerned about their legacy. Obama? He had Obamacare. I think that if we could get Trump in that situation, he could help the country come together. I told everyone when he got elected, all over Facebook, let's just try to unite. Let's try to work together and support the President. I would have done the same thing if Hillary had won.

I hope that there can be more unity. I feel bad that people have defriended me on Facebook or they don't like me because I'm an outspoken conservative.

I have a lot of problems with a lot of hypocrisy that comes out of the left, but I know there's hypocrisy that comes out of the right, too. When someone brings up a good point, I acknowledge it and I just say, "Yeah, you know, you're right." I just feel like it's not the same on the other side. Believe it or not, my mom hates Donald Trump and has been blue no matter what for her entire life. My uncle worked on John Kennedy's campaign, and picked him up when he flew into T.F. Green to campaign in Rhode Island before he was president. That's how close my family was with the Kennedy's. But my father, my brother, and myself are huge Donald Trump supporters.

We don't even talk about it with my mom anymore, because my mom watches CNN all day every day and whatever they say, she just repeats. That's all she sees. She truly, honestly believes Donald Trump's done absolutely nothing right in four years. Even though we try to tell her that the reason why my father's 401(k) that they are living off of (which, mind you, is not very large) has *increased* as they've drawn off of it for the last four years is because of the strong economy under Trump.

If there's a kink in Trump's armor, it's only with the pandemic. He could've dealt with it differently; I agree with that. Now do I think that it would've saved a hundred thousand lives? No. I do not think that. Do I think it could've potentially saved some lives and potentially made the country a little bit more unified through it? Yes. I think it would have been better if he stood up there and said, "I'm wearing a mask. We should all wear masks" So – pardon my French – Trump fucked up. He should've put a mask on.

Dan, thank you again and I apologize for being so long winded. I'm very passionate about this. And no matter what happens, I'll support whichever president that we do have.

CHAPTER FIFTY-TWO
The Liberal Feminist (Again)

October, 2020
Tulsa, Oklahoma

Victor sure had a lot to say, and I have to commend him for his promise to support whichever candidate is elected in November of 2020. I certainly could not make that same promise in 2016. He doesn't seem to mind Biden, but sticks by Trump for the pages and pages and pages of reasons filling the last chapter.

I'm coming to the close of my virtual visits for this project, and I still haven't found anyone willing to go on the record as having turned their back on Trump… until now. For a final commentary, let's hear from Babs. She is the pizza-delivery feminist who I first met in a doughnut shop at the extreme end of a long Tulsa night, and she's the only one here not willing to vote for Trump again in 2020.

###

BABS: If I'm honest, I'm nervous about being quoted. I'm just really grateful for what you're doing. My position in the "extreme center" constantly leaves me trying to help each side see the other's perspective, and that's becoming increasingly difficult as we become more polarized. If your book helps liberal New Yorkers like yourself at least understand some rational thoughts in the minds of conservative (and, at least in my case, moderate) Midwesterners, even if they disagree, then I think it will do some good. This isn't about convincing anyone that Trump is a good person or that he was the right choice, it's about helping people who didn't vote for him understand that not all of us who did are as awful people as he is. Right?

I'm a feminist because no one ever told me that I couldn't do anything just because I was a woman. In other words, I grew up a lot like you: really unable to understand the other side. From my perspective, Republicans always seemed very fear-based and greedy, always using the emotional appeal to control people with fear. I never got it.

And then I moved to Oklahoma, unenthusiastically. A year after that, I left academia and ended up staying in Tulsa for financial reasons. When you met me, I was probably the most educated pizza delivery driver in the State of Oklahoma. Most people that I talked to or associated with at the time had a completely different background from me. That did have some effect, but I was also moved by my experience working for minimum wage. In some ways you would think that would make me more progressive, but hearing conservative people's perspectives helped me understand the logic behind where they were coming from on that side. It made me more *economically* conservative, but not along the Republican party lines or anything. It just brought me more toward the center.

At the time of the last presidential election, I was thinking that wherever the next president took the economy was going to be what had the most effect on America and our day-to-day lives. I thought at the time that Trump was the option to go to for that reason. I knew Trump was an asshole and I honestly hoped that might inspire people to get more involved in politics. And I knew that anything bad he would do would be effectively front and center; he's not very good at hiding anything. Hillary Clinton would be more two-faced. Again, I don't know how much of that was influenced by the people I was around, but those were some things that I thought through, and that's why I voted the I did.

After the 2016 presidential election, I did get frustrated struggling to find a job. I'm a college-educated individual, I'm very smart, I have great attitude, and yet I was a pizza delivery driver. So I ended up joining the Army, the Oklahoma National Guard. I'm the first person in my family to enlist in the military; I'm really proud of that. I had one grandfather who was drafted for the Air Force, but he was colorblind so that didn't really last. There's even more exposure here to different points of view, and it's really cool to finally do something that no one in my family prepped me for.

I'm an IT specialist for the Army. And I was, like, top of my class and got a bunch of civilian certifications and came out of that able to get a job, a real big-girl job and not even entry level. I'm a network administrator at a cybersecurity firm now. I, like, have a salary and everything, like for real, just what my dad wanted for me. Two years ago, I met my husband, I'm now married and for the record, I do now largely go by my legal name, Diana. I don't know a whole lot of people who still call me Babs, not that I mind it.

My husband and I bought a house in a middle-class neighborhood outside of Tulsa. My lifestyle is almost unrecognizable now compared to where I was just three years ago when you met me, when I was subletting a room from a guy that I met off Craigslist in the ghetto part of town and working for minimum wage; it's just unrecognizable. But I'm not a different person. I'm very thoughtful about everything around me, politically. Effectively, it's made me an extreme moderate. I'm neither liberal nor conservative, I'm just an extreme moderate at this point.

Exactly what I hoped for has come to pass: Trump is terrible at being sneaky and I feel like we pretty much know everything that he's about. We know everything that he's done, we know everything he's trying to do. I don't feel like there are any secrets.[112] The media doesn't want to admit that Trump can do anything positive, but if you look for it, it's all there.

What upsets me though, is the way some people have become involved in politics. Maybe *some* are leaning toward the importance of some of those liberal ideas that I thought were good, and that's what I wanted. But the problem is how the left has handled President Trump. I remember at the very beginning, I was really frustrated because he seemed to be doing enough on his own that could be criticized, but then instead of harping on those things, there was a scandal over Trump's starving seniors because a small percentage of money he eliminated made up a small portion of the budget that went to Meals on Wheels. A very, very weak argument, but they were trying to paint him more negatively than I think he was. They were trying to get him to look bad for a few cases where he wasn't making himself look bad, instead of giving him the rope to let him hang himself. It was just poorly handled.

What that led to was me getting completely pissed. I really was; I was very upset during the impeachment hearings because I

---

112 He *is* still hiding those tax returns.

really do believe that Trump did exactly what he was accused of and I do think that using his position of power to influence the next election is bad; it's really, really not okay. And I do think that it is an offense worthy of a president being removed from office. And acquitting him does set the precedent that a president can get away with whatever he wants. On the other hand, because of the rhetoric the left has been using about the 2016 election, it would have been worse to remove him from office. For years, rather than coming together and saying, "We don't have to like him, he's not from our party, but he's the president," we're saying things like, "Not my president." And so, if Democrats had actually removed him from office, in my opinion, it would have set an even worse precedent: that one party – if they don't like the president – can effectively overturn an election.

As far as policy, I'm unhappy with how Trump rolled back environmental protections, but I expected that. On the other hand, his tax reform really did help lower middle-class and middle-class individuals like myself and my husband. As far as the trade war, I really can't tell from my perspective if that worked. It seems like one of those things that was probably a good idea that would hurt at first – like getting braces – but ultimately make things better. But I haven't heard an unbiased analysis of it his trade policies. I know the Biden campaign says the policies are a disaster, but their job right now is to make Trump look bad.

Trump is unnecessarily inflammatory, but he is pointing out a few real problems with how things traditionally have been done. I recently heard on NPR an interesting perspective about killing Qasem Soleimani: that many presidents before Trump had the opportunity to attack him, but they hemmed and hawed and decided not to because they were afraid of unintended consequences and degrading that region into a worse situation. Like, "Yes, he's bad, but killing him would be worse." Then Trump just goes out and does it and shocks everybody. And all of those consequences we were afraid of didn't happen. From what the reporter was saying on NPR, presidents from all parties going forward will actually get something positive out of that move, learning that we don't have to hem and haw as much. We kind of can do what is in our interests without having to worry so much about the consequences.

In a nutshell, Trump is about like any president: I agree with some things he's done and disagree with others. My favorite thing about him is that he is more transparent than any other president we've had for a long while. He is who he is and is unapologetic about it. We know his agenda, good and bad, and I really wish that that came standard. Because knowing what he's done and what he stands for and where he's going, some of it's just really bad and I can't...

You asked the question, why has he got my vote again? And effectively, he does not. But please let me explain here. I learned a handy trick in relationships some time ago in deciding whether or not to stick with a person based not on their best qualities, but on their worst. In other words, figure out not what you like best about them, but what is your least favorite thing about them? And if that's really, really bad, no matter how good their good stuff is, you should probably not be with them. In the case of my husband, for example, my least favorite thing about him is that in his youth he mis-learned pronouns and now uses *him* and *her* where he should use *he* and *she*. I come from a family of grammar Nazis, and it drives me nuts. But you know what? That isn't a reason not to marry him. And we have an incredibly healthy, positive, happy relationship.

On the other hand, with Trump the worst things started happening when he started calling the media, "fake news."[113] And now what scares me, coming close to the election, is that he's refusing to commit to a peaceful transfer of power. He is sowing fear and doubt into our election system when there's no call for that. The FBI has assured us that everything's fine, mail-in ballots are fine. There's no reason to doubt it. Transparent as he is, he's also very effective and that's scary.

I guess some people say they saw this coming. Back in 2016, to me, the worst thing about Trump was that he was an asshole, and he's largely blocked from putting that attitude into policies! *Now* the worst thing about him is that he's undermining our very system of democracy, and I can't vote for that. That's just really not okay. I realize that other people out there are probably saying, "*That's* the reason you're not going to vote for him?! Not all these other long lists of terrible things?!" And don't get me wrong, I don't agree with him on all policy – I don't agree with anybody on all policy at this point – but his sowing doubt about our election system is the reason I can't vote for Trump. Because even if I agreed with him 100% on policy and I disagreed with other candidates 100% on policy, we can only debate policy when we have a system. We have to have the democratic system, and he's undermining the democratic system.

---

[113] An interesting reminder: Trump co-opted the phrase "fake news" for the first time in January 2017, one week before his inauguration.

Even if I can't vote for President Trump, I'm really frustrated because, applying the same logic to the Biden campaign, I don't know if I can vote for them either. For a lot of the same reasons I didn't want to vote for Hillary back in 2016, what bothers me about Biden and Harris is this classic politicking, this two-faced talking. In the vice presidential debate, Kamala Harris said to the camera, "Joe will not raise taxes on anyone making less than $400,000 a year," and I really appreciated that Mike Pence just dropped all pretense, dropped the performance aspect of the debate, and just said, "That directly contradicts what you stated a sentence before, that the first thing you want to do is roll back Trump's tax reforms." They're painting this picture that Trump's tax reforms only benefited the rich, but I know from personal experience that they've benefited middle-class people as well.[114] And I don't know what the ratio is. I'm not an economist, I haven't looked at it. Maybe it helped me a little bit, and it really did help the rich a whole lot more and maybe there really are reasons why we should be repealing them; I'm not arguing that. If that's the case, tell me that my taxes are going up and we'll work with it. But she said to my face a *lie* and that really bothers me. It's like in sales: some people don't mind negatives; they just don't like surprises. And I don't like being lied to my face.

Likewise, I think that the Democratic party as a whole, and certainly the campaign, is lying to the American public very blatantly by saying that their reasons for wanting to delay the Supreme Court nomination are because they really think that the people deserve the right to choose the nominee. First of all, that is not how it works. Whether you like Trump or not, he was elected for four years – not three – and that is his prerogative. Lindsey Graham might be an asshole, but he was right when he said that if the Dems were in his shoes, they would be doing exactly the same thing. And they *did* the same thing four years ago, when Obama did a nomination to the Supreme Court right before his election. In that case, the Senate wasn't on his side so that person was not confirmed, but they literally did the exact same thing. The Biden campaign is lying so obviously.

Unfortunately, the lying is very effective, just like how Trump's lies about mail-in ballots being unreliable is effective. People believe it; people believe these lies.

People worry that Biden would step down and then Kamala Harris will be president. And I don't think that she's not presidential,

---

[114] I agree with this assessment.

I don't think that she wouldn't do a great job… but as a woman, I would love if the first woman president was someone that we actually directly voted for. So, here's a solution.

If I can't vote for Trump because he's undermining democracy, and I really have a major problem with Joe Biden for the same reason I had a problem with Hillary Clinton – they're two-faced – at this point my husband and I are both going to vote for Jo Jorgensen. I think the most negative thing about her – I mean besides the fact that third parties are effectively non-viable at this point – is that she's totally inexperienced. But compared to the other two? If that's the worst thing about her, people would help her.

But I don't just quite want to leave it there because I'm not content with this idea that we're stuck two elections in a row with most people feeling like they have to choose between the lesser evil, or else go for a third-party candidate who's "non-electable." I'm tired of elections that seem to come down to two highly objectionable options, so I'm trying to actually do something about it. It won't solve all our problems, but I think a "single transferable vote" system would go a long way toward reversing the polarization in the country. I'm starting research on how to actually introduce that at the local and state level. That kind of ranked voting has several benefits, one of them being that it actually makes third-party candidates viable. And if you vote for a candidate that doesn't get enough support, your vote would transfer to your second pick. You can actually vote your conscience.

I know that there's a lot of people who'll cry "tin foil hat" here, but I really do believe in Yuri Bezmenov's warning from decades ago that the way enemy countries will attack free nations like the United States is from within. And us tearing ourselves apart like this? There's no one who's going to win here. Maybe Russia wins, maybe China wins, but certainly we're not going to win by tearing ourselves apart like we're doing now.

I really want to thank you for allowing me the opportunity to follow up. I think this is a really good project. I ended up at the middle myself from trying to understand the other side. If you're able to help people who cannot conceive of why anybody would ever vote for Donald Trump unless they're a racist, xenophobic, horrible person, then this project is worth it. You can at least help them understand what the logic is behind it. We don't have to agree, but I do want to protect our ability to disagree safely and nonviolently.

THE FINAL CURTAIN

I've fulfilled the obligation I placed on myself. I've listened, fully and deeply. I've strained to follow opposing arguments and I've researched every anecdote. I've given voice to the opposition, limiting my own voice to these interpolated passages of written commentary and the selective editing of thousands of hours of recordings. My goal has never been to change minds, but to understand them.

There is a populist movement in America, and it will not end when Trump is out of office. Republican advisor Amanda Carpenter said to the *Los Angeles Times*, "People are laying the groundwork to consolidate that Trump base…he will still be the kingmaker of the Republican party in many senses." Liberals will be side-to-side with this Trump base for a long time, so it is imperative that we understand where they find their passion and reason. It is imperative that we learn to speak their language.

Trump kept many campaign promises that his supporters care about. Trump championed tax cuts that decreased the personal income tax burden on the vast majority of Americans. Trump presided during a Wall Street boom that hit the highest levels of all time. Is that enough? For many, yes. But for me? After a grand listening tour and legitimate deep dive, decidedly not.

My sincere hope is that liberal readers will read these chapters with empathy, attempting to understand explicitly where our neighbors differ from us and why. We can empower ourselves this way. My other sincere hope is that the conservative folks documented in these pages give more attention to empathy when empowering their next leader, giving credence to the fact that a politician's words can cause tangible harm and incite real violence. Black lives matter beyond the economic talking points and choosing the directive "stand back and stand by" demonstrates a lack of emotional comprehension of race relations on a human level, and no acknowledgment of the pain that many Black citizens feel.

Political leadership demands more than business leadership. Elected representatives should be financially savvy, open-minded strategists willing to upset the status quo in order to make American lives better, but they should also listen with care. They should also reign in any act of divisiveness. They should also check any tendency toward dismissiveness.

It's October 24th, 2020 and I'm putting on shoes to go cast my early vote. Though my physical trek has ended, my commitment to understanding shall continue. There's no substitute for empathy, and mine is a work in progress.

www.ingramcontent.com/pod-product-compliance
Lightning Source LLC
Chambersburg PA
CBHW051244250726
48656CB00004B/1123

* 9 7 9 8 5 5 6 7 4 6 2 0 6 *